Essays on Key Issues of Development in Nepal

Ramesh C. Paudel

Essays on Key Issues of Development in Nepal

Macroeconomic Perspectives from an LDC Graduating Landlocked Country

palgrave
macmillan

Ramesh C. Paudel
Central Department of Economics
Tribhuvan University
Kirtipur, Kathmandu, Nepal

ISBN 978-981-95-7714-9 ISBN 978-981-95-7715-6 (eBook)
https://doi.org/10.1007/978-981-95-7715-6

This Palgrave Macmillan imprint is published by the registered company Springer Nature Singapore Pte Ltd.
The registered company address is: 152 Beach Road, #21-01/04 Gateway East, Singapore 189721, Singapore

Competing Interests The author has no competing interests to declare that are relevant to the content of this manuscript.

Contents

About the Author

Ramesh Paudel is Associate Professor of Economics at the Central Department of Economics, Tribhuvan University, Kirtipur, Kathmandu, Nepal. He served as a member of the National Planning Commission and a member of the Board of Trade, Government of Nepal on different occasions. He holds a PhD in Economics from the Australian National University and a Master of Research in Economics from the University of Wollongong, Australia. Paudel worked as an academic in Australia and Nepal for about 20 plus years. He brings an excellent combination of experiences in academia, research, and policymaking relevant to macroeconomics, financial economics, development economics, international trade, human resources development, and the governance quality issues of developing countries. His list of publications includes, but is not limited to, well-ranked peer-reviewed journals, book chapters of Oxford University Press, Springer, and other outlets, and a few books in the Nepalese context. He has worked as a consultant to the World Bank, the Asian Development Bank, the United Nations, and the Nepalese government on different occasions. During his tenure in NPC, he led a team in various stages to draft a few chapters related to Education, Health, Urban Planning, and Infrastructure Development of the 16th National Plan of the government of Nepal.

Abbreviations

ADF	Augmented Dickey-Fuller
ARDL	Autoregressive Distributed Lag
BCPS	Banks' credit to the Private Sector
BDS	Bangladesh
BWA	Botswana
BS	Bikram Sambat
CCMC	COVID-19 Crisis Management Center
CHN	China
DF	Dickey-Fuller
EVI	Economic Vulnerability Index
ECM	Error Correction Model
FDI	Foreign Direct Investment
FE	Fixed Effect
GDP	Gross Domestic Product
GDPPC	GDP per capita
HAI	Human Assets Index
IMF	International Monetary Fund
IND	India
INFL	Inflation
JEL	Journal of Economic Literature
KEN	Kenya
KOR	South Korea
LAO	Laos (Lao PDR)
LDC	Least Developed Country
LR	Long Run Relationship
NLR	No Long Run Relationship
NPL	Nepal

PDR	People's Democratic Republic
PP	Philips and Perron
RE	Random Effect
REM	Remittances
SFA	Stochastic Frontier Analysis
SITC	Standard International Trade Classification
SLK	Sri Lanka
UK	United Kingdom
USD	United States Dollar
WITS	World Integrated Trade Solution

List of Figures

List of Tables

CHAPTER 1

Introduction

1.1 Background

Nepal, a landlocked least developed country (LDC), stands at the crossroads of a significant transition, poised to graduate from the list of LDCs in 2026. This moment is not merely symbolic but carries profound economic and policy implications that need to be discussed systematically, based on the facts and figures in a macroeconomic perspective. The political economy not only guides but also directs overall economic activities and leads the nation toward a higher level of productivity, coordinating the factors of production for the betterment of all stakeholders. Fiscal policy is the primary domain where the political economy is actively engaged in the macroeconomic perspective, even coordinating with monetary policy issues to create employment and increase national output. However, has it worked in Nepal? It is a challenging question.

Nepal stands as a unique country in the key macroeconomic and political figures in the global context because of its geographical location, climate, and untapped natural endowments, but with poor economic performance than the expectations from the stakeholders. The poor economic performance is said to be largely affected by the poor quality of governance led by the political turmoil that has prevailed every one or two decades in the last five decades, causing systemic instability in the country, creating doubt for the potential growth contributors in the nation. In

R. C. Paudel, *Essays on Key Issues of Development in Nepal*,
https://doi.org/10.1007/978-981-95-7715-6_1

recent history, Nepal witnessed a nationwide students' movement against the party-less Panchayat System in Bikram Sambat (BS) 2036 (1979) that laid the path for the restoration of the democratic system in BS 2046, that is, in 1989/1990 (Snellinger, 2007).

From 1996, the Nepal Communist Party (Maoist) started an armed conflict that paved the path to abolish the about two-and-a-half-century-old monarch system in the country in 2006, and then the monarch was abolished in 2008 (Paudel, 2013). Recently, in 2025, a two-day Gen-Z uprising resulted in toppling the Nepal government elected based on the parliamentary composition of more than two-thirds majority, and the parliament was dissolved, and an interim government if formed. Notably, the main demand of the protest was about the bad governance, corruption, and bad governance in the country and the ban on social media by the government. The bad governance resulted from the rooted inefficiency of the leadership of the major political parties and their poor governance within their own political parties (Koirala, 2025). Once again, this political movement has also resulted in political instability in the country. All these political scenarios have always created a dilemma in political paths in the country, but not meaningfully different in the sector of systemic reform and proper execution of a quality governance system to achieve the expected level of economic development in the country; however, each of these movements has a positive contribution to making the country more inclusive, transparent, and raising social awareness.

Because of these facts, Nepal has been unable to meet its development expectations. Even Nepal has failed to achieve the potential success in the economic development aspects as compared to its close neighbours and other neighbouring countries. This may be because of many political revolutions, not the industrial or agricultural revolutions in the country. The industrial or agricultural revolution could enhance productivity and national output, unlike the political revolution occurring every decade or so.

As of 2025 in the global rank, Nepal stands in 95th position in geographical areas, 52nd position in population, 100th position in gross domestic product (GDP), as found in different pages of Worldometers.info (2025). It means that Nepal has 0.36 percent of the World's population but only 0.04 percent of the World's GDP.

Having this background, Nepal is graduating from LDC status in 2026. Among the three criteria: income criteria, Human Assets Index (HAI), and Economic and Environmental Vulnerability Index (EVI), Nepal has passed the last two criteria and, by 2026, hopefully will pass the income criteria too, though this is not mandatory at this stage. Because of the poor quality of governance, it seems no sincere preparations are made to sustain the LDC graduation, particularly to recover the loss and extend the trade with major partner countries via bilateral trade agreements and so on. Doing so will not only recover the potential loss of trade, which is estimated at four percent because of LDC graduation, but also will open new venues for trades and other opportunities from financial flows and sovereign ratings in the global context.

1.1.1 *Current Key Macroeconomic Issues in Nepal*

In the background mentioned above, Nepal's development is not as expected by the stakeholders, specifically the youth generations' aspiration is very high as they compare the country with neighbouring countries, and feel frustrated to migrate for jobs, leaving families and friends in the country. This is because of the lack of jobs in the country, as the youth unemployment rate in the country has soared to above 20 percent, as mentioned in O'Neill (2025), however, the increased remittances have played a crucial role in running the government as well as managing the external sector of the national economy (Nepal Rastra Bank, 2025). I capture a few, but the most important current issues in the development field of Nepal; however, there are many issues. As these are not possible to cover in a book, I selected the most important linking with the governance, trade and economic development. Nepal has a serious economic structural problem created by the political turmoil and led by the poor quality of governance in the country (National Planning Commission, 2024).

To correct the structural problem of Nepal's economy, probably, one way to improve the base of agriculture-based manufacturing so that more employment can be generated on a mass scale of the labour force, both unskilled and semi-skilled, and would provide a solid base to the service sector too. This would help boost exports, which can be achieved by mobilizing remittances and banks' credit to the private sector in a more efficient manner, focusing on credit flows to productive sectors. This has been discussed in detail and systematically in Chap. 2 of this book.

To redirect remittances through formal channels into productive sector loans, a reliable governance system trusted by domestic and foreign investors is essential. Therefore, Chapter 3 discusses these issues, examining the impact of overall governance quality on the export performance.

Yes, export performance is an essential task of the economy in the liberalization and reform era. Still, Nepal has not been able to boost exports, even though Nepal is known as one of the earlier entrants in the liberalization and reform era in the region. In this regard, Nepal's focused sector did not work much to boost exports and accelerate economic growth. While looking to answer the question, such as what went wrong in boosting exports in Nepal, probably agriculture-based manufacturing did not get much focus in the past. If it were the case, the economic growth of Nepal can also be enhanced because of the synergy created by the integration of the agriculture and manufacturing sectors, as this would create a sound ecosystem for industrialization, absorbing many backward and forward linkages of the products in the process from agriculture to manufacturing. This linkage is elaborated in Chap. 4.

Another important macroeconomic issue in the current situation in Nepal is the slower-than-expected growth of revenue collection. As revenue is a lifeline for any country, the capacity to collect revenue and its proper spending largely determines the quality and quantity of welfare activities in the country. A sustainable source of revenue would be a solid base of exports, but current revenue largely comes from the import trade. Therefore, Chapter 5 analyzes the revenue efficiency of Nepal, highlighting the current scenarios, problems, and paths to solve the issues of revenue efficiency in the country.

The concept of participatory democracy enhances the quality of governance in the country. This fact is well considered in analyzing the role of democracy and economic development in enhancing the governance quality in Chap. 6. This chapter elaborates on the importance of governance, finding major determinants of the quality of governance, which has been a major issue of economic development in the country for a long time.

Fiscal policy is the main domain of political economy that, overall, guides and determines the level of economic activities in the country. Considering this role, Chapter 7 investigates what can be done in the context of enhancing export efficiency, highlighting that fiscal policy does not directly affect a country's export efficiency unless it is tied to a better quality of governance.

The major contribution of this book lies not only in its coverage of current macroeconomic issues in Nepal, but also in the methodological aspects applied in different chapters. In this context, Chaps. 2, 4, and 6 employ an annual time series-based Auto-Regressive Distributed Lag (ARDL) approach of cointegration after observing the time series properties of the data. Chapter 3 is a panel data-based gravity modelling technique, Chapter 5 employs the Stochastic Frontier Analysis (SFA) in time series data, observing the time series properties of the data, and Chap. 7 again employs the SFA version of the gravity modelling technique in unbalanced panel data.

1.1.2 What Does Nepal Have?

Nepal, located in South Asia, is well-known for its history of never being colonized and having unexploited natural resources. Nepal is positioned between two rapidly growing global economies, China and India, where more than one-third of the global population resides. Another six percent population lives in nearby neighbours, such as Bangladesh, Bhutan, Pakistan, Myanmar, and Sri Lanka. This means that Nepal is surrounded by about 40 percent of the global population, indicating a big potential for Nepal in this era of globalization and reform, as this points to a big market for Nepal. A few questions come to mind: how can Nepal tap those potentials? Being located near a large population should have opened an avenue for development and prosperity, but why has it not happened in Nepal yet? Unless the narration is changed from "landlockedness" to "market lockedness", the destiny would remain the same. But, how? These questions create pressure on policymakers, stakeholders, and sometimes on the political system, too. The market in the globalization era is one fundamental aspect, particularly it represents the demand side; the supply side factors are equally crucial. Then, we may think about what Nepal has in the supply-side factors.

Not only the market prospects, but also many other things that the rest of the world does not have. First, Nepal has a total of eight out of the top 10 mountains in the world (Paudel et al., 2011). Doubtlessly, these mountains are the major sources for clean water and environment, energy, adventure tourism, and many more potentialities for living beings and human civilization. Nepal's biodiversity is very unique, with different climatic zones, and the landscapes are considered as biodiversity hotspots with heterogeneous topography suitable for different species linked with climatic zones based on forest, rivers, landscape, plants, and animals, making a unique place for tourism and recreation, research, innovation, and invention potential (Bhattacharjee et al., 2017). Nepal's richness in cultural diversity is widely discussed in the literature (Tamang, 2001).

Second, Nepal has several iconic places in spiritual perspectives, including Pashupatinath and many more, for about 1.3 billion Hindus in the world, Lumbini and other such places for about 520 million Buddhists in the world, Janakpur-Mithila for about 75 million population of the world, making it a unique country for its kind (Waseerman, 2024). This makes Nepal a country with a direct connection for almost 22 percent of the world's population from a religious perspective.

Third, Nepal's demographic dividend for another two decades is very pivotal, when the dependency ratio is very small compared to that of the working age population that can directly contribute to economic activities and national output (Navaneetham and Dharmalingam, 2012). Nepal's window of demographic dividend will not last forever, though. There is a time to manage it and extend the benefits, but ample exercises are required in a timely fashion (Chalise, 2018). Inclusiveness has been increasing rapidly in recent decades that will maintain the momentum for a few more years. Because of low manufacturing activities in the country, our human resources have been contributing overseas and sending remittances to the country for a few decades now.

There are a few other things that are not only in Nepal but are very important for development perspectives. For example, openness helps to maximize the national welfare in many respects. Openness provides an avenue to trade excess global goods and services markets, allows us to participate in the global value chain (producers' welfare) on one hand, and on the other hand, it allows us to import goods and services from overseas at a cheaper price and better quality (consumers' welfare). We cannot imagine how many generations would have passed without seeing a computer if Nepal were a closed economy. The openness is maintained by policy, which was initiated in the 1990s, making Nepal one of the earlier entrants in the liberalization and reform era in the region (Paudel, 2019, 2020). In this process, tariffs were reduced massively, a mixed economy management philosophy was adopted, and many reforms were made in banking and financial sectors, industrial relations, and overall economic policies.

Nepalese labour forces are praised as hard-working, honest, and adaptable. A new image is building from global warriors to global workers (Yamanaka, 2000). It is a major concern of policymakers at this time that the outflow migration pattern is increasing (Adhikari et al., 2023), indicating comparatively cheap labour force is available in the country. Because of this situation and demographic dividend, the labour force is comparatively cheaper for production activities.

Nepal has a long tradition of food, shelter, clothes, and culture. Therefore, Nepal had its own style of products and production systems, construction systems and materials, consumption patterns, and food items. These items could have been linked with tourism industries, including natural beauties, scenes, and suitable places for diverse sectors of tourism, as the country has a long history of tradition for these potentialities Paudel (2013).

This background presents a solid foundation for economic development. Despite all the positive attributes and potential of the economy discussed above, Nepal has remained a poor country for a long time, and policymakers, stakeholders, and sometimes the political system have also been heavily criticized within and beyond the country. It naturally raises the question, what went wrong?

1.1.3 What Did Go Wrong?

Nepal's problem in terms of economic development seems to be multifaceted. First, the poor economic growth can be linked to poor governance quality, political instability, no focus on trade, particularly the export trade, etc. Second, the growth itself is blamed for jobless growth. Policy inconsistency is where those issues can be linked to these problems.

Table 1.1 presents some indicators to say what went wrong from a comparative perspective. A total of six indicators are presented (depending on data availability from a single source) for nine countries, including Nepal, such as Bangladesh, Botswana, China, India, Kenya, South Korea, Lao PDR, and Sri Lanka, for the years 1965, 1990, 2010, and 2023. The years have been chosen to make a fair air for all countries, excluding pandemic or any kind of crisis years. The countries are either Nepal's close neighbours in the region, or similar features covering East Asia and Sub-Saharan Africa.

Let's start to discuss with per capita gross domestic product (GDP/head), which shows an increase for all countries, including Nepal. The speed seems to low for Kenya and Nepal. An interesting point is that Nepal's per capita GDP (USD333) in 1965 was higher than that of China (USD233) and India (USD329), which by the year 1990 had overtaken Nepal's per capita GDP. Since the year 1990, Nepal's per capita GDP has remained the lowest among countries per capita GDP. The last row of the same table shows how these countries' GDP per capita is recorded in 2023 compared to that of 1965, indicating that Nepal is the lowest performer. The fact is that China, which had the lowest per capita GDP in 1965, increased its per capita GDP in 2023 to 52.3 times that of 1965, whereas Nepal was able to increase by 3.4 times only. Not only China, but also India has achieved remarkable progress, taking this ratio to 6.80 times that of 1965 in 2023. Therefore, the growth perspective for Nepal went wrong; this is the first point.

Then, let's move to two other important indicators measured in per capita (export/head and import/head), shown in the same table. Both figures are important for national welfare issues, as discussed earlier. In these terms, if we look at the 2010 data, Nepal's per capita export is the lowest among the countries, that is less than USD60 annually, while the second lowest is that of Bangladesh with USD148. In terms of import per capita, Nepal's is the second lowest, that is USD218 and USD210 of Bangladesh, the lowest among the selected countries. In 2023, Nepal's per capita exports remained the lowest among the selected countries, but in terms of imports per capita, it is the third lowest. Both in terms of exports and imports per capita, South Korea tops the list, but has more exports compared to imports. Sri Lanka's position remains top in the South Asia region. Nepal's per capita trade is very low, and that is import-dominant rather than export-dominant. This is another point that went wrong for Nepal.

The country that trades more and grows faster seems to be a fact to be established from this table. Nepal trades less and grows slower is a problem. Import-based trade cannot provide the extensive employment that export-based trade does. So, 'Nepal's growth is jobless' is a true statement in one sense, as Nepal's international trade is dominated by the import trade, even though this is very low compared to many other countries, indicating a low level of integration, plus several hindrances in the arena of

Table 1.1 Major indicators of Nepal and few other countries

Year	*Indicators*	*BDS*	*BWA*	*CHN*	*IND*	*KEN*	*KOR*	*LAO*	*NPL*	*SLK*
1965	GDP/head	466.3	480.5	232.6	329	768.3	1274	.	333.2	678.3
	Export/head	14.8	.	.	9.13	195.5	17.08	.	.	.
	Import/head	179.7	.	.	16.7	182	57.66	.	.	.
	Life expec.	46	54	53	46	52	56	42	41	63
	Literacy Rate	.	.	.	.	.	.	.	.	.
1990	GDP/head	473.4	4039	905	538	1329	9367	635	422.7	1389
	Export/head	14.62	2407	.	31.9	204.3	1141	.	.	.
	Import/head	35.58	1454	.	36.1	127.6	1748	.	.	.
	Life expec.	56	60	68	59	58	72	54	55	69
	Literacy Rate	.	.	78	.	.	.	.	.	.
2010	GDP/head	943.7	5585	5647	1235	1340	25456	1565	721.3	2995
	Export/head	148.6	2331	.	263	232.1	9804	434	56.8	.
	Import/head	210.4	2396	.	336	343.1	8662	636	218.5	.
	Life expec.	68	59	76	67	61	80	64	67	74
	Literacy Rate	.	.	95	.	.		.	.	91
2023	GDP/head	1885	7236	12175	2236	1808	34121	2649	1136	3969
	Export/head	294.7	2240	.	483	192.1	15514	.	78.56	890.8
	Import/head	414.3	2550	.	560	385	13324	.	443.1	843.2
	Life expec.	74.67	69.16	77.95	72	63.65	83.43	69	70.35	77.48
	Literacy Rate	.	.	.	77	.	.	.	.	.
GDP/head ratio: 2023/1965		**4.04**	**15.06**	**52.34**	**6.79**	**2.35**	**26.78**	**.**	**3.41**	**5.85**

Source: Author's calculation using the data from World Bank (2025)

Note: BDS = Bangladesh, BWA = Botswana, CHN = China, IND = India, KOR = South Korea, LAO = Lao PDR, NPL = Nepal, and SLK = Sri Lanka. GDP, Export, and Import are in USD, Life expectancy is in years, and literacy rate is in % of the population aged over 15 years and above. The dot (.) represents that the data is not available

international trade. One of the major constraints comes from the geographical condition, landlockedness, which results in expensive imports due to transportation costs and loss the export competitiveness in the international market.

In terms of life expectancy, Nepal's reported progress is remarkable. This was just 41 (the lowest one) years at birth in 1965, it has reached more than 70 years in 2023. The data for 2023 stands in a better position than that of Kenya (52 years in 1965 and 64 years in 2023), Botswana (54 years in 1965 and 69 years in 2023), and Lao PDR (42 years in 1965 and 69 years in 2023). South Korea's and China's progress in this respective area is high.

The data for literacy rate are not reported well in the common source of data for all countries, but Nepal has made satisfactory progress in the literacy rate (Lal, 2025) and the South Asian region needs to focus on more inclusiveness, as discussed in Bhul (2025). In terms of the source of energy, Nepal's consumption pattern has changed from domestic to an imported one dramatically; most of the consumable goods are imported, and our domestic and endogenous types of food items are declining and being replaced by imported ones. Our traditional methods of herb-based medicines are being replaced by imported ones (Basnett et al., 2014). This has also hampered economic growth. Instead of updating the technology to produce endogenous products, we replaced them. Producing our endogenous goods with updated technology would help to grasp the comparative advantages from the global market, but in the wrong way, we replaced them with imported items, which have not been suitable for nature, climate, and health in many respects. This is another point that went wrong in Nepal.

As stated earlier, despite being surrounded by big markets, around 40 percent of the global population, and several favourable situations, Nepal's trade performance is poor. It seems because of the supply side constraints rather than the demand side constraints. Nepal has become unable to do what it has to do to boost trade, which is another point to consider, as it has gone wrong by now. Because of these backgrounds, the youth generation has lost confidence and beliefs in the state and system, which is a challenging situation currently.

1.2 Objectives

The major objectives of this research book are to make a systematic analysis of the key political-economic issues related to the economic development of Nepal from a current macroeconomic perspective and to document suitable policy inferences in the respective areas. To achieve this major objective, chapter-wise specific objectives are set in the respective key Chapters (Chaps. 2, 3, 4, 5, 6, and 7), which are given as below:

1. To analyze the circular nexus of remittances, banks' credit to the private sector, and trade deficit (Chap. 2),
2. To analyze the role of government quality on expert performance, considering the COVID-19 pandemic period in Nepal (Chap. 3),
3. To analyze the role of integrated agriculture and manufacturing sectors for potential high economic growth in the background of jobless slow economic growth, and to highlight the synergy effects from agriculture and manufacturing sectors in the background of economic structural problems of the Nepalese economy (Chap. 4),
4. To analyze the revenue efficiency, examining its determinants in the background of poor revenue collection compared to the target of the government (Chap. 5),
5. To analyze the role of democracy and economic development in the quality of governance, considering the transitional (transition in economic policy, administration, and political system) phase of the country (Chap. 6), and
6. To examine the determinants of export performance from fiscal policy perspective and to analyze the technical efficiency of exports in the situation of poor export performance of Nepal (Chap. 7).

1.3 Major Issues

There are number of major issues of the Nepalese economy at present times, which deserve specific chapters, even a book, such as data management and cyber security issues, climate change and its financing issues, financial literacy issues, energy issues, circular economy issues, many microeconomic issues related to welfare economics, trade and economic diplomacy issues, and many more. However, these are not all possible to cover in a book. Therefore, this research book is written on the most crucial issues of the Nepalese economy at this time, as limited by the title, that is, political economic issues of economic development in a macroeconomic perspective, focusing mostly on the fiscal policy context. In this background, I selected six such issues that are captured in Chaps. 2, 3, 4, 5, 6, and 7 as listed in the organization of this book.

1.4 Research Design

This book employs qualitative and quantitative analytical frameworks for a systematic analysis to achieve the research objectives. In this process, a systematic desk review is conducted following standard procedures of academic research. This review is conducted for the key chapters (Chaps. 2, 3, 4, 5, 6, and 7). Chapter 1 is the introduction of the research book, and the final Chapter is the conclusion of the studies in the book. Doing this has helped to find the research gap and choose the estimation methods for the quantitative analysis.

The quantitative analysis is based on secondary data sets, each designed to be set in the model of each chapter. This book has used both time series and panel data-based quantitative research frameworks relevant to the respective chapters, which contain a separate section for research methodology. A brief overview of each chapter's research methodology is discussed here.

A total of six essays in the form of complete research articles are covered from Chaps. 2, 3, 4, 5, 6, and 7. Chapter 2 employs a proper time series analysis and autoregressive distributed lag (ARDL) approach to cointegration as the econometric method to investigate the determinants of trade deficits. Chapter 3 is based on a panel data framework, and the gravity modelling technique is applied as the econometric method of research to examine the role of governance quality in export performance. Again, a proper time series technique is adopted in Chap. 4 to examine the synergy effect of integrated agriculture and manufacturing sectors in the economic growth of Nepal. The econometrics employed here, based on the test of time series properties, is the ARDL approach to cointegration. Chapter 5 employs stochastic frontier analysis (SFA) in time series data after testing the time series properties of the data to examine the determinants of revenue efficiency and for a technical analysis of the revenue efficiency.

Chapter 6 uses the time series data, and after testing the time series properties, the ARDL approach to cointegration is employed to examine the determinants of governance quality. Finally, Chapter 7 employs the SFA version of the gravity modelling technique in panel data to examine the determinants of export efficiency of Nepal, along with a technical efficiency analysis to estimate the untapped export potential with Nepal's trading partners.

This research book incorporates different econometric approaches as discussed above to make the study more robust and credible findings from the analysis. The different methods of econometric estimation to cover a wide range of fiscal issues are one major strength of this book, in my opinion.

1.5 Roads Ahead

The issue of how Nepal should proceed ahead for the economic development path is clear, that all those wrong ways should be corrected so that the direction would be sensible and the speed of growth can be maintained as expected. In this regard, to come out of slow jobless growth, Nepal should correct the economy's structure, focusing on the agriculture-based manufacturing sector, so that the growth speed can be increased and jobs can be created in the economy. Then, the country would have speedy growth with jobs at hand. This would increase per capita export, per capita import, and per capita GDP simultaneously. But the issue is how we do this. For this purpose, the following roads ahead are presented based on the key findings from the main chapters of this research book.

First, the remittance, the main source of a foreign reserve and household expenditure, to be directed towards more productive sectors and investment so that it would help to reduce the alarming trade deficits. The dominance of import trade turns to be export dominance. Probably, focusing on manufacturing activities based on endogenous products, updating their production technologies is the best way of mobilizing the remittance into investment for cottage, small, and medium-scale industries, as in Chap. 2 of this book.

Second, the governance quality is very critical for enhancing the export performance. The export market (supply side) needs to be reformed well and be disciplined, as the export volume has indicated that it increased during the peak time of COVID-19. Without improving the quality of governance, the exports do not flourish as concluded in Chap. 3.

Third, a synergy effect is to be created by a proper integration of the agriculture and manufacturing sectors for a speedy growth rate in the country. The agriculture sector, as it is now, for consistency and the scattered manufacturing sector, cannot contribute to accelerating economic growth. Here, the synergy from the integration of agriculture and manufacturing is important, and this synergy can be linked to service sectors, such as tourism, financial, health, and education sectors, too, in rural to urban areas. It will also help to upgrade the production technology in the country, as found in Chap. 4 of this book.

Fourth, as of now, revenue collection is not as expected, and the development needs cannot be fulfilled, as the other sources of government income are very limited in the country, at least for a few more years. The heavy requirements of development resources are not possible to manage, unless revenue is increased substantially. Therefore, the revenue base needs to be expanded, and numerous policy shifts related to governance quality are necessary to enhance revenue efficiency (Chap. 5).

Fifth, as the quality of governance is a multifaceted determinant of economic development, this needs to be enhanced throughout the country with priority. Therefore, strengthening the local democracy and civil society participation are major tools to improve the quality of governance. This suggests investing more in building institutions and second-generation reform, with priority in the country (Chap. 6).

Sixth, export efficiency is one of the most crucial issues in this globalization and reform era. To improve export efficiency, all fiscal policy variables must be integrated with the regulatory quality of governments; without enhancing governance quality, fiscal policy instruments have become ineffective. Therefore, a special focus is needed to improve the regulatory quality and, side-by-side, a thorough analysis of the potential market dynamics with the trading partners' income status. Nepal can do better in terms of export performance using the untapped potential from its close neigbhbour, China, and other emerging trade partners, such as Saudi Arabia, Brazil, Israel, Russia, Korea Republic, Poland, Indonesia, etc. Human resources should be provided with an understanding of these needs of trade and growth (Chap. 7).

1.6 Organization of this Book

This research book has a total of eight chapters divided into different sections and subsections covering the relevant contexts. The brief organization of the book is as follows:

1.6.1 Chapter 1: Introduction

Chapter 1 includes the background of the book to support the importance of the book. It covers the strengths and weaknesses of the Nepalese economy from the given perspective, then moves to the objectives, major issues addressed, research design, and structure of the book to get the readers familiar with the contents of the book.

1.6.2 Chapter 2: The Circular Nexus of Remittances, Banks' Credit and Trade Deficits

Chapter 2 is about the analysis of the association of workers' remittances, banks' credit to the private sector, and trade deficit in a set of journal articles format, which includes an introduction, trends and patterns of major variables, and a brief literature review covering remittances, banks' credit, and trade deficits. Then, it moves to the research methodology of the chapter, covering the model, variables, data, data sources, time series properties' tests, and econometrics of the chapter, with a brief conclusion and policy recommendation.

1.6.3 Chapter 3: Governance Quality and Export Performance: A Lesson from COVID-19

This chapter examines the role of governance quality in export performance concerning the COVID-19 pandemic. This is divided into seven sections in a set of academic articles, incorporating background of the study, research methodology, global export scenario during the COVID-19 period, COVID-19 scenario in Nepal, and export scenario pre- and after origin of the COVID-19, making them contextual. Then, conclusions and policy recommendations are presented in the final section.

1.6.4 Chapter 4: Integrated Agriculture and Manufacturing Sectors for Speedy Growth

Chapter 4 examines the synergy impact of the integration of the agriculture and manufacturing sectors on economic growth. It contains a general introduction followed by a literature review and presents some casual observations in the Nepalese context of the relevant economic variables. This further disaggregates the research methodology section, followed by results and discussion, before concluding in the final section.

1.6.5 Chapter 5: Revenue Efficiency in Nepal: The Key Determinants

Chapter 5 also follows a similar structure to Chap. 4, which presents the trends and patterns of revenue. The literature review section is divided into theoretical foundation, empirical foundation, and Nepalese context. The research methodology section is divided into research design, descriptive framework, and quantitative framework. The results are discussed in qualitative analysis and quantitative analysis subsections. The final section concludes with a summary of the chapter and presents some findings in a consolidated form.

1.6.6 Chapter 6: Democracy, Governance Quality, and Economic Development

This chapter is about the role of democracy and economic development on the quality of governance, which incorporates the introduction of the chapter, then highlights some observations about the modern history and economic system of Nepal, discusses the democracy and governance issues together, and presents some discussion about the linkage between per capita GDP, trade openness, and education. In the next section, a brief literature review is presented with an appropriate research gap. The results are presented and discussed with the relevance of the literature, and then the final section presents the summary, conclusions, and policy recommendations.

1.6.7 *Chapter 7: Export Efficiency from the Perspective of Fiscal Policy in Nepal*

Chapter 7 has examined the determinants of export efficiency of Nepal from the perspective of fiscal policy and identified the untapped export potential with the trading partners of Nepal. This chapter is also organized into a set of academic journal articles. The introduction covers the materials to introduce the importance of this chapter, and some export and fiscal policy-related variables' trends and patterns are discussed before moving to the literature review. The research methodology section is divided into model and variables, data and their sources, and econometrics. Then, the results are discussed with economic interpretation, robustness check, and the export efficiency and export potential are described. The final section concludes with major findings and some policy inferences.

1.6.8 *Chapter 8: Conclusions*

The final chapter presents a summary of this book in very brief terms, consolidates the findings from the key chapters of this book, and presents the policy recommendations based on those findings. In the concluding form, this book highlights some limitations of this book itself and discusses the avenues of future research.

The Abstract, Key Words, Journal of Economic Literature (JEL) classification codes, and references are given in the key chapters, as necessary.

References

Adhikari, J., Rai, M. K., Baral, C., & Subedi, M. (2023). Labour migration from Nepal: Trends and explanations. In *Migration in South Asia: IMISCOE regional reader* (pp. 67–81). Springer International Publishing Cham.

Basnett, Y., Henley, G., Howell, J., Jones, H., Lemma, A., & Pandey, P. R. (2014). Structural economic transformation in Nepal. *A diagnostic study submitted to DFID Nepal. Document consulté de,* https://www.odi.org/sites/odi.org.uk/files/odi-assets/publications-opinion-files/9019.pdf.

Bhattacharjee, A., Anadón, J. D., Lohman, D. J., Doleck, T., Lakhankar, T., Shrestha, B. B., Thapa, P., Devkota, D., Tiwari, S., & Jha, A. (2017). The impact of climate change on biodiversity in Nepal: Current knowledge, lacunae, and opportunities. *Climate*, 5(4), 80.

Bhul, B. R. (2025). Inclusive Governance in Nepalese Civil Service: A Comparative Study in South Asia. *PAAN Journal, 31*, 1841–1853.

Chalise, H. N. (2018). Demographic window of opportunity in Nepal. *Nepal Population Journal, 18*(17), 133–140.

Koirala, J. (2025). Gen Z Protests and Role of Social Media in Nepal (September 8–10, 2025).

Lal, S. (2025). Nepal's National Education Policy: Challenges, Progress and Future Directions. *Political Science Journal, 3*(1), 95–107.

National Planning Commission. (2024). The Sixteenth Plan (Fiscal Year 2024/25–2028/29). In: National Planning Commission, Government of Nepal, Singha Durbar, Kathmandu, Nepal.

Navaneetham, K., & Dharmalingam, A. (2012). A review of age structural transition and demographic dividend in South Asia: Opportunities and challenges. *Journal of Population Ageing, 5*, 281–298.

Nepal Rastra Bank. (2025). *Current Macroeconomic and Financial Situation of Nepal Based on One Month Data (Ending Mid August).* Nepal Rastra Bank, Kathmandu, Nepal: https://www.nrb.org.np/contents/uploads/2025/09/Current-Macroeconomic-and-Financial-Situation-English-Based-on-One-Month-data-of-2025.26-2.pdf

O'Neill, A. (2025). *Youth unemployment rate in Nepal 1991–2024*, https://www.statista.com/statistics/812273/youth-unemployment-rate-in-nepal/, Issue. Statista.

Paudel, P. K., Bhattarai, B. P., & Kindlmann, P. (2011). An overview of the biodiversity in Nepal. *Himalayan biodiversity in the changing world*, 1–40. Springer

Paudel, R. C. (2013). *Growth and export performance of developing countries: is landlockedness destiny?* Australian National University, Canberra, Australia].

Paudel, R. C. (2019). Exports Performance of Nepal: What Can Be Done? *Applied Economics and Finance, 6*(5), 92–103.

Paudel, R. C. (2020). The Role of Financial Development in Economic Growth of Nepal: ARDL Approach of Cointegration with Structural Break Analysis. *Journal of Economics and Business, 3*(4), 1372–1386.

Snellinger, A. (2007). Student movements in Nepal: their parameters and their idealized forms. *Contentious politics and democratization in Nepal*, 273–295. Sage

Tamang, M. S. (2001). Democracy and cultural diversity in Nepal. *HIMALAYA, the Journal of the Association for Nepal and Himalayan Studies, 21*(1), 12.

Waseerman, P. (2024). World Population by Religion: A Global Tapestry of Faith. *Population Education*, https://populationeducation.org/world-population-by-religion-a-global-tapestry-of-faith/ (access 16/06/2025).

World Bank. (2025). World Development Indicators. https://data.worldbank.org/ *(accessed 25 January 2025)*.
Worldometers.info. (2025). *Worlometer*
Yamanaka, K. (2000). Nepalese labour migration to Japan: from global warriors to global workers. *Ethnic and racial studies*, *23*(1), 62–93.

CHAPTER 2

The Circular Nexus of Remittances, Banks' Credit, and Trade Deficits

2.1 Introduction

In Chap. 1, I discussed and identified the major macroeconomic issues, one of which is the role of remittance, banking credit to the private sector, and trade deficit, which seems to be an issue to investigate and analyze for better policy recommendations, as the alarming trade deficit is one of the major concerns of Nepal at this time. Poor trade performance has been an issue to focus on as a major step in economic development. As discussed in Chap. 1, the trade history of Nepal for the last six decades shows that trade deficit is our tradition, and it is increasing every year, with some exceptions, as can be seen from the data from Nepal Rastra Bank (2025a). Therefore, the poor trade performance of Nepal has become one of the major macroeconomic issues in this era of globalization.

On the other hand, increased remittance has contributed to substantially increasing the banking sector's credit to the private sector, encouraging consumerism rather than production, resulting in more trade deficits every year. These trends have caused heavy pressure from time to time on the foreign currency reserve, which has forced the central bank of Nepal (Nepal Rastra Bank) to impose restrictive measures on imports in recent months (Nepal Rastra Bank, 2022).

Since the restoration of democracy in 1989/1990, the number of out-migrant workers from Nepal has increased gradually, following the trend of many developing countries. In addition, this out-migration trend

R. C. Paudel, *Essays on Key Issues of Development in Nepal*,
https://doi.org/10.1007/978-981-95-7715-6_2

increased substantially since 2001 because of the city-focused armed struggle by the Nepal Communist Party (Maoist), resulting in increasing remittance, which reached around 30 percent of Nepal's GDP. Many research works have found a positive impact in enhancing economic growth and uplifting the living standard of people from different countries' perspectives (Hasan et al., 2019). Yet, the channel of the contribution of remittance to economic growth is a topic of much interest. It has various dimensions for doing so. First, increasing consumption improves the quality of human resources of the country, so that a substantial contribution to the economy is possible. Second, if the remittances are utilized properly and linked with entrepreneurship, they can help to increase export trade and generate employment, from which an increment in national output is possible.

On the role of remittance, Sapkota (2013) stated that remittances have caused a kind of Dutch Disease in Nepal. In the same year, Bhatta (2013) stated that remittances have a strong long-run relationship with the trade deficit. It seems that the scenario is getting worse in recent years as both of these variables (remittances and trade deficits) are increasing substantially since then, as shown by the data, that is trade deficit is almost 28 percent of Nepal's gross domestic product (GDP) as of the fiscal year 2019/2020, which was about 21 percent in 2010/2011. Paudel et al. (2020) stated that remittances have a strong negative impact on export performance. This means that remittances are fueling import promotion and export distortion, which may be the reason for the alarming trade deficit. A huge flow of remittances can lead to the appreciation of a country's exchange rate and hurt its competitiveness on one hand, and on the other hand, it will boost the imports, which is an adverse economic phenomenon known as the Dutch disease.

Even, the financial development has hurt export performance that led to the trade deficits (Paudel and Alharthi, 2021). Against this crucial background of the remittances, the inflows into Nepal have reached more than 25 percent of the country's GDP consistently in the years 2013 to 2016 and have reached around 28 percent in recent years (World Bank, 2025), while the trade deficits have recorded the apex numbers in recent years (Nepal Rastra Bank, 2025a).

On the other side, Nepal's banking sector has faced liquidity problems from time to time and vice versa making the financial situation very vulnerable. This scenario pushes toward the scarcity or insufficiency of loanable funds to the private sector, which lacks sufficient capital required for manufacturing activities, which require longer-term financing strategies. So, banks' role in managing credit financing may also be responsible somehow for alarming trade deficits. A long time back, Timsina (2014) investigated the relationship of bank credit to the private sector and economic growth and concluded that there is a positive relationship. Paudel and Acharya (2020) have concluded in almost similar way while analysing the role of financial development in the economic growth of Nepal. However, these papers also do not discuss from which channel this relationship exists. One such channel might be from credit to the productive private sector, such as manufacturing will boost exports to economic growth.

Therefore, still in the Nepalese context, the doubt of whether these variables (remittance and banking sectors' credit to the private sector) play any role in improving the export performance of Nepal and thereby minimizing the trade deficits remains unsolved. This chapter aims to remove this doubt, clarifying the circular nexus of remittance, banks' credit to the private sector, and trade deficits.

For this purpose, this chapter documents the relevant macroeconomic variables trends and patterns to show how these variables have emerged and moved over time. Then, the role of selected variables in trade deficits has been investigated using annual data from Nepal from 1996 to 2023, employing the time-series technique. The main finding from this chapter suggests that Nepal should move away from the remittance-based economy to boost export performance or should make provisions to utilize the remittances towards saving and investment to boost the manufacturing sector. Also, the lending agencies, including the commercial banks and finance, should prioritize the manufacturing sectors for financing their needs to increase the output, and via which the export performance can be improved. Doing so will only help to reduce the alarming trade deficits. The main concern of the economy is how to mobilize the remittances towards more productive sectors. For this purpose, banks' credit also should be responsible for directing the financial packages to fulfill the requirements of manufacturing sectors so that this triangular nexus (remittances to banks' credit, banks' credit to trade deficits, trade deficits to outflow migrations and then to remittances) can be built for the export promotion soon.

The following section of this chapter presents brief trends of trade deficits, remittances, and banking credit to the private sector following a review literature in Sects. 2.2 and 2.3. Section 2.4 presents the research methodology of this chapter. Section 2.5 discusses the results of the empirical study, and the final section concludes.

2.2 Major Relevant Variables: Trends and Patterns

2.2.1 Trends

Remittance, Banking Credit, and Trade Deficits

Figure 2.1 illustrates the trends of remittances, banking credit to the private sector, and trade deficits in Nepal from 1996 to 2023, all measured as percentages of GDP. Looking at the trends of remittances, banking credit to the private sector, and trade deficits, all these three variables have upward trends. The remittances have experienced a sharp incline since 2001. Starting at around two percent of GDP in 2001, remittances rose significantly to about 11% within a year. This rapid increase is linked to the political turmoil in Nepal, which led to a substantial outflow of youth from the country in search of better opportunities abroad. The upward trend continued with some fluctuations, reaching approximately 28 percent in 2015 and maintaining a high level since then.

In the case of the banking sector's credit to the private sector, the most notable increase occurred between 2008 and 2011, coinciding with the global financial crisis, which had a massive negative impact on several countries. This period saw the most substantial hump in the graph, indicating a significant rise in banking credit. This variable has increased much more quickly than the remittances and trade deficits and remains always higher than the other two variables in the graph throughout the period except for the initial two years. This variable has a record high in 2021 with a value of 103.5 percent of GDP.

The trade deficit trend reveals more ups and downs compared to remittances. There was a gradual decline up to the first half-decade of the millennium and then recorded the highest, that is 34.6 percent, in the year 2021 then had a bit of decline in 2022 and 2023. The overall trends suggest that remittances and banking credit to the private sector have both increased over the selected period, while trade deficits have shown significant fluctuations. The increase in remittances and banking credit suggests an influx of financial resources into the country, but the persistent and rising trade deficits highlight an ongoing challenge in balancing trade,

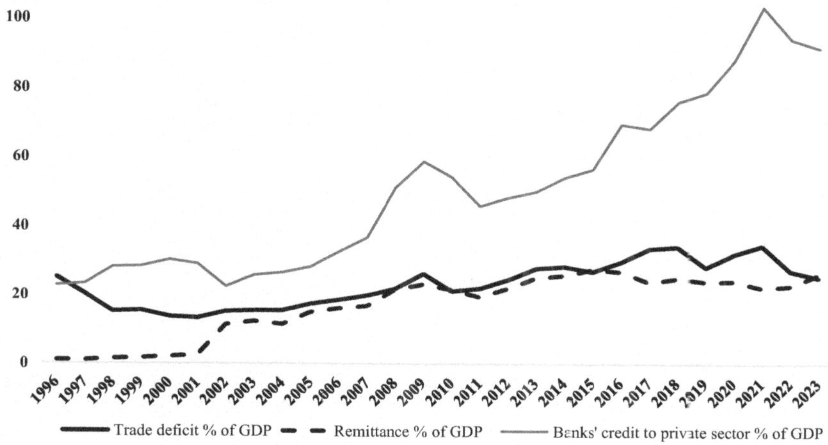

Fig. 2.1 Remittances, banking credit to the private sector, and trade deficits. (Source: World Bank (2025) for remittance and Banking credit to the private sector, and Nepal Rastra Bank (2025a) for the Trade deficits)

potentially exacerbated by these financial trends. This indicates that there is a circular nexus among remittance, banking credits to the private sectors, and trade deficits in Nepal.

Import, Export, and Remittances

Figure 2.2 shows the imports, exports, and remittances measured as a percent of GDP for the period from 1996 to 2023, which shows that Nepal's imports have been higher than exports even since earlier than 1965, and the gap has widened since 2001, when remittances increased sharply. Exports increased slightly up to 1999, then gradually declined with minor fluctuations. Overall, the export's share went just 5.1 percent in 2021 and showed a bit upward trend. The fluctuations in imports are more visible than exports. Interestingly, with some exceptions, the trend of imports follows the trend of remittances. Remittances have increased sharply since 2001, with visible fluctuation, maintaining an overall increasing trend. In the case of imports, it is almost the same level as in 1996, and the exports overall trend is declining, indicating that the imports are fuelled by remittance in the later decades. Understanding these dynamics

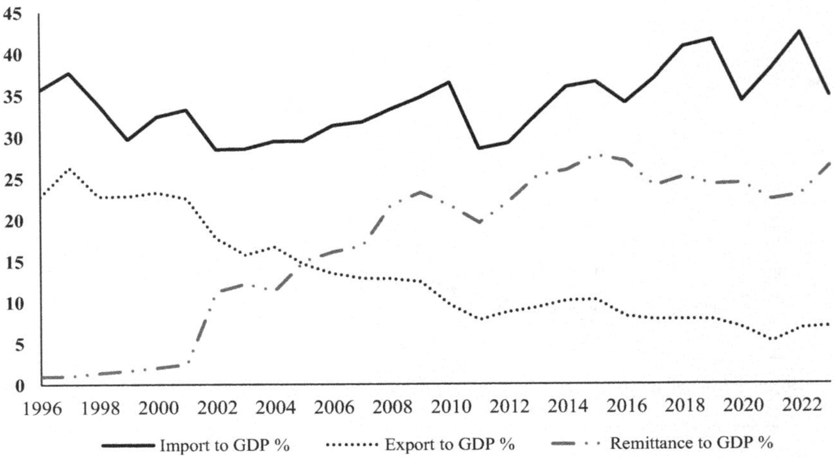

Fig. 2.2 Import, export, and remittances. (Source: World Bank (2025))

is crucial for policymakers and stakeholders aiming to address the trade deficit and improve economic stability in the country.

Figure 2.3 shows the trends of interest rates, inflation, and foreign aid. These three macroeconomic variables directly impact, as discussed in the literature, the international trade environment; either favourable to imports or exports. If these are more favourable to import, then the trade deficits increase. Interest rates and inflation were recorded at about eight percent in 1996 and until 2002, they seem to move in the opposite direction. Then, it seems inflation-induced interest rates rise and they move in the same direction but at different speeds. Again, since 2018, they seem diverging in the opposite direction indicating that a declining interest rate caused inflation as in the literature. As of 2020, the interest rate is recorded just above two percent and the inflation is around four percent. The peak of inflation was in 2008 with a record high above 12.5 percent, while the peaks of the interest rate were in 1998 and 2010 with 11.4 and 12.6 percent. The same figure shows the foreign aid, which was just above two percent in 1996, then gradually increased to above three percent in 2009, the peak time of political transition, and then gradually declined to below half a percent of GDP in 2023. For the overall period, it has a negative trend.

Fig. 2.3 Interest rate, inflation, and foreign aid. (Source: Nepal Rastra Bank (2025a) and Nepal Rastra Bank (2025b))

2.2.2 *Patterns of Banking Credit to the Private Sector*

Banking credit to the private sector measures loanable funds and is one of the major variables in development and financial economics. Lenders and policymakers aim for growth in the productive sector. Credit provided in the unproductive sectors weakens the economy, indicating a kind of misallocation of loanable funds in the banking system. Table 2.1 shows the percentage distribution of banking credit to the private sector in different economic sectors. Manufacturing and other productive sectors are assumed to contribute more to employment and national output. The general assumption is that the manufacturing and other productive sectors would contribute more to generating employment and increasing the national output on a much larger scale.

As seen in the table, all economic sectors are classified into 13 sectors (note: not classified as in the government account). Among them, others refer to the combination of small sectors, meaning the rest of all these 12 sectors listed in the rows above. In the individual sector, the largest sector of financing seems to be wholesalers and retailers, which hold more than 20 percent of total bank credit to the private sector, which has always remained above 20 percent and reached around 22 percent for a few years.

The second-largest sector in this context seems to be the production sector, which has around 20 percent in a few years and then declined to

Table 2.1 Sector-wise distribution of banking credit to the private sector (%)

Sectors	*2011/2012*	*2012/2013*	*2013/2014*	*2014/2015*	*2015/2016*	*2016/2017*	*2017/2018*	*2018/2019*	*2019/2020*	*2020/2021*
1. Agriculture	3.6	4.2	4.5	4.8	4.7	4.5	5.6	6.6	6.9	7.8
2. Mines	0.3	0.4	0.3	0.3	0.2	0.2	0.2	0.3	0.2	0.2
3. Productions	19.8	19.9	19.6	18.8	17.6	16.6	16.4	16.4	16.3	15.4
4. Construction	10.4	10.1	10.5	11.2	10.9	10.7	10.4	10.6	10.6	9.9
5. Metal Productions, Machinary, and Electrical Tools and fitting	1.4	1.4	1.2	1.2	1.2	1.3	1.4	1.3	1.4	1.5
6 Transportation Equipment Production & Fitting	2.2	1.9	2.0	1.7	1.8	1.7	1.5	1.5	1.5	1.3
7 Transportation, Communications & Public Services	4.6	4.6	4.2	4.4	5.0	5.3	5.5	6.1	6.4	6.1
8 Wholesaler & Retailers	20.4	20.8	21.6	21.8	22.3	21.9	22.0	21.1	20.3	20.1
9 Finance, Insurance & Fixed Assets	10.1	8.9	8.0	7.9	8.0	8.3	8.4	8.0	7.7	8.1

10 Service Industries	7.6	7.5	7.7	7.9	7.5	7.9	8.1	8.4	9.2	8.7
11 Consumable Loan	4.4	4.7	4.6	4.3	3.9	4.3	3.6	3.1	2.8	3.7
12 Local Government	0.2	0.1	0.1	0.1	0.1	0.1	0.1	0.1	0.0	0.0
13 Others	14.9	15.7	15.6	15.6	16.9	17.3	16.8	16.5	16.5	17.4
Total (1 to 13)	100	100	100	100	100	100	100	100	100	100

Source: Author's calculation from the data by Confederation of Banking and Financial Institutions (CBFIN), unpublished data, adopted from Paudel (2022)

around 15 percent in the fiscal year 2020/2021 from around 20 percent in the fiscal year 2011/2012. This sector has a significant reduction in its share in total bank credit.

The construction sector stands as the third largest sector, with about 10 percent of bank credit, and it reached its peak time in 2014/2015, then began to decline gradually. The fourth sector is service industries, and its share is increasing over the period, as of 2020/2021, it is recorded at around nine percent in the later years.

The agricultural sector's share has increased to more than twofold, which was just 3.6 percent in 2011/2012, and it has increased to 7.8 percent in 2020/2021. Also, it has gradually increased in every fiscal year except in 2015/2016 and 2016/2017. Transportation, communication, and public services have been increasing impressively to reach above six percent in 2020/2021.

Other sectors worth noting, including financial intermediaries, have maintained a relatively stable share of around 10 percent, reflecting the sector's crucial role in the economic framework. The consumable loan has declined but hovers around four percent of GDP.

Overall, the distribution of banking credit reveals the dynamic nature of economic development and the shifting priorities in terms of sectoral growth slightly but largely this has not gone to the productive sector. Mostly, the credit seems to be distributed to boost imports rather than promoting exports as most of them are focused on increasing consumption rather than on production. Therefore, policymakers and financial institutions, including other relevant stakeholders, must continuously adapt to these changes to ensure the optimal allocation of resources and support sustainable economic progress.

2.3 Literature Review

Several studies have focused on different dimensions of remittance but have not directly investigated the role of remittances and banks' credit to the private sector on trade deficits in the context of Nepal. The literature suggests two important points in the association of remittances and international trade based on different methodologies, countries' cases, and qualitative analyses. One string of literature suggests it boosts imports and results in trade deficits. Another string of literature shows the negative association between remittances and export performance linking the literature with the Dutch Disease story as found by Sapkota (2013) and Paudel and Bhusal (2021) in the Nepalese context.

2.3.1 *Remittances and Export Performance*

The role of remittances in promoting export performance is not the same in country-to-country and region-to-region contexts and cases. For example, León-Ledesma and Piracha (2004) empirically analyze the impact of remittances, estimating the productivity equation in a panel data set of 11 transition countries from 1990 to 1999, and find that the remittances have a positive impact on productivity and employment both directly and indirectly through their effect on investment, which can be helpful to boost exports.

Kandil and Mirzaie (2008) found contradictory results on the role of remittances on export performance, for example, a positive contribution of remittances in export growth in the case of Tunisia, but a negative impact in other countries, such as Jordan and Egypt. Another study by Bayangos and Jansen (2011) examined the impact of remittance on export competitiveness and performance using the data from the Philippines and found a negative impact on export performance.

In a study in the context of Bangladesh, Chowdhury and Rabbi (2014) analyzed the impact of workers' remittance and suggested that the remittance inflows caused to loss the export competitiveness in line with the story of Dutch disease, similar to the doubts of the Nepalese context raised by Sapkota (2013) and Paudel and Bhusal (2021).

Shamim et al. (2015) found a negative effect of remittances on export performance in the long run in the case of Pakistan. Recently, Jena and Sethi (2019), using the annual data for South Asian countries from 1993 to 2017, suggested that remittance inflows are affecting export performance negatively during the study period in the region. Hien et al. (2020) found support for the Dutch Disease story in a panel of 32 countries covering the period from 2006 to 2016. The main reason is that it hurts exports, making them uncompetitive.

Recently, Pacheco et al. (2024), using a panel data set for Portuguese trade with 187 countries from 2008 to 2017, investigated the role of remittance remittances on international trade, both import and export. This study found a significant impact of remittances on bilateral trade both in terms of exports and imports.

2.3.2 Remittances, Import Boost, Banks' Credit, and Trade Deficits

A few research works have shown the positive impact of remittances on economic growth, largely via imports and foreign currency earnings. Okodua and Olayiwola (2013) studied the impact of the remittance on trade balance using the panel data from Sub-Saharan Africa and found that remittance has a negative impact on trade balances (increases trade deficits) but the results are not statistically significant. Bhatta (2013) stated that remittances have a strong long-run relationship with the trade deficit, boosting imports and deterring exports. This study employed a vector error correction model (VECM) using Nepal's monthly data for the period of 2001 August to 2011 May.

stated that remittances increase purchasing power within the receiving economy, which promotes domestic demand and preferences here may be in favour of imported goods and services based on those amount of remittances. This situation often results in the increment of trade deficits. Similarly suggested that government should adopt appropriate policy actions to reduce imports while drawing remittances in the country in the case of the Fiji Islands. found a strong positive impact of remittances on imports in the context of Vietnam.

Ahmed et al. (2014) noted that remittances boost purchasing power, which increases domestic demand and often leads to higher imports and trade deficits. Similarly, Makun (2018) recommended policies to reduce imports while attracting remittances in Fiji. Minh (2020) observed a strong positive impact of remittances on imports in Vietnam. Farzanegan and Hassan (2020) found that the remittance inflows have caused trade deficits in the Middle Eastern and North African (MENA) region. Regmi (2022) found that remittances have a significant negative impact on trade balances, though it has a positive impact on trade openness, and hence import increases faster than exports, resulting in a trade deficit.

Overall, a brief literature review provides an insightful impression in the role of remittance on trade deficits either we take a note from the Dutch Disease story by hurting the export performance or boosting imports in the country. Also, there are many concerns about the growing trade deficits despite the increase in remittances and banks' credit to the private sector. Paudel (2022) analysed the determinants of trade deficits in Nepal considering the role of remittances and banks' credit to the private sector covering the data until 2019. A clear research gap is that the role of remittances and banks' credit in rocketing trade deficits in the country for the recent period has not been investigated by employing the advanced econometric technique. Our approach will be different from that of Bhatta (2013) in three aspects: first, the data coverage will be longer when the various dynamics than in the past have been seen in this nexus, for example, the COVID-19 lag effect. Second, our methodology differs broadly from a macroeconomic perspective, employing annual rather than quarterly data. Third, we look at the cointegration order of the variables by analyzing the time-series properties of the data. This chapter is an updated version of Paudel (2022) in terms of data and methodology. The data are updated in this chapter to identify the impact of COVID-19 covering the data up to 2023, and the time series properties of the data are analyzed using structural break analysis and incorporating the role of governance in the story. Therefore, this chapter has a strong research agenda to justify the need for research explaining the circular nexus of remittance, banks' credit to the private sector, and trade deficits.

2.4 Research Methodology

The major objective of this chapter is to measure the impact of remittance inflows and bank credit to the private sector on trade deficits analyzing the circular nexus among these variables. In the modern economy of the least developed or developing countries, remittances have become one of the major sources of income, but it has a long-run opportunity cost in the economy. On the other hand, the bank credit to the private sector can contribute to running production activities in the country to help improve export performance via which to reduce the trade deficits.

To do so, this chapter employs annual data for the period from 1996 to 2023 as some of the crucial variables can go back only up to 1996. As the covered period is 28 years, time-series data may have different orders of cointegration. Considering this fact, the time series properties are analyzed by testing the structural break employing Gregory and Hensen (1996) test and stationarity of the data. Then, standard modeling techniques for the time-series data are applied. The estimations are conducted employing alternative specifications of the model so that the findings are robust. There are several methods for unit root tests with and without structural breaks. Even for the structural break test, there are several methods. The Chow Test is appropriate for identifying a known structural break within a linear regression model. In contrast, the Zivot-Andrews

Test is designed to detect an unknown breakpoint in the mean of a time series, making it useful when the exact timing of a suspected break is uncertain. For multiple unknown breaks in the mean of a time series, the Bai-Perron Test is more suitable as it can determine both the number and the locations of these breaks. However, these three methods do not apply to our issue as they are inadequate when the breakpoint is unknown or when there is a doubt of multiple breakpoints. Therefore, I employ the Gregory and Hansen (1996) test in this chapter. This test examines a break in the cointegrating relationship between two or more time series and is particularly beneficial for analyzing long-term relationships between variables.

2.4.1 Model, Variables, and Data

This chapter employs an econometric model largely influenced by Okodua and Olayiwola (2013), Hien (2017), and Farzanegan and Hassan (2020). Here, the main concern is whether remittances and bank credit to the private sector have fueled to trade balance deficit, and if yes we are interested to know their elasticities. For this purpose, a simple model is developed as in Equation (2.1).

$$LTDEF_t = \beta_0 + \beta_1 LREM_t + \beta_2 LGDPPCG_t + \beta_3 INFL_t + \beta_4 INTR_t + \in_t \quad (2.1)$$

where L represents the natural logarithm of the variables. The TDEF (trade deficit) is the dependent variable, REM (remittances) is the main variable of interest in this paper, GDPPC is per capita GDP, and INFL (inflation) and INTR (interest rate) are other controlled variables. All the variables related to the amounts are measured in the United States Dollar (USD) and then converted to a natural logarithm scale. Here, INFL and INTR are measured in their annual rate percent. The first variable of the right-hand side (β_0) is constant, $\beta_1 - \beta_4$ are coefficients of the independent variables to show the elasticities, t is the year, and the last term ($\in_t$)is the error term.

Based on the literature, we expect β_1 to be both positive and negative. In the case of positive, we mean that remittances have caused to import more leading to trade deficits and vice versa. These expectations are based on literature, such as Stiglitz and Charlton (2006). The variable GDPPC is used as the proxy of infrastructure quality and capital stock that would contribute to improving the trade balance motivating the export factors. Therefore, we expect β_2 to be negative. Inflation (INFL) causes a decline in the consumer's purchasing capacity, lowering the import and reducing the trade deficits. It supports the coefficient of β_3 to be negative. The value for β_4 is can be both positive and negative the higher interest rate decreases consumption at the household level to reduce import and trade balance, on the other hand, the higher interest rate demoralizes the investment causing to decline in export and increasing trade deficits.

We want to know the impact of banks' credit to the private sector in trade deficits, so a variable of interest BCPS (bank credit to the private sector) is added and REM is replaced in Eqn. (2.2). The coefficient for β_1 is expected to be negative as the bank credit to the private sector could help to develop entrepreneurship and economic activities in the economy. Equation (2.3) is just an alternative specification to know the robustness of our model.

$$LTDEF_t = \beta_0 + \beta_1 LBCPS_t + \beta_2 INFL_t + \beta_3 INTR_t + \in_t \quad (2.2)$$

$$LTDEF_t = \beta_0 + \beta_1 LREM_t + \beta_2 LGDPPC_t + \beta_3 INFL_t + \in_t \quad (2.3)$$

Then, as we doubt that there is a circular relationship between trade deficits, banks' credit to the private sector, and remittance, we want to test the impact of remittances on Banks' credit to the private sector. Therefore, the Eqns (2.4), (2.5), and (2.6) are developed and tested in this chapter. The dependent variable is the natural log of banks' credit to the private sector and the independent variables are as explained earlier, and the expected sign for INFL and INTR on these occasions are negative.

$$LBCPS_t = \beta_0 + \beta_1 LREM_t + \beta_2 INFL_t + \beta_3 INTR_t + \in_t \quad (2.4)$$

$$LBCPS_t = \beta_0 + \beta_1 LREM_t + \beta_2 INTR_t + \in_t \quad (2.5)$$

$$LBCPS_t = \beta_0 + \beta_1 LREM_t + \beta_2 INFL_t + \in_t \quad (2.6)$$

2.4.2 Data Sources

The data used in this empirical analysis are collected from the world development indicators as given in World Bank (2025) except interest rate from Nepal Rastra Bank (2025).

2.4.3 *Structural Break Analysis*

As explained earlier, the best suited method for structural break in this chapter seems to be the Gregory-Hansen test, which is specifically designed for cointegrated time series and used for the model as discussed in Gregory and Hansen (1996) test.

Here, null hypothesis, H0: no-cointegration at the breakpoint
Alternate hypothesis, H1: there is cointegration at the breakpoint

Table 2.2 shows the results of a structural break using Gregory-Hansen method, which shows that no structural break/s are detected for Eqns. (2.1), (2.2), (2.3), (2.4), (2.5), and (2.6) by all methods at the significance level of five percent. These values are calculated by choosing the lags based on the Bayesian Information Criterion (BIC). As the breaks are not detected, we need to test the unit root for the variables to detect whether I(0) or I(1). Identifying the variables' integration order will help us to choose the cointegration method.

2.4.4 *Unit Root Tests*

As the breaks are not detected in the structural break test, our next step is to test the stationarity of the series. For this purpose, we conduct unit root tests using the Dickey-Fuller test (DF), augmented Dickey-Fuller (ADF) test, and Phillips and Perron (PP). Test results are achieved, assuming the presence of a unit root (non-stationary variable) in the null hypothesis (H0) and no unit root (stationary variable) in the alternative hypothesis (Ha). In this process, a decision is made based on the calculated statistic and McKinnon's critical value; that is, if the calculated statistic is higher than McKinnon's critical value, then H0 is not rejected, and considered the variable is non-stationary (has a unit root). To make the test systematic and reliable, we observed in the level form and then in the first difference, including the intercept and time trend, because this is the most flexible specification of the test, as illustrated in Eqn. (2.7).

$$\Delta Z_t = \alpha_1 + \alpha_{2t} + \gamma Z_{t-1} + \sum_{j=1}^{k} \beta_j \Delta Z_{t-j} + \varepsilon_t \tag{2.7}$$

Table 2.2 Structural break analysis, Gregory-Hansen Cointegration test

	ADF		Z_t		Z_a	
	Statistics	*Break Year*	*Statistics*	*Break Year*	*Statistics*	*Break Year*
Equation (2.1)						
Intercept shift	−5.03	2002	−4.53	2003	−24.58	2003
Intercept shift with a trend	−5.01	2002	−4.76	1999	−25.71	1999
Intercept shift with slope	−6.36	2001	−6.35	2001	−35.11	2001
Equation (2.2)						
Intercept shift	−5.06	2002	−4.56	2003	−24.97	2003
Intercept shift with a trend	−5.22	2002	−4.65	2003	−24.96	2003
Intercept shift with slope	NA	NA	NA	NA	NA	NA
Equation (2.3)						
Intercept shift	−4.56	2009	−4.65	2009	−24.38	2009
Intercept shift with a trend	−4.90	2009	−4.99	2009	−26.09	2009
Intercept shift with slope	−5.09	2001	−5.19	2001	−28.34	2001
Equation (2.4)						
Intercept shift	−4.74	2010	−4.79	2009	−22.13	2009
Intercept shift with a trend	−4.49	2006	−4.57	2006	−24.43	2006
Intercept shift with slope	−5.04	2001	−5.13	2001	−27.92	2001
Equation (2.5)						
Intercept shift	−4.95	2010	−4.64	2010	−22.15	2010
Intercept shift with a trend	−5.18	2006	−5.28	2006	−28.19	2006
Intercept shift with slope	−5.04	2010	−4.97	2000	−26.89	2000
Equation (2.6)						
Intercept shift	−4.74	2010	−4.19	2010	−21.13	2010
Intercept shift with a trend	−4.35	2005	−4.03	2006	−22.49	2006

(*continued*)

Table 2.2 (continued)

	ADF		Z_t		Z_a	
	Statistics	*Break Year*	*Statistics*	*Break Year*	*Statistics*	*Break Year*
Intercept shift with slope	−4.54	2017	−4.36	2010	−21.84	2010

Note: (1) **indicates the variables are significant at 5 % significance level. NA refers the figures are not available

(2) The results detect no structural breaks as indicated by *ADF* and *Zt* results at 5% significance level as none of the variables are significant at this table

where, Δ is the first difference operator, Z is the variable of interest, α_1 is the intercept, *t* is the period, ΔZ is the augmented terms, *k* is the appropriate lag length of the augmented terms and ε is the white noise error term, β_j is the coefficient of the variable of interest in j^{th} lag. The ADF test is essentially the test of the significance of the coefficient γ in the above equation. The DF test is performed without the augmented term. To select the lag length *k*, we start with a maximum lag of 1 considering a relatively small sample of observations and pare it down to the appropriate lag by examining the Schwarz Information Criterion (SIC) following standard procedures.

Table 2.3 presents the unit root test results of all six variables for which DF, ADF, and PP tests were conducted with 1 lag selected from the lag selection criteria. The results of the unit root tests show that three variables, namely, LTDEF, LBCPS, and LGDPPC are stationary at the first difference indicating these variables as I(1). The rest of the variables are recognized as I(0) as they have cointegrated at the level. Therefore, it is concluded that the set of variables is mixed with I(0) and I(1) order of integration.

2.4.5 Correlation Among the Variables

Table 2.4 presents the correlations among the variables, which shows that remittance (LREM), banks' credit to the private sector (LBCPS), and trade deficits (LTDEF) have a strong positive relationships among them. Also, per capita GDP (LGDPPC) has a strong positive relationship with trade deficits (TDEF). Also, LBCPS and LREM have a strong positive

Table 2.3 Unit root test results of the variables

Tests at level						
	Test with constant			*Test with constant & trend*		
Variable	DF	ADF	PP	DF	ADF	PP
LTDEF	−1.51	−0.47	−0.44	−2.05	−2.14	−2.14
LREM	0.75	21.35***	−3.14**	2.95*	−12.83***	−0.76
LBCPS	−0.35	−0.32	−0.36	−1.68	−1.65	−1.94
INFL	−3.46***	−3.66**	−3.66**	−3.66**	−3.63**	−3.64**
LGDPPC	−0.02	−0.23	−0.25	−1.76	−1.76	−1.76
INTR	−2.58**	−3.98***	−3.98***	−3.28**	−3.83**	−3.83**
Critical value @ 5%	**−1.950**	**−2.943**	**−2.943**	**−3.190**	**−3.536**	**−3.537**
Tests at first difference						
	Test with constant			*Test with constant & trend*		
	DF	ADF	PP	DF	ADF	PP
LTDEF	−1.14	−4.85***	−4.83***	−4.85***	−3.85**	−4.63***
LBCPS	−3.81***	−3.79***	−3.79***	−3.87***	−3.68**	−3.68**
LGDPPC	−4.14***	−4.09***	−4.04**	−4.16***	−3.98**	−3.93**
Critical value @ 5%	**−1.95**	**−2.94**	**−2.94**	**−3.19**	**−3.548**	**−3.540**

Note: *, ** and *** indicate the values are significant at 10%, 5% and 1% level of significance

Table 2.4 Correlation matrix

	LTDEF	*LREM*	*LBCPS*	*INFL*	*LGDPPC*	*INTR*
LTDEF	1					
LREM	0.93	1				
LBCPS	0.98	0.91	1			
INFL	0.14	0.12	0.13	1		
LGPPC	0.99	0.92	0.99	0.12	1	
INTR	−0.09	−0.22	−0.07	0.01	−0.13	1

Source: Author's calculation

relationship. These figures indicate that there is a strong relationship between remittance, banking credit to the private sector, and trade deficits, meaning that remittance has contributed to an increase in BCPS, and also BCPS has caused to increase in remittance and trade deficits. Therefore, the relationship seems to be a circular in nature.

2.4.6 Econometrics

Now as the standard procedure, the next step is to conduct the cointegration tests. As the variables are of a different order of integration, that is, the set of I(0) and I(1) variables in the model, we conduct the empirical tests using the autoregressive distributed lag (ARDL) approach of cointegration. The reasons for using ARDL in our data situation are widely discussed in the literature (Paudel and Jayanthakumaran, 2009; Pesaran et al., 2001). For this purpose, the benchmark model as stated in Eqn. (2.1) will be modified as in Eqn. (2.7) to represent the ARDL version of the specification.

$$\begin{aligned}\Delta LTDEF_t = {} & \alpha + \beta_1\, LTDEF_{t-1} + \beta_2 LREM_{t-1} + \beta_3 LGDPPC_{t-1} \\ & + \beta_4 INFL_{t-1} + \beta_5 INTR_{t-1} + \sum_{i=1}^{28} \gamma_i \Delta LTDEF_{t-i} \\ & + \sum_{i=1}^{28} \delta_i \Delta LREM_{t-i} + \sum_{i=1}^{28} \varphi_i \Delta \mathrm{L}GDPPCG_{t-i} \\ & + \sum_{i=1}^{28} \lambda_i \Delta INFL_{t-i} + \sum_{i=1}^{28} \theta_i \Delta INTR_{t-i} + v_t\end{aligned} \tag{2.7}$$

Here, Eqn. (2.7) captures the dynamic impact in the form of the Auto-Regressive Distributed Lag Model, in which, Δstands for the first-order differential variable, α is the intercept, β_1, β_2, β_3, β_4 *and* β_5 are the coefficients of first-order variables. Similarly, γ_i, δ_i, φ_i, λ_i, and θ_i, are the parameters of the error correction model, and the final term v_t is the vector of random error terms. Similarly, the equations are developed for Eqns. (2.2), (2.3), (2.4), (2.5), and (2.6) in the estimations process but are not listed here.

2.5 Results and Discussion

This section is about the results of the econometric estimation. Table 2.5 presents the bound test results based on the F-statistics value of all equations in the model, such as Eqns. (2.1), (2.2), (2.3), (2.4), (2.5), and (2.6) respectively. As seen in the table, if the F-statistics are higher than the upper bound critical values, we conclude there exists a long-run relationship in the model. If the F-statistics are lower than the lower bound of the critical values we conclude that no long-run relationship exists in the

Table 2.5 Bound test results

Details	*(1)*	*(2)*	*(3)*	*(4)*	*(5)*	*(6)*
F-tests statistics	3.37	0.99	5.23	2.27	2.85	2.79
Critical values: Upper Bound	3.52	3.77	3.77	2.72	4.14	4.14
Lower Bound	2.45	2.72	2.72	3.77	3.17	3.17
Decisions	Amb.	NLR	LR	NLR	NLR	NLR

Note: Critical values are considered based on at least a 10 percent level of significance. Amb. refers to the results being ambiguous and needing further investigation, LR refers to the long-run existence in the respective specifications of the model, NLR refers to no long-run relationship exists

model, and if the F-statistics are in between the lower and upper bound of the critical values, we conclude the results are ambiguous, meaning that the long-run relationship may or may not exist in the model. For this purpose, we consider the critical value range at a 90 percent level of confidence level (10 percent level of significance). Based on the results, for model (3), the F-statistics are higher than the upper bound indicating there exists a long-run relationship in the models. For model (1) the values lie in between the lower and upper bound of critical values indicating that the results are inconclusive at this stage, and we cannot say any without estimating the long-run relationship coefficients. For the rest of the model, the results indicate not long-run relationship.

In the next step, we conduct the cointegration test to find the long-run coefficients. Tables 2.6 and 2.7 present the long-run relationship results for the model of different specifications in columns (1) to (3) of both tables for each Equation from (2.1), (2.2), (2.3), (2.4), (2.5), and (2.6) respectively. Similarly, Tables 2.8 presents the results for the ECM (Error Correction Model) version in different specifications.

These tables show the long-run and short-run coefficients of ARDL with different lags as shown in their bottom row for the given model. Schwartz-Bayesian Criteria (SBC) is selected due to the relatively small size of the series used for the econometric analysis of this chapter.

The results in column (1) of Table 2.6 show that the remittances (REM) have a strong positive impact on trade deficits in Nepal. The results suggest that a one percent increase in remittance causes to increase in trade deficit on average by more than half a percent holding other variables in the model constant. This result reflects the picture in Fig. 2.1, where remittances and trade deficits both have moved upward together and maintain almost a similar trend. Further, per capita GDP (GDPPC),

Table 2.6 ARDL Long run relationship coefficients-1

Dependent variable: Trade deficit (LTDEF)-log	*(1)*	*(2)*	*(3)*
Remittance (LREM)-log	0.189***		0.173**
	(0.069)		(0.069)
Credit to private sector (LBCPS)-log		0.966***	
		(0.105)	
Per capita GDP (LGDPPC)-log	1.241***		1.280***
	(0.173)		(0.177)
Inflation (INFL)-%	−0.018	−0.060	−0.022
	(0.019)	(0.086)	(0.021)
Interest (INTR)-log	0.028	0.008	
	(0.020)	(0.075)	
Number of observations	*27*	*27*	*27*
R-squared	*0.71*	*0.37*	*0.41*
Root MSE	*0.13*	*0.18*	*0.17*
Log Likelihood	*22.96*	*12.27*	*13.11*
ARDL Lags	*(1,1,1,1,1)*	*(1,1,1,1)*	*(1,1,1)*

Note: ***, **, and * indicate that the statistics are significant at 1%, 5%, and 10% levels of significance. The figures in the parenthesis are the standard error

inflation (INFL), and interest rate (INTR) are included in the estimations and the results are presented in the same column. The result for the per capita GDP is statistically significant, indicating the elasticity of more than one and a quarter percent. The results for the rest of the variables in the model are not statistically significant but they have indicated the direction of the association with the trade deficits.

Column (2) of the same table presents the results for the banking credit to the private sector (BCPS). Here, the results for BCPS are statistically significant at a one percent level of significance indicating that a one percent increase in the bank credit to the private sector causes to increase in the trade deficits by an average of about one percent if other things remain the same in the model. It means that the banks' credit policy is also responsible for the alarming trade deficit in the country. The results from the interest rate (INTR) are positively associated with the trade deficits, indicating that the increased interest rate discourages investment in the producing sector and boosts imports (easy consumption).

Therefore, based on the results of LGDPPC, LREM, and LBCPS, it can be concluded that there is a common role played by these variables in alarming trade deficits in the country. The results of column (3) of the same table show the estimated results in column (1)

Table 2.7 presents the results for the role of remittances in banks' credit to the private sector. Here, the results show that remittances have a statistically significant role on Banks' credit to the private sector, and the magnitude of this variable's coefficient is more than half a percent consistently in all estimations, as can be seen in the columns (1), (2), and (3) of the table.

Overall, remittances can contribute to reducing the trade deficit and improving the trade balance, if a substantial portion of remittances is used to import capital and technology products that can contribute to increasing national output and exports, as discussed in Saadi (2020), the condition is that only if a significant proportion of available funds from remittances is used for investment purposes or to increase the productivity of the production forces. Directing the remittances and bank credit to the productive sector largely depends on the policy, which is determined by the quality of governance.

Table 2.8 presents the short-run results of the model, in which columns (1), (2), and (3) are for the trade deficits in lag as the dependent variable, and columns (4), (5), and (6) have the results for the banks' credit to the private sector as the dependent variable. In all specifications, ECM (−1) results are statistically significant with the expected negative sign, with

Table 2.7 ARDL Long run relationship coefficients-2

Dependent variable: Credit to Private sector (LBCPS)-log	*(1)*	*(2)*	*(3)*
Remittance (LREM)-log	0.535***	0.571***	0.535***
	(0.115)	(0.106)	(0.124)
Inflation (INFL)-%	−0.050		−0.078
	(0.082)		(0.093)
Interest (INTR)-log	0.093	0.097	
	(0.085)	(0.083)	
Number of observations	*27*	*27*	*27*
R-squared	*0.55*	*0.45*	*0.48*
Root MSE	*0.11*	*0.11*	*0.11*
Log Likelihood	*27.75*	*25.21*	*26.05*
ARDL Lags	*(1,1,1,1)*	*(1,1,1)*	*(1,1,1)*

Note: ***, **, and * indicate that the statistics are significant at 1%, 5%, and 10% levels of significance. The figures in the parenthesis are the standard error

Table 2.8 Short Run-ECM results

	Dependent variable: LTDEF (−1)			*Dependent variable: LBCPS (−1)*		
	(1)	*(2)*	*(3)*	*(4)*	*(5)*	*(6)*
LREM(-1)	−0.19		−0.22	−0.32***	−0.28***	−0.32***
	(0.11)		(0.139)	(0.084)	(0.082)	(0.083)
LBCPS(-1)		0.49				
		(0.13)				
LLGDPPC(-1)	0.44					
	(0.43)					
INFL(-1)	0.02	0.01	0.02	0.02*		0.02**
	(0.01)	(0.013)	(0.013)	(0.008)		(0.008)
INTR(-1)	−0.001	0.01		0.01	0.01	
	(0.013)	(0.017)		(0.009)	(0.012)	
ECM(-1)	−0.74***	−0.29	−0.25***	−0.12***	−0.12***	−0.11***
	(0.220)	(0.26)	(0.077)	(0.042)	(0.04)	(0.04)

Note: ***, **, and * indicate that the statistics are significant at 1%, 5%, and 10% levels of significance. The figures in the parenthesis are the standard error

exception in column (2), indicating the disequilibrium that occurred in the previous year is corrected in the current year following a short-run shock at a relatively slow to moderate pace as the coefficients are in between −0.11 to −0.74. The remittances have a significant negative impact on the trade deficit in the short run with one lag in column (1) and (3) but statistically not significant, while in columns (4), (5), and (6) this has a statistically negative impact on Banks' credit to the private sector. It turns out to be negative in the same scenario indicating the results are inconsistent for one lag.

Considering the post estimation tests statistics, we say that the R-square shows the overall goodness of fit of the model and is moderate about half percent but within the acceptable range. The diagnostic test results show that the model passes the tests for serial correlation, functional form, normality, and heteroscedasticity. Further, the stability test results (CUSUM and CUSUMSQ) plotted against the critical bounds of 5 percent level of significance are within the range, indicating that the model is structurally

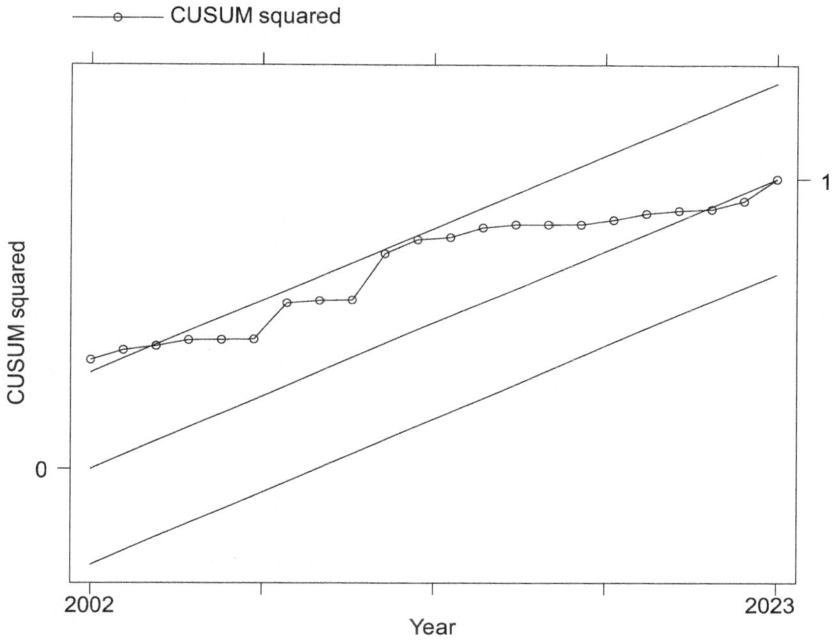

Fig. 2.4 Plot of CUSUM and CUSUM squared Figure for Eqn. (2.1)

stable (Figures 2.4, 2.5, 2.6, 2.7, 2.8, and 2.9). The stability tests show the estimated results lie within the boundary of a 5 percent level of significance (95 percent level of confidence). These results indicate no evidence of misspecification and instability during the period covered for the estimation in the econometric modelling process of this paper.

2.6 Conclusions and Recommendations

The main objective of this chapter is to analyze the circular nexus, that is from remittances to the banks' credit to the private sector, from remittance to trade deficit, and from banks' credit to the private sector to trade deficits. Descriptive and time series-based econometric analyses are made to conclude. The conclusions drawn both from descriptive analysis and econometric analysis move together indicating the analysis is robust.

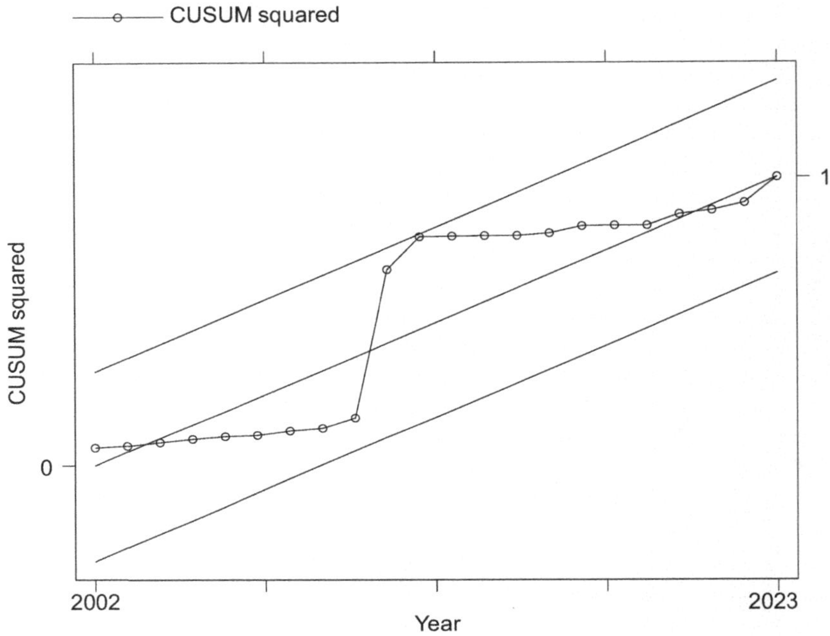

Fig. 2.5 Plot of CUSUM and CUSUM squared Figure for Eqn. (2.2)

The major findings of this chapter are threefold. First, remittances have a significant positive impact on trade deficits. The correlation between these variables is very high and the elasticity is about half a percent. The second, bank credit to the private sector also has a strong association with the trade deficits. The correlation between these variables is also very high and the elasticity is just below one percent. It means a 100 Rupees increase in bank credit to the private sector causes to increase in the trade deficit by almost 97 Rupees in the long run. This association in the short run is not consistent. These results are supported by the credit flows to the private sector as the majority of the credits are absorbed in the unproductive sector. For example, almost one-fifth of credit goes to wholesale and retail services followed by other service sectors substantially.

The third, the remittance also has a strong positive association with the banks' credit to the private sector. These results indicate a circular nexus

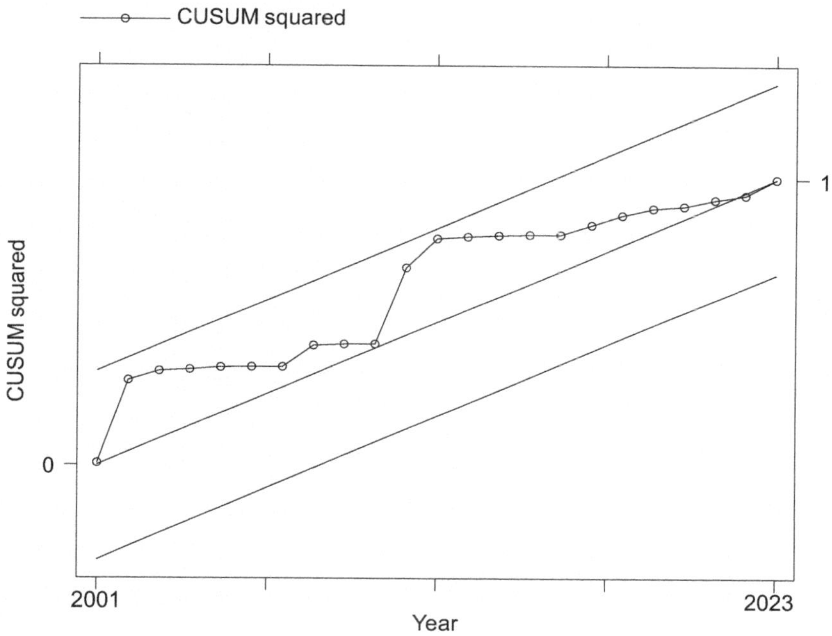

Fig. 2.6 Plot of CUSUM and CUSUM squared Figure for Eqn. (2.3)

of these variables, trade deficit, remittance, and banks' credit to the private sector.

Based on these findings, a few policy recommendations can be made for the policy inferences related to improving the alarming trade deficit situation. First, an increase in the remittance inflow to Nepal is observed to increase the trade deficits in the long run. Therefore, the appropriate policy may not be to limit the remittance flows but to learn to enhance exports by developing compulsory saving and investment provisions.

Second, looking at the nature of bank credit and considering the positive impact on trade deficits, it is probably a good time to develop a sound credit policy for the private sector with some provisions to maintain compulsory flows to the productive sector, such as manufacturing and industries. In addition, focusing on these types of credit flows to agriculture, hospitality, import of capital goods such as machinery and types of equipment, healthcare and hygiene, and small and medium scale industries to be

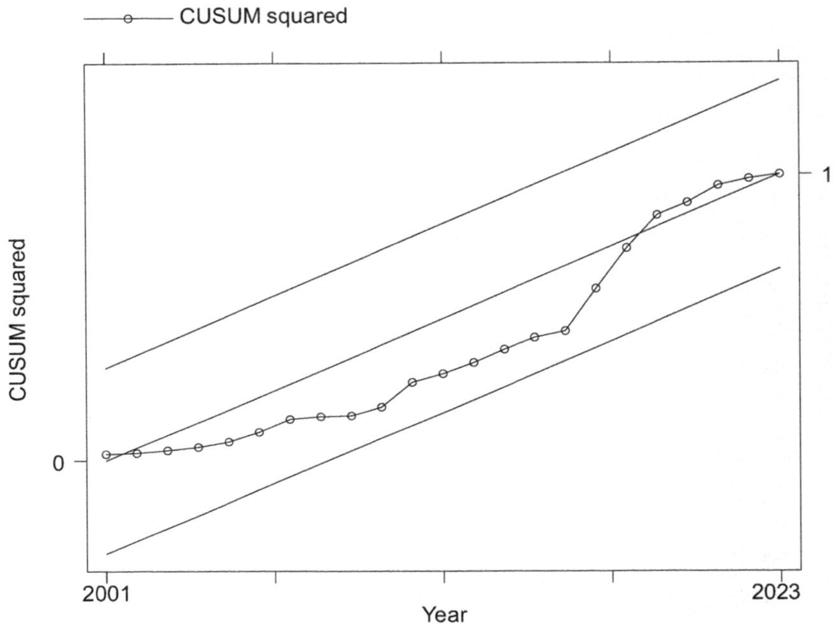

Fig. 2.7 Plot of CUSUM and CUSUM squared Figure for Eqn. (2.4)

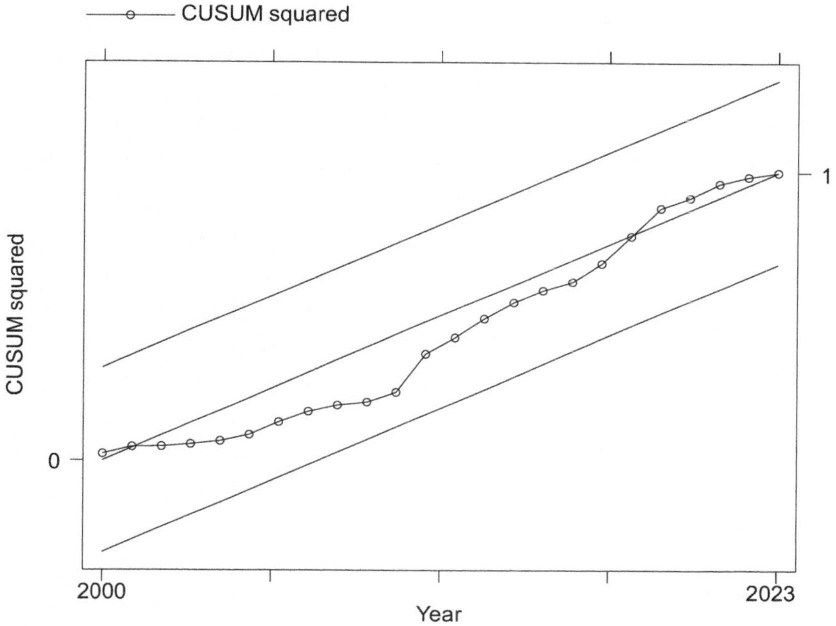

Fig. 2.8 Plot of CUSUM and CUSUM squared Figure for Eqn. (2.5)

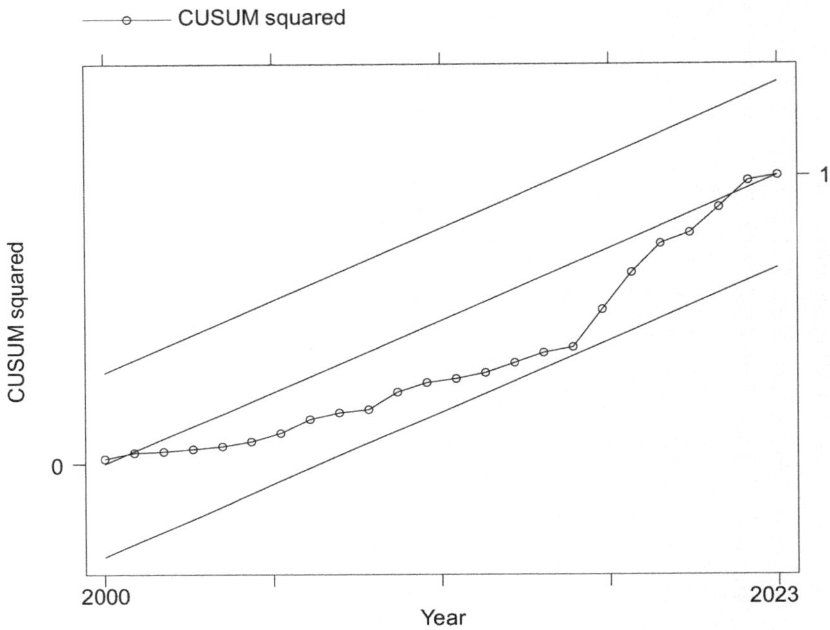

Fig. 2.9 Plot of CUSUM and CUSUM squared Figure for Eqn. (2.6)

specially considered. Doing this will help to increase exports and control imports.

In sum, trade deficits can be reduced in two ways, one by increasing exports and the other by reducing imports. Both of these ways should be practiced simultaneously for a quick response to the economy.

References

Ahmed, R., Vishnu, P., & Ahmad, N. (2014). Causal relationship between worker's remittances and imports in Pakistan. *European Journal of Scientific Research, 120*(1), 177–188.

Bayangos, V., & Jansen, K. (2011). Remittances and competitiveness: The case of the Philippines. *World Development, 39*(10), 1834–1846.

Bhatta, G. R. (2013). Remittance and trade deficit nexus in Nepal: A VECM approach. *NRB Economic Review, 25*(1), 37–50.

Chowdhury, M. B., & Rabbi, F. (2014). Workers' remittances and Dutch disease in Bangladesh. *The Journal of International Trade & Economic Development, 23*(4), 455–475.

Farzanegan, M. R., & Hassan, S. M. (2020). How does the flow of remittances affect the trade balance of the Middle East and North Africa? *Journal of Economic Policy Reform, 23*(2), 248–266.

Gregory, A. W., & Hansen, B. E. (1996). Residual-based tests for cointegration in models with regime shifts. *Journal of Econometrics, 70*, 99–126.

Hasan, S. B., Akhter, R., & Saha, S. (2019). Impact of remittance on economic growth in Bangladesh. *American Journal of Trade and Policy, 6*(1), 41–48.

Hien, N. P. (2017). The impact of remittance on trade balance: The case of Malaysia. *Journal of Economics and Public Finance, 3*(4), 531–540.

Hien, N. P., Vinh, C. T. H., & Mai, V. T. P. (2020). Remittances, real exchange rate and the Dutch disease in Asian developing countries. *The Quarterly Review of economics and finance, 77*, 131–143.

Jena, N. R., & Sethi, N. (2019). Does inward remittance lead to export performance in South Asian countries? *International Journal of Social Economics, 47*(2), 145–172.

Kandil, M., & Mirzaie, I. (2008). The impact of capital and remittances flows on economic performance in MENA countries. *World Economics, 10*(3), 159–192.

León-Ledesma, M., & Piracha, M. (2004). International migration and the role of remittances in Eastern Europe. *International Migration, 42*(4), 65–83.

Makun, K. K. (2018). Imports, remittances, direct foreign investment and economic growth in Republic of the Fiji Islands: An empirical analysis using ARDL approach. *Kasetsart Journal of Social Sciences, 39*(3), 439–447.

Minh, C. H. (2020). Remittances, Foreign Direct Investment, Imports and Economic Growth: Empirical Evidence from Vietnam. *Asian Journal of Economic Modelling, 8*(2), 133–140.

Nepal Rastra Bank. (2025). *Weighted Average Treasury Bills Rate (91–day)*

Nepal Rastra Bank. (2022). *Circular No 15 and 20.* Nepal Rastra Bank

Nepal Rastra Bank. (2025a). *Current Macroeconomic and Financial Situation.* Baluwatar, Kathmandu, Nepal

Nepal Rastra Bank. (2025b). *Weighted Average Treasury Bills Rate (91–day)*

Okodua, H., & Olayiwola, K. (2013). Migrant workers' remittances and external trade balance in Sub-Sahara African countries. *International Journal of Economics and Finance, 5*(3), 134–142.

Pacheco, L. M., Maldonado, I., & Lobo, C. A. (2024). Migration and export performance: the role of diaspora remittances. *International Journal of Trade and Global Markets, 19*(2), 174–192.

Paudel, R. C., & Bhusal, T. P. (2021). Role of Workers' Remittances in Export Performance of Nepal: Gravity Modelling Approach. *NRB Economic Review, 33*(1 & 2), 1–13.

Paudel, R. C., & Jayanthakumaran, K. (2009). Financial Liberalization and Performance in Sri Lanka: The ARDL Approach. *South Asia Economic Journal, 10*(1), 127–156.

Paudel, R. C. (2022). *Remittances, Banking Credit to Private Sector, and Nepal's Trade Deficits*, Study Report, Confederation of Banking and Financial Institutions, Nepal

Paudel, R. C., Acharya, C., & Thapa-Parajuli, R. (2020). The Role of Cooperatives, Remittances, and Infrastructure in Export Performance of Nepal: ARDL Approach of Cointegration. *Sumerianz Journal of Economics and Finance, 3*(10), 151–159.

Paudel, R. C., & Acharya, C. P. (2020). Financial development and economic growth: Evidence from Nepal. *NRB Economic Review, 32*(1), 15–36.

Paudel, R. C., & Alharthi, M. (2021). Role of financial development in the export performance of a landlocked developing country: The case of Nepal. *Cogent Economics & Finance, 9*(1), 1–18. https://doi.org/10.1080/23322039.2021.1973653

Pesaran, M. H., Shin, Y., & Smith, R. J. (2001). Bounds testing approaches to the analysis of level relationships. *Journal of Applied Econometrics, 16*, 289–326. https://doi.org/10.1002/jae.616

Regmi, R. H. (2022). Remittances and trade balance: A new transfer problem. *Remittances Review, 7*(1), 3–19.

Saadi, M. (2020). Remittance Inflows and Export Complexity: New Evidence from Developing and Emerging Countries. *The Journal of Development Studies, 56*(12), 2266–2292. https://doi.org/10.1080/00220388.2020.1755653

Sapkota, C. (2013). Remittances in Nepal: boon or bane? *The Journal of Development Studies, 49*(10), 1316–1331.

Shamim, M. A., Panhwar, I. A., Rizvi, S. M. A., & Shaikh, E. A. (2015). Impact of remittances on export performance: Time series evidence from Pakistan. *IBT Journal of Business Studies (JBS), 11*(2), 123–135.

Stiglitz, J. E., & Charlton, A. (2006). Aid for trade. *International Journal of Development Issues, 5*(2), 1–41.

Timsina, N. (2014). Bank credit and economic growth in Nepal: An empirical analysis. *NRB Economic Review, 26*(2), 1–24.

World Bank. (2025). *World development indicators.* World Bank Group. Retrieved January 25, 2025, from https://data.worldbank.org/

CHAPTER 3

Governance Quality and Export Performance: A Lesson from COVID-19

3.1 Background

In this chapter, I discuss the role of governance quality in improving export performance so that it will help to reduce or eliminate the trade deficits, which is the main concern raised in Chap. 2. In this regard, the question is whether the quality of governance contributes to boosting export performance. I tried to highlight this issue with an example of a trade association during the COVID-19 pandemic.

Nepal's exports began to increase visibly and maintained the trend largely up to the end of the second quarter of 2022 (the peak period of the COVID-19 pandemic), and then after, with some exceptions. The World was facing the challenge of the second wave of COVID-19 and fearing potential third and next waves in different forms and variants of COVID-19. As seen from the experiences of various countries in the global context, the pandemic resulted in severe negative impacts on the health and economic sectors. Many scholars compared the threat of this pandemic with the century-old Spanish flu that infected around 500 million people between 1918 to 1920 and killed about 50 million people (Baker et al., 2020). As the world is much integrated due to expanded tourism industries, international trade, cultural exchange, technological advancement, people-to-people connectivity, corporate-to-corporate and government-to-government relationships, the potentiality of the severe effect of

R. C. Paudel, *Essays on Key Issues of Development in Nepal*,
https://doi.org/10.1007/978-981-95-7715-6_3

COVID-19 seems higher than that of the Spanish flu (Baker et al., 2020). Probably, this has become the single subject of concern for all people in the world for a long time

As of the end of June 2022, the fear of the pandemic has declined, but it is still in existence around the corners of the globe. Nepal is also one of the severely affected countries by the pandemic, with a record of about a million infected cases and deaths of about 11500 due to the pandemic. However, about 80 percent of the population is fully vaccinated against the pandemic, and the country was in a state of fear of a series of waves of the pandemic in the future.

Nepal imposed several lockdowns of different natures for about 11 months since the first wave of the pandemic in two phases until the end of July 2021. Since then, the situation remained a sort of neo-normal for about two more years. The economic sectors, such as tourism and hospitality, education, and entertainment, were either out of business or compelled to change their business modality for almost one and a half years until the end of July 2021. Then, gradually, tourism and education were taking a neo-normal path but at the given national and international scenario, predicting the future of the Nepalese economy was a difficult task.

In brief, the literature suggests that the COVID-19 pandemic has had a substantial negative impact on both import and export segments of international trade globally. Hayakawa and Mukunoki (2021a), Gössling et al. (2020), and Vidya and Prabheesh (2020) state that both export and import trades have a substantial negative impact from the Covid-19 pandemic, and the magnitude of the negative impact varies from country to country. However, at this current stage, a light of hope about the future is raised by Hayakawa and Mukunoki (2021a) who further explain, based on an empirical investigation, that the first wave of the pandemic had a more severe adverse impact on trade, and that negative impact has started to decline gradually.

Despite the heavy decline of both imports and exports in the first year of the pandemic, Nepal has shown some silver lights on export trade with a remarkable increase in digital literacy, exports of technology-based services, medicinal herbs, health and hygiene products, spices, and other light-processed food items have gained momentum after the emergence of the pandemic (Paudel, 2021).

Baldwin and Tomiura (2020) suggest that the shocks of this pandemic can be in both the demand and supply sides, that is, both imports and exports of international trade. In the Nepalese context, in import, from experience of almost two years in Nepal, it had created a hurdle disturbing the supply chain, breaking the poor production sharing networks, and regular supply of raw materials and labour forces to the industries. Because of lockdowns and other types of restrictions imposed for mobility in the country, they have further limited the supply-side factors and have created difficulties in maintaining the regular supplies to export. Following all these backgrounds, Gruszczynski (2020) states that the crisis can be managed by a huge effort from different stakeholders and policymakers. There is another side to a coin too, for example, Goyal (2020) suggests that the post-COVID-19 macro-financial package may provide some supportive base for better economic performance as in some occasions in the past, this study indicates that the various efforts made by the relevant governments can contribute to faster economic growth in the years to come.

Nepal has supply-side constraints in its export trade because of many reasons, such as the poor scale of economies and technologies led by low level of investment, insufficient and poor quality of infrastructure, constraints of landlockedness and difficult geographical features for trade, poor quality of governance and doing business environment, mismatch of education and production, etc., as discussed in Paudel (2019). Some of these constraints are further extended because of COVID-19. In addition, there are some demand-side constraints created by this pandemic, such as most of Nepal's top 15 trading partners were badly affected by the pandemic, resulting in a slight decline in their imports from Nepal. More than 95 percent of Nepal's exports are imported to these countries in the year 2019 and 2020. The top five countries that import more than 85 percent of Nepal's exports are intensively affected by COVID-19 in the first and second waves. Therefore, most of these partner countries were still in a difficult position because of the pandemic fuming trade futures (Table 3.1). The table also shows that the total exports of Nepal have declined by more than six percent in 2020 compared to 2019.

In the given background, this chapter attempts to investigate the impact of COVID-19 on Nepal's export trade, noting the new dynamics in international trade, and then examines the role of the quality of governance in the export performance. Nepal's trade costs and supply capacity seem to be going in the wrong direction due to the reasons discussed in Hayakawa and Mukunoki (2021a). This has already been one and a half years of COVID-19 globally, and about 16 months (as of June 2021) in Nepal of

Table 3.1 Nepal's top 15 partners: exports (Rs. Millions) and share (%)

Rank as of 2019		*2020*		*2019*		*2018*		*Covid-19 Global Rank- 2021 June*
	Importers	*Imports*	*Share*	*Imports*	*Share*	*Imports*	*Share*	
1	India	73910	72.9	74268	68.7	50542	59.1	2
2	U.S.A.	10288	10.2	11077	10.3	10156	11.9	1
3	Germany	2800	2.8	3188	3.0	3224	3.8	12
4	Turkey	1456	1.4	2715	2.5	3849	4.5	6
5	U.K.	2031	2.0	2494	2.3	2854	3.3	7
6	China P. R.	681	0.7	2040	1.9	2430	2.8	100
7	Bangladesh	478	0.5	1364	1.3	1298	1.5	30
8	France	1144	1.1	1353	1.3	1278	1.5	4
9	Japan	931	0.9	1052	1.0	1058	1.2	34
10	Italy	663	0.7	1015	0.9	1234	1.4	9
11	Canada	756	0.7	845	0.8	888	1.0	23
12	Australia	736	0.7	713	0.7	663	0.8	125
13	Netherlands	435	0.4	435	0.4	417	0.5	20
14	Vietnam	81	0.1	363	0.3	462	0.5	140
15	U.A.E.	279	0.3	363	0.3	259	0.3	41
	Total exports	101333	95.4	108054	95.6	85489	94.3	

Source: Trade and export promotion centre (2021) and Johns Hopkins University & Medicine (2021)

COVID-19's direct cases and casualties. Therefore, it seems reasonably needed work to evaluate its impact on trade, particularly on exports, not only showing the difficulties of the pandemic but also trying to open the avenues of export trade in the changing scenario with a systematic analysis of the exports. With this background, this paper aims to assess COVID-19's impact on Nepal's international trade, focusing on export trade.

This chapter has seven sections. The following section presents the research methodology adopted in the chapter. Section 3.3 presents a contextual scenario of COVID-19 and world trade, focusing on exports. Section 3.4 analyses new dynamics in global trade due to the pandemic. Section 3.5 highlights the export scenario of pre- and post-COVID-19 in Nepal, Sect. 3.6 presents results and discussion, and the final section concludes with contextual policy recommendations.

3.2 Research Methodology

This chapter employs data-based descriptive and quantitative analysis of Nepal's exports before and after the emergence of the COVID-19 pandemic. In the first instance, a systematic desk review is performed. The desk review of the literature, policy briefs, and relevant documents is noted carefully with a standard critical approach following research ethics. The relevant information is collected from the publications of different bodies of the Nepal Government, Nepal Rastra Bank, newspapers, and other international agencies' databases. For credible policy inferences, this study presents the figures and tables to explain the different scenarios of trade flows. The comparative analysis attempted to compare the period before and after COVID-19's emergence.

As seen from the literature, the COVID-19 pandemic has hurt global trade. The elasticity is not unique, and it is assumed that the pandemic has different levels of impact on international trade in many countries and industries, as discussed in Hayakawa and Mukunoki (2021b). As per our knowledge, there are no such studies that identified the pandemic's elasticity in the export performance in the case of Nepal, which this chapter aims.

For this, a model developed by Hayakawa and Mukunoki (2021b) is employed, but this chapter is slightly different from this paper in terms of coverage, measuring the pandemic severity, and estimation methods. In terms of coverage, this chapter only covers Nepal's context. Also, in terms of measuring the pandemic's severity, we cover only the number of cases of COVID-19 and ignore the deaths, as the number of effective cases is far higher than the number of deaths, which is around 0.5 percent. Also, in terms of the estimation method, Fixed and Random effect estimation methods are used instead of the Poisson Pseudo Maximum Likelihood (PPML) estimation method, as the data gaps are not an issue in this chapter for the covered period.

The benchmark (baseline) model is as in Equation (3.1) below:

$$\begin{aligned} LEXPORT_{i,j,y,m} &= \alpha + \beta 1 LCOVID_{i,y,m} + \beta 2 LCOVIDPTR_{j,y,m} \\ &\quad + \delta_{i,j,y,m} + \delta_{i,j,m} + \delta_{y,m} + \varepsilon_{i,j,y,m} \end{aligned} \tag{3.1}$$

Where the dependent variable is the natural log of exports measured in Nepalese Rupees. This variable is in the gravity modeling framework, which is the flow of exports from Nepal to partner countries each month. The first term on the right-hand side is the constant to represent the fixed cost of trade, β1 and β2 are the coefficients of the regressors, LCOVID is the natural log of the number of COVID-19 cases in each month for Nepal, and LCOVIDPTR is measured similarly to LCOVID but for partner countries. The terms $\delta_{i,\,j,\,y,\,m}$, $\delta_{i,\,j,\,m}$, and $\varepsilon_{i,\,j,\,y,\,m}$ are the number of fixed effects (first partners and months of the year-specific effect, and second partners and month-specific effect) and an error term. The term i refers to Nepal, j to partner, y to year, and m to month. We use different sources of data, for example, TEPC (2021) for exports, CEPII (2025) for gravity variables, Ritchie et al. (2021) for the COVID-19 cases in Nepal and partners. We cover the period from January 2020 to June 2021 (18 months).

Once we estimate the benchmark model, we move to estimate the alternative specifications of the model, including the distance and border dummy variable. Here, distance is measured in the natural log of kilometers between the most populous cities of the traders, and border is a dummy variable that is 1 if the partner country is bordered by Nepal, and zero if otherwise. So, China and India have the values of 1.

Then, we want to estimate the role of governance in export for the longer term (not only for the COVID-19 period). For this purpose, the data from 2010 to 2022 are used in gravity modeling approaches for the Eqns. (3.2), (3.3), (3.4), and (3.5).

In these equations, the dependent variable is the natural log of exports from Nepal to its partner countries. On the side of the independent variables, other than the governance index (GOVIN) and Covid-19 dummy (COVID) are measured in natural logarithm scale. These variables are Nepal's GDP, Nepal's population, Nepal's trading partners' GDP and Population, and the distance between Nepal's most populous city and its trading partners' most populous cities. GOVIN is an index and COVID is a dummy variable that takes 1 for the years 2020, 2021, and 2022; and zero for the rest of the years. The subscript i refers to Nepal, j refers to the trading partner, and y refers to the year.

These equations are estimated using robust standard errors for fixed effect estimations (FE) and random effect estimations (RE) employing gravity modeling techniques.

$$LEXPORT_{i,j,y} = \alpha + \beta 1LGDP_{i,y} + \beta 2LPOP_{i,y} + \beta 3LPGDP_{j,y} + \beta 4LPPOP_{j,y} + \beta 5LDIST_{i,j,y} + \varepsilon_{i,j,y} \tag{3.2}$$

$$LEXPORT_{i,j,y} = \alpha + \beta 1LGDP_{i,y} + \beta 2LPOP_{i,y} + \beta 3LPGDP_{j,y} + \beta 4LPPOP_{j,y} + \beta 5LDIST_{i,j,y} + \beta 6GOVI_{i,y} + \varepsilon_{i,j,y} \tag{3.3}$$

$$LEXPORT_{i,j,y} = \alpha + \beta 1LGDP_{i,y} + \beta 2LPOP_{i,y} + \beta 3LPGDP_{j,y} + \beta 4LPPOP_{j,y} + \beta 5LDIST_{i,j,y} + \beta 6GOVI_{i,y} + \beta 7COVID_{y} + \varepsilon_{i,j,y} \tag{3.4}$$

$$LEXPORT_{i,j,y} = \alpha + \beta 1LGDP_{i,y} + \beta 2LPOP_{i,y} + \beta 3LPGDP_{j,y} + \beta 4LPPOP_{j,y} + \beta 5LDIST_{i,j,y} + \beta 7COVID_{y} + \varepsilon_{i,j,y} \tag{3.5}$$

3.3 Covid-19 and Exports in a Global Context

From 2020 to 2022, COVID-19 along with its different variants, became a pandemic threatening human lives and challenging the global economy. The first case affected by this virus was detected in Wuhan Town, Hubei Province of the Peoples' Republic of China On 31st December 2019 and since then, it became not only a global phenomenon in the healthcare industries but also became a top of the issues of policymakers, development activists, entrepreneurs, and people of all walks of life. It has exposed the global healthcare system and challenged the leading figures in the fields to reshape the healthcare mechanism to cope with such pandemics in the future.

As of June 2022, more than 600 million cases of COVID-19 are recorded globally with total deaths of about six million (Johns Hopkins University & Medicine, 2022). Different vaccination options are found but they have not become easily available to ordinary people, particularly, in the poor and developing countries. Therefore, scholars have compared the threat of this pandemic with a century-old Spanish flu, which infected around 500 million people between 1918 to 1920 and killed about 50 million (Baker et al., 2020). Further, the world is much more integrated due to expanded tourism industries; international trade, cultural exchange, technological advancement, people-to-people connectivity, corporate-to-corporate connectivity, and government-to-government relationships, the potentiality of the severe effect of COVID-19 may be even higher than that of Spanish flu (Baker et al., 2020), and we do not know how long it will take to fully control yet.

Overall, COVID-19's economic impact on the worldwide economy is negative as stated in Alon et al. (2020). For example, one of the fastest-growing regions before the pandemic was Developing Asia that region also faced a negative growth of 0.2 percent in the year 2020. The global economy faced a 3.5 percent contraction due to pandemics in 2020 (World Bank, 2021a). The situation in 2020 was very devastating because of the pandemic, Kristalina Georgieva, the Chief of the International Monetary Fund (IMF) indicated that 2020 is likely to be the most difficult, devastating, and failed year in terms of economic performance since the great depression of the 1930s, she also feared that more than 170 countries at that time in the world may have negative per capita growth because of this pandemic in 2020 (Dev & Sengupta, 2020). Despite this fear, the contraction remained below four percent, which increased confidence in the global economy to converge.

COVID-19 had a net negative shock in global exports specifically in 2020. The reasons for this situation to happen are numerous. Verities of restrictions on mobility of people, social distancing, lockdowns, etc., were imposed to break the virus chain in many countries. Closer of many businesses related to entertainment, transportation, aviation, physical fitness, schools, etc., were made for the same purpose. The closure of the schools put many parents either out of jobs or had to reduce their workload to care for their children at home and online education. Sick people cause by the virus had to deal with many kinds of health problems even after the post-Covid-19 infection. The closure of transportation resulted in many people's mobility restrictions and remained out of jobs. These all scenarios led to lower production of many goods imposing a condition on the industry of *producing less and supplying less*. This condition caused to downgrade to a low scale of production for many producers.

However, the effect is of different degrees based on the nature of the goods produced, the technologies used, and the consumption patterns of the produced goods. The producers of those goods that can be produced from home or possibly produced by lowering the physical presence of the labour force did a good job but others had to lose in such a situation. Hayakawa and Mukunoki (2021a) state that the food, medical, and hygiene industries have seen a positive shock, and some other products that are needed for human beings but not urgent have negative shocks in the global market. They also suggest that the negative effect may decrease as the span of the pandemic gets longer over time when people and entrepreneurs learn to deal with the pandemic using technologies, medicines, working styles, and other ways from the experience. If we have a look at the market, there are certain sectors largely benefited by the increased government spending on health, Medicare, and entire healthcare issues.

3.3.1 New Dynamics in Global Trade

Governments' heavy spending on health and hygiene products, medical, and the entire healthcare system has resulted in this sector boom globally because of the pandemic, which has changed the consumption habits of many people raising the demand for some consumable products like herbs, spices, noodles, and soups. Lin and Zhang (2020) stated that the agriculture business experienced difficulties during the pandemic but in the case of the light products market has been very favorable because of their medicinal attributes. For example, edible fungus and horticultural products faced a sharp decline in the market but the exports of grains and oils have increased substantially. In addition to these, medicinal products, hygiene products, and herbs have increased globally. The study also suggests that small firms are in a difficult position than larger firms (Devan et al., 2021).

Erokhin and Gao (2020) suggested that food security and food supply chain issues were crucial along with health threats caused by the pandemic in developing countries. This is true as the countries imposed different types of restrictions, lockdowns, and closures, breaking the existing channel of distribution in the locality. This paper shows the urgency as well as a new avenue of international trade, that is, focus on quality food products and systematic distribution with an alternative at difficult times so that it will work smoothly to fulfill domestic consumption at the time of much needed and help a quicker resilience of the respective economies.

Barichello (2020), in the context of agriculture trade in Canada, found the minimal impact of COVID-19 on agricultural products and suggests that the agricultural trade will be less affected due to relatively low elasticities of demand. Gregorioa and Ancog (2020), using the case of Southeast Asian economies, discussed that a systemic transformation of the agriculture sector making it a more resilient, sustainable, productive, and inclusive food system is essential. Doing so would help to get their people sustained at such a difficult time.

Elsayed and Khan (2020), following many studies of a similar nature, explained the findings of the study highlighting the role of spices and herbs to improve the immunity of people and helping to fight against the pandemic, such as COVID-19. This research says further investigation is needed on how it contributes to the immune system but in the meantime, this opens an avenue for Nepal's potential trade. This clearly shows the silver lights in the dark clouds, indicating agriculture may be a roadway and focus point for economic prosperity and a better future in many respects.

3.4 COVID-19 Incidents and Government Responses in Nepal

Nepal has three layers of government; federal (central) government, provincial governments, and local governments. These governments were actively fighting against the pandemic in terms of restricting the mobility of people and limiting some of the economic activities to break the chain of the virus, providing and administering vaccinations, establishing health care system including test labs, temporary hospitals and beds, rehabilitation, and quarantine centers, and several relief packages in their capacity. Initially, Nepal did not have any lab to test the Covid-19 infection. Even in such a devastating stage, these governments were engaged in controlling the pandemic with very limited resources, poor and unorganized healthcare infrastructure, and poor and insufficient human resources in hand. There may be different verdicts on the role played by the governments of Nepal in dealing with this pandemic, but they had to start with a variety of scarcities and scary situations in the system. As a country and a civilized society, we faced verities of transmissible diseases in the past, but the nation had only one hospital in hand in the country to face any type of transmissible diseases. This scenario shows the negligence or unplanned action in the past about the healthcare system and healthcare delivery mechanism of the country. Table 3.2 shows the evolution of the pandemic's incidents and the major responses of the government to control the pandemic.

Table 3.2 Covid-19's evolving incidents and the government's response

Date	*Incidents*	*Remarks*
January 23, 2020	First case of COVID-19 was found in Nepal.	A 32-year-old male student had returned to Kathmandu from Wuhan on 9th January and tested positive for the disease.
March 1, 2020	A High-Level Coordination Committee for the Prevention and Control of COVID-19 is constituted by the Government of Nepal.	This commission committee has the leading role in planning and implementing leadership to control the pandemic in the country. This committee has worked under the name of COVID-19 Crisis Management Center (CCMC), which has held a series of meetings to decide on the immediate situation. In the process, decided verities of restrictions on mobility and economic activities, issues different rules and regulations to control the spread of the pandemic.
March 23, 2020	Suspension of international flights and Visit Nepal 2020 national program, schools and educational institutions were closed.	Some rescue international flights were arranged in between, few flights with restrictions were allowed only after 1st of September 2020. Schools and education institutions particularly classroom teachings are not allowed yet as of October 1st, 2020.
March 24, 2020	Country-wide lockdown started (first round lockdown)	The lockdown ended on 21st July 2020 with restrictions on mobility and economic activities, no public transportation until 1st of September 2020.
April 4, 2020	First case of local transmission was detected.	In the Kailali district of Far Western province. This means the infected was not from overseas but infected by the infected incomer from India.
May 17, 2020	First death from COVID-19	A 29-year-old woman from Kavrepalanchowk died from the novel coronavirus. She was tested positive after a few days of discharge from the hospital after giving birth to a baby boy.

(*continued*)

Table 3.2 (continued)

Date	*Incidents*	*Remarks*
Until October 1st, 2020	Extension of testing labs in different hospitals	A total of 57 (government 40 and the private sector's 17) labs in different districts covering all provinces of the country have been established to date. Testing facilities was hardly in existence in only one hospital, that is, Teku Hospital (Sukraraj Tropical & Infectious Disease Hospital) in the federal capital city (Kathmandu).
November 24th, 2020	Further relaxation of economic activities and visas to foreigners	Authority delegated to local government for relaxing the economic activities based on the infection cases, also, visa process to foreigners was normalized with some condition to follow the COVID-19 protocol issued by Nepal's government. Air travelers were allowed but the travelers via land transportation were still restricted.
December 22nd, 2020	Restrictions imposed to visitors from the UK in the fear of the new variant of the virus in Europe	The visitors from and via the UK were restricted, and recently arrived were put in contact tracing. A compulsory quarantine was imposed on visitors from Europe.
January 3rd, 2021	Relaxed the restriction imposed on film industry with strong provision of monitoring	Relaxation on the restrictions imposed on the film halls and industries was made with the strong monitoring mechanism to follow up the protocols via the Ministry of Communication and Information Technology. Also, the relaxation of the restriction was made for other businesses such as restaurants and other businesses.
March 18th, 2021	13 routes from India opened with strict protocol	With COVID-19 negative report within 72 hours, visitors were allowed from India's 13 routes via land transportation. Also, vehicles with Indian number plates were allowed with the same protocols.
April 10th, 2021	Monitoring was made tighter	In the fear of the increasing number of infected cases in Nepal and overseas (EU, India, and other countries), the business and economic activities with mass gatherings were monitored strictly and discouraged to do so. The protocol of COVID-19 was imposed further limiting the number of gatherings for social, entertainment, religious, and fitness purposes. Online classes were encouraged, contact tracing was speeded up, focus on isolation centres and quarantines were made to control the pandemic.

(*continued*)

Table 3.2 (continued)

Date	*Incidents*	*Remarks*
April 26th, 2021	The nationwide lockdown was imposed	As the number of infected people was increasing and created fear from the growing number of infected cases (particularly in India and outmigrant for workers destination countries), the lockdown was imposed in all districts with more than 200 infected cases in the country. Land transportations from overseas were restricted, a compulsory quarantine was imposed on all air passengers, and schools and teaching methods were compelled to be virtual. Other various restrictions were imposed on economic activities. This situation remained for almost two months.
May 27th, 2021	The highest number of infected cases, i.e., 238115 during this month.	Scarcity of ICU beds, hospital beds and ventilators, oxygen cylinders, and shortages of health workers. The government tried to install oxygen plants and concentrators, established hospital beds, and extended the capacity of ICU and ventilators using different sources. The situation remained tense till mid-June.
July 30th, 2021	Working procedures for smart lockdown were approved and implemented.	The lockdown was released, and the smart lockdown was started. In this modality, transportation, and business with no gatherings were allowed. Strict lockdowns were imposed in some districts where the infected cases were in substantial numbers.

Source: CCMC (2021) and Government of Nepal (2020)

3.5 Exports Scenarios: Some Observations

3.5.1 Before Covid-19

Despite many policy and strategic efforts, Nepal's export performance has not been satisfactory for a long period. We present the growth rate and share in GDP of exports of goods and services in Fig. 3.1 to show the overall progress situation of Nepal's exports. The exports of goods and services compared to Nepal's GDP have always remained below 30 percent. This was at the highest point in the year 1997. On the other hand, exports have many fluctuations, maximum with 111 percent growth in 1975, 42 percent in 1995, and negative growth in a few years, such as in

Fig. 3.1 Exports of Goods and services scenario, 1966–2019. (Source: author's presentation using the data from World Bank (2021b))

2002, 2010, and 2016 in recent years. The fitted line shows that the annual growth of exports for the selected period is negative as it is sloped downwards right.

Being a landlocked least developed country, Nepal's exports have many supply-side problems. First, most of the time it must rely on India's infrastructure and route for road transport to Kolkata port, the nearest port at about 1000 kilometers. This creates additional constraints to increase the price of exports. Further, with a small scale of economies and production technologies, Nepal's exporters face a high amount of cost of production. These entirely make exports uncompetitive, which we can replace by improving doing business environment, good governance, and other ways to increase productivity as well as the quality of the products. Shortage of investment/capital is another issue that has resulted in poor progress on technological innovation and productivity. There are a few infrastructure-related issues for some types of exports such as organic cold crops and products from the northern part of the country (products in the Himalayas, mountains, and nearby areas).

A known fact is that Nepal is located in between two big markets of two of the fastest-growing economies in the world. Grabbing the opportunity from these two markets is an important issue, for which Nepal's supply-side factors are not enough developed yet. In this background, Nepal needs to work hard and smart for graving opportunities from these large markets in line with the cheap labour force with the demographic dividend, abundant natural and other resources in the country, sound climate for unique agriculture (both tropical and cold crops), and other geographical benefits, such as eight of the top ten mountains, Pashupatinath-pivotal place for Hindus, Lumbini-pivotal place for Buddhists, Janaki Mandir-pivotal place for Mithila culture, forests with the potential benefits from the non-timber forests and bio-diversities.

Against these backgrounds, a rapidly increasing trend of trade deficit is one of the major concerns in the country. Nepal is also unable to diversify its trade in terms of countries and commodities as the concentration is in India with more than 60 percent. Even with the diversification of the products, not much consistent success has been achieved. Therefore, until and unless Nepal increases its trade competitiveness by adopting different policies, it cannot reduce its ever-increasing trade deficit. Doubtlessly, considering the costs factor, priority should be given to the high-value-to-weight products not only based on agriculture but also high-tech light products.

Nepal's trade deficit was widening every year as shown in Fig. 3.2, which presents the share of exports and imports in the gross domestic product (GDP). This figure shows the trends of imports and exports that have been changing from 1990 to 2018. The figure shows that something went wrong as exports have declined even since 2004 but imports as a share of GDP are growing at a much faster pace. The trend of imports share as a percent of GDP substantially increased from 2001 onwards. A noteworthy point is that this increment of imports is fed by the

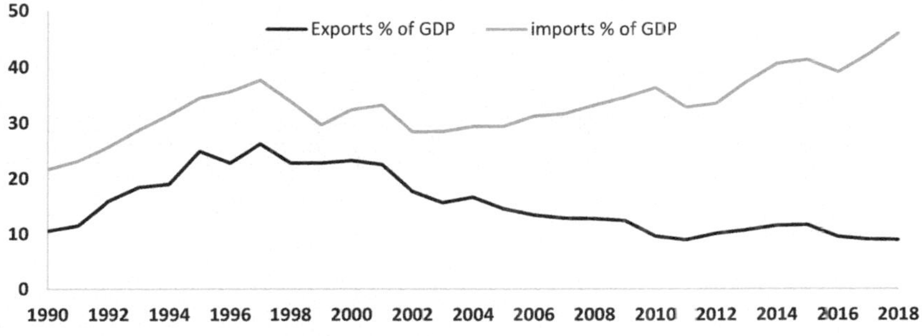

Fig. 3.2 Imports and exports, 1990–2018. (Source: WITS (2021))

remittances, which have particularly increased since the same year, making the gap wider.

3.5.2 After the Origin of Covid-19

Nepal's exports decreased during the months when the lockdowns were imposed because of the pandemic. However, if we look at the entire duration from the origin of the pandemic to the end of 2021, an overall average growth of exports is recorded at about 12 percent of the monthly average. Figure 3.3 shows several fluctuations during the months. Particularly, the negative shocks were given when the lockdowns and other mobility restrictions were imposed to control the pandemic. The data show that exports declined by nine percent during March 2020 when the pandemic was rising in the global context. Because of lockdowns in most of the major cities of trading partners and Nepal, the exports heavily declined, such as 77 percent lower exports in April 2020, which was the biggest shock in the export sector after the origin of the pandemic. During May, the piled exports during March also were exported because of the relaxed provision to exporters during April, so was the highest amount of growth, that is 129 percent. It seems that the exports from the second

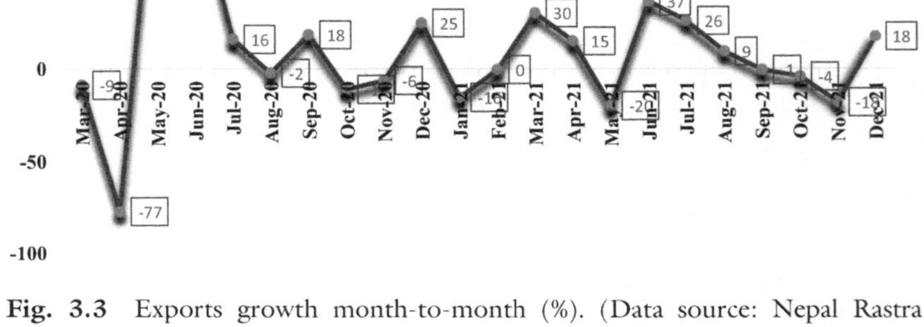

Fig. 3.3 Exports growth month-to-month (%). (Data source: Nepal Rastra Bank (2025))

quarter of 2020 maintained growth in most of the months. Overall, the growth of exports in total seems impressive in this period.

Figure 3.4 also tells a similar story, more clearly visible that the export growth during the same months of the fiscal years 2020/2021 and 2021/2022 are higher in general.

Table 3.3 presents the top 20 products exported from Nepal to different countries for 2018/2019 to the first three months of 2020/2021. The half of 2019/2020 and the three months of 2020/2021 cover the COVID-19 period. There are two key messages from this table. First, few products' shares in total exports have grown in the first quarter of 2020/2021 to the maximum share over three years. For example, the shares of Cardamom, Pashmina, Medicine (Ayurvedic), Noodles, Toothpaste, Ginger, and Tea have increased visibly. Second, the share of these top 20 products in the total exports has declined during the first quarter of 2020/2021 compared to that of the previous years but remains higher than that of the year 2018/2019. This indicates that our export ground was deemed even pre-COVID-19 period but has not substantially lost the ground of export diversification.

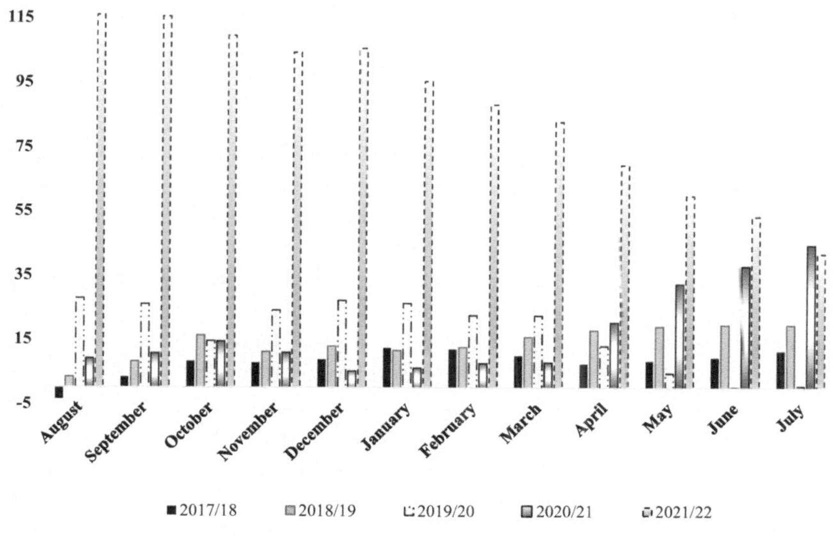

Fig. 3.4 Exports growth month-to-month (%). (Data source: Nepal Rastra Bank (2025))

Table 3.3 Export dynamics over the period from 2018/2019–2020/2021

S.N.	*Items*	*2018/2019*	*2019/2020*	*2020/2021*
1	Woolen Carpet	7.6	6.3	6.6
2	Polyster Yarn + Threads	7.1	5.6	6.0
3	Jute Goods	6.0	5.4	5.2
4	Cardamom	4.4	4.1	4.7
5	Readymade garment	4.3	2.9	3.3
6	Juice	4.7	3.5	3.2
7	Textiles	3.5	2.9	2.5
8	Pashmina	2.0	1.8	2.5
9	Medicine (Ayurvedic)	0.8	1.0	1.9
10	Noodles	1.0	0.8	1.5
11	Oil Cakes	1.7	1.6	1.4
12	Herbs	1.4	1.5	1.1
13	Toothpaste	0.8	0.8	1.0
14	Zinc Sheet	3.0	1.0	0.8
15	Shoes and Sandles	0.9	0.8	0.6
16	Wire	2.2	0.6	0.6
17	Silverware and Jewelleries	0.5	0.4	0.6
18	Rosin	1.4	0.8	0.5
19	Ginger	0.5	0.4	0.5
20	Tea	0.3	0.3	0.5
	Other Products	*45.9*	*57.4*	*55.0*
	Total exports share	100	100	100

Data source: Nepal Rastra Bank (2021)

As stated earlier, globally, there are few positive marks on international trade. However, these positive marks are not enough to neutralize the negative marks on trade, but can be a sort of avenue for potential trade scope in the future in the Nepalese context.

Because of the pandemic, globally, the consumption and demand of products related to medicine, herbs, spices, health, and hygiene have increased substantially (Shahrajabian et al., 2020) and Nepal seems to have grabbed the opportunity. This trend has been reflected in the case of Nepal, as seen from the data of the cardamom exports, which have increased substantially in this period. Similarly, Ayurvedic medicinal products' export is increased by more than 60 percent, exports of herbs have increased by 66 percent, and ginger and tea exports have increased by more than 29 and 45 percent, respectively, during 2020 (Nepal Rastra Bank, 2020). This trend has been consistently realised in the first half of 2021.

It has been noticed from the data in the global context that the consumption trend of Asian foods, including Asian noodles, soups, juices, and other processed foods has increased substantially because of COVID-19. Nepal also seems to get some benefits in this regard, for instance, the export of Juice, Noodles, Oil cakes, etc. have made significant growth, that is more than 100 percent growth in some cases as stated in Nepal Rastra Bank (2020).

As suggested by the literature, agriculture products have the largest backwards and forwards linkages in Nepal. The data shows that the agriculture products as raw materials to produce the finished products have contributed a lot to increase some products' export value in the past. For example, Jute goods, Pashmina, toothpaste, handmade wooden items, edible products, herbs, ginger, etc. have a strong linkage with agriculture. These products have performed well during the pandemic too.

Export of garments products has increased substantially in the pandemic period too. The database of Nepal Rastra Bank (2020) shows that exports of Polyester yarn and threads, Readymade garments, Textile have increased to some extent. More importantly, the Readymade Garments' import has declined by more than 35 percent indicating that import has been substituted creating more employment in the domestic economy, and this trend has remained consistent during the first half of 2021.

For almost one and a half years now, teaching methodology has had a regime shift. Because of the pandemic, most of the schools and colleges are teaching online. Most of the business meetings, seminars, conferences, and discussions are held virtually using different platforms provided in gadgets by different vendors. Much of the office work is performed from home using a variety of software, applications, and platforms. Banking transactions have shifted towards online payments speedily; there seems to be an increasing trend for shopping payments using digital payments aided by various applications and software, making habitual digital transactions. Even ordinary people also have increased their time with digital devices while being in isolation or at the stage of facing lockdowns and other restrictions in mobility. These activities have resulted in to increase in internet use by more than 50 percent (Singh, 2020). This may ultimately change the way of transactions and entertainment in the future as the habit of coping the digital transactions has increased substantially in the first half of 2021.

3.6 Results and Discussions

The estimation results are presented in Table 3.4, in which the first column results are from the fixed effect estimation method. The second, third, and fourth columns' results are based on the random effect estimation method. First, we estimate the benchmark model using the fixed-effect estimation method, and then the same model is estimated based on the random-effect estimation method. As seen in the first and second columns, the results consistently indicate a statistically positive association of COVID-19 with Nepal's exports and a statistically significant but negative impact of COVID-19 cases on the partner countries' imports from Nepal. The results of the Covid-19 cases in Nepal expose a few important facts about Nepal's export behaviour. The results suggest that a one percent increase in COVID-19 cases in Nepal is associated with an increase in

Table 3.4 Impact of Covid-19 on the Export performance of Nepal

Dependent variable: EXPORT	*(FE)*	*(RE1)*	*(RE2)*	*(RE3)*
LCOCIDNPL: Covid cases in Nepal-log	0.217***	0.196***	0.187***	0.198***
	(0.035)	(0.032)	(0.033)	(0.032)
LCOVIDPART: Covid cases in partner-log	−0.22***	−0.19***	−0.17***	−0.18***
	(0.045)	(0.041)	(0.042)	(0.041)
BORD: Border-Dummy			2.81	6.81***
			(2.336)	(1.432)
LDIST: Distance between most populated cities			0.37	0.95
			(0.623)	(0.663)
Number of observations	*242*	*242*	*242*	*224*
Number of groups	*14*	*14*	*14*	*13*
F-statistics/Wald Chai-squared	*21.07*	*47.40*	*61.25*	*223.59*
R-Squared	*0.61*	*0.61*	*0.55*	*0.57*
corr	*−0.53*	–	–	–
Partner-year-month fixed effect	*Yes*	*Yes*	*Yes*	*Yes*
Partner-month fixed effect	*No*	*Yes*	*No*	*No*

Note: ***, **, and * refer to the coefficients that are significant at 1%, 5%, and 10% levels of significance. The figures in the parenthesis are robust standard errors

Nepal's exports by an average of about 0.20 percent holding other variables in the model constant. This result generally seems against general expectation, but this also reflected from the data as mentioned in Figs. 3.3 and 3.4, and Table 4.1 on which the exports in the later months have increased visibly, and the average growth rate of the top 10 products that capture about 86 per cent of Nepal's exports is impressive for the selected period.

This result raises many questions and doubts about the exports and the pandemic. Therefore, we intend to observe the product-wise exports scenario during this period and found that the growth of soyabean oil is remarkable that has increased by more than three folds during June 2020 to June 2021 (around 2.5 billion to 8.6 billion Rupees) which is skewing Nepal's overall export performance during the pandemic. Similarly, carpet, knotted of wool or fine animal hair, woven fabric of jute or bast fibres and yarns increased visibly in large during the same period. These data remove the doubt of dominating export growth by soyabean oil and other seasonal fluxes of the products. This scenario shows export growth in total. However, we cannot say all sectors have performed this well. Some sector-specific big players may have done to lead overall export growth, which is beyond the scope of this research. It does not mean that all sectors benefited but the few selected products have done better in this period, though the diversifications, both in terms of destination and products, have been narrowed down is a point of worry.

Then, we can say four main reasons might have played a role in this favourable situation for exports during this difficult time. First, lockdowns and other restrictions controlled the informal export (export without record, which normally is not recorded in the normal time) and that turned out to be formal recording in the export account. It has not been proved but it seems highly possible (this opens a new horizon of research to knowing the volume of exports without record in normal time). It means, the pandemic lowered the informal exports that were mainly because of not properly recording exports in normal situation, and the pandemic's restriction and strict monitoring of the economic activities on the Indian border side forced to record such exports, which resulted in to increase in the export volume.

Also, as noted, export to India has increased tremendously in this period. Further, this is supported by the results of the fourth column of the same table in which another bordering country, China, is dropped from the sample and the border variable turned out to be statistically significant with a very high degree of coefficient.

Second, the lockdowns with the provision of allowing production forces to run the manufacturing sector increased the productivity of those forces, which had a difficult situation due to traffic congestion and other crowds in the major cities during normal times. Even in the validation workshop held in Kathmandu, few representative participants raised the difficulty in accessing their factories and outlets in Kathmandu during the daytime on normal days.

The third reason is potentially the effort of returnee migrant workers due to the pandemic. Notably, many of these returnees engaged in the agriculture sector, small industries related to health care items, garments, food items like noodles and species, tea, and so on. The fourth potential reason is that there is an increased demand for some products that have a comparative advantage and are in favour of Nepalese exporters in the pandemic (for example in textiles due to disruptions in supply chains due to lockdowns in China).

The results also show that the pandemic in the partner countries caused to decline in Nepal's exports by almost 0.20 percent. It means if Nepal's partners are heavily impacted by the pandemic, it will have to severe adverse impact on Nepal's export trade (especially because Nepal is a landlocked country and has a reliance on neighbouring countries for transit). In the third column, we added two gravity variables: distance and border dummy. Even, in this case, the results for the Covid-19 cases in Nepal and partner countries remain consistent with very negligible changes in the coefficients.

These estimated results for the short term raise the confidence to say that the role of governance quality is a very important determinant of the export performance of Nepal. Therefore, the role of governance quality in export performance is examined by employing the gravity dataset for the period from 2010 to 2023, and the results are presented in Tables 3.5 and 3.6, which show some important points about the export performance of Nepal.

Table 3.5 Gravity modeling results, determinants of exports (2010–2022)

Dependent variable: EXPORT-log	*(FE1)*	*(RE1)*	*(FE2)*	*(RE2)*
LGDP: Nepal's GDP-log	0.865*	0.788*	0.921*	0.852*
	(0.481)	(0.445)	(0.476)	(0.437)
LPOP: Nepal's population-log	−3.441	−3.597	−6.10***	−6.10***
	(2.438)	(2.463)	(2.195)	(2.268)
PLGDP: Partner's GDP-log	−0.744*	−0.559	−0.796*	−0.606
	(0.432)	(0.452)	(0.410)	(0.440)
PLPOP: Partner's population-log	0.871	1.106**	1.064	1.149***
	(1.606)	(0.438)	(1.645)	(0.433)
LDIST: Distance-log	Dropped	0.706	Dropped	0.768
		(0.751)		(0.737)
GOVIN: Nepal's governance index			2.159***	2.053***
			(0.565)	(0.654)
Number of observations	*195*	*195*	*195*	*195*
Number of groups	*15*	*15*	*15*	*15*
F-statistics/Wald statistics	*1.59*	*20.49*	*14.43*	*94.32*
R-squared	*0.11*	*0.11*	*0.14*	*0.13*
Correlation	*−0.43*	-	*−0.51*	-

Note: ***, **, and * refer to the coefficients that are significant at 1%, 5%, and 10% levels of significance. The figures in the parentheses are robust standard errors

Table 3.5 demonstrates the role of governance quality in the export performance of Nepal from 2010 to 2023. The results underscore the critical importance of governance in enhancing export activities in both estimation methods (FE and RE). Specifically, improved governance quality is shown to be a significant determinant that positively influences Nepal's export performance, reinforcing the need for strong institutional frameworks and effective policies to sustain and boost exports.

These results are robust, even another variable (Covid-19) is added to the estimations (Table 3.6). Consistently, it is found that Nepal's exports can be improved by improving the quality of the governance of Nepal and it is largely determined by Nepal's GDP and its partner countries' population. As expected, the coefficient of the COVID-19 dummy is negative and statistically significant at a 10 percent level if the quality of governance variable is controlled.

These results, overall, validate our doubt that the export data reported in normal times do not replicate the true story of export episodes. Improving the quality of governance will improve the quality of data of export on one hand, and other and most important side, the enhancement

Table 3.6 Gravity modeling results, robustness check

Dependent variable: EXPORT-log	*(RE3)*	*(RE4)*
LGDP: Nepal's GDP-log	0.129	0.374
	(0.323)	(0.328)
LPOP: Nepal's population-log	−0.631	−0.038
	(2.958)	(2.930)
PLGDP: Partner's GDP-log	−0.620	−0.555
	(0.447)	(0.460)
PLPOP: Partner's population-log	1.142***	1.093**
	(0.437)	(0.442)
LDIST: Distance-log	0.772	0.694
	(0.749)	(0.758)
GOVIN: Nepal's governance-index	2.841***	
	(0.508)	
Covid-19: Covid year-Dummy	−0.434*	−0.240
	(0.238)	(0.238)
Number of observations	195	195
Number of groups	15	15
Wald statistics	367.19	22.02
R-squared	0.16	0.11
Correlation	–	–

Note: ***, **, and * refer to the coefficients that are significant at 1%, 5%, and 10% levels of significance. The figures in the parentheses are robust standard errors

of the quality of the governance would motivate investors, attract domestic and foreign investment, and boost economic activities to improve the export performance of Nepal.

3.7 Conclusions and Recommendations

As an attempt to assess COVID-19's impact on Nepal's international trade and to identify the role of governance quality in export performance, this chapter documents the COVID-19 scenario in global and Nepal's prospects, then analyses the impact of the pandemic on Nepal's export trade and investigates the role of the quality of governance in the export performance. In doing so I review the relevant literature, policies, opinions expressed in different outlets, data, and responses from people of different walks of life in Nepal in the background of COVID-19's economic impact on the global economy is very serious and negative in many respects. The threat of the pandemic is explained as seen in the health, restricted mobility of production forces, various restrictions of different governments, closure of schools and education institutions, and limited operation of markets and other economic activities. The crisis in the economies can be seen not only in employment, output, productivity, and growth but also in overall macroeconomic indicators with some exceptions in the context of Nepal.

An encouraging scenario is that few dynamics in export trade have been realized in Nepal's export case due to the pandemic. The exports of agriculture-based products, such as herbs and medicines, health and hygiene, spices, Pashmina, and a few edible products have grown. These can be noted as the Silverlight in the dark cloud and can open potential avenues for export. But it depends on how efficiently and timely, we grab these opportunities from the international market. The major paradigm shift in the transaction behavior of the people seems to be digital literacy forced by the pandemic. Digital literacy has been accelerated by practice in the workplace, market, and financial institutions, economic activities, and digital entertainment. This has been a point of attraction even in the transportation sector, where digital transactions seem to grow for online tickets and seat bookings in the days to come.

As noted from various shocks of the COVID-19 global pandemic to most economies, there may be other global, regional, and national pandemics and shocks creating hurdles for national and international mobilities, and other varieties of restrictions to be imposed at the national level. Therefore, we need our economic system to consider what option could be used in such a situation.

The evidence suggests that the priority in the vaccination against the virus and trade based on domestic products with backward and forward linkages should get the national priority because such trade helps to sustain the economy in times of crisis. Relying on imports for food and garment products does not seem reasonable, reliable, and sustainable in such a situation. Therefore, domestic agriculture should be closely linked with small and medium-scale industries so that it can help to substitute the imports as well as to improve the bases for exports.

There are some potential avenues for export trade exposed by the pandemic. These avenues are in favor of the comparative advantage of Nepal too. Therefore, timely and efficient grabbing opportunities from the market should be the national priority so that export performance may be better than even the pre-COVID-19 situation. Also, developing the industry base for Asian foods with light weight-to-value, such as herbs, spices, tea, coffee, juice, and drinks, medicines with different methods, and health care and hygiene products should be the priority of the industrialization system. Doing so will help at the easy time to boost exports and in the difficult time including the pandemics, this will help to sustain the economy and minimize the risk of being without food, medicines, and garments. We suggest developing the programs and policy considering this fact in practice with priority.

Proactive and strategic efforts to promote exports in neighboring and regional markets are another way to sustain the economy in the time of crisis. India is the market for more than half of Nepal's exports which is governed by the bilateral trade treaty. Exploring exports to China, which is the largest market in the world and is not a significant player in the case of Nepal's exports, is another way to boost exports in the background of Nepal's weak export diversification for a long time now.

Another point of recommendation is to focus on connectivity and trade capacity building, which can help to promote exports both at a time of crisis and in normal situations. Nepal's weak connectivity to neighbouring and regional markets has always been a challenge in flourishing trade and reducing trade costs. Therefore, it is very important to focus on improved connectivity, quality infrastructure, quality of governance, and trade capacity building so that the supply chain for both imports and exports would not be an issue, and export performance can be improved.

References

Alon, T., Doepke, M., Olmstead-Rumsey, J., & Tertilt, M. (2020). The impact of the coronavirus pandemic on gender equality. *Covid Economics Vetted and Real-Time Papers*(4).

Baker, S. R., Bloom, N., Davis, S. J., Kost, K. J., Sammon, M. C., & Viratyosin, T. (2020). *The unprecedented stock market impact of COVID-19* (0898–2937).

Baldwin, R., & Tomiura, E. (2020). Thinking ahead about the trade impact of COVID-19. In R. Baldwin & B. W. di Mauro (Eds.), *Economics in the Time of COVID-19* (Vol. 59). CEPR Press.

Barichello, R. (2020). The COVID-19 pandemic: Anticipating its effects on Canada's agricultural trade. *Canadian Journal of Agricultural Economics/Revue canadienne d'agroeconomie*, *68*(2), 219–224. https://doi.org/10.1111/cjag.12244

CCMC. (2021). *COVID-19 Related Documents.* COVID-19 Crisis Management Center, Kathmandu, Nepal

CEPII. (2025). *The CEPII Gravity Dataset*

Dev, S. M., & Sengupta, R. (2020). Covid-19: Impact on the Indian economy. Indira Gandhi Institute of Development Research, Mumbai April, 1–43. http://www.igidr.ac.in/pdf/publication/WP-2020-013.pdf

Devan, A. R., Nair, B., Kumar, A. R., Gorantla, J. N., & Nath, L. R. (2021). Unravelling the Immune Modulatory Effect of Indian Spices to Impede the Transmission of COVID-19: A Promising Approach. *Current Pharmaceutical Biotechnology*.

Elsayed, Y., & Khan, N. A. (2020). Immunity-Boosting Spices and the Novel Coronavirus. *ACS Chemical Neuroscience, 11*(12), 1696–1698. https://doi.org/10.1021/acschemneuro.0c00239

Erokhin, V., & Gao, T. (2020). Impacts of COVID-19 on trade and economic aspects of food security: Evidence from 45 developing countries. *International journal of environmental research and public health, 17*(5575), 1–28.

Gössling, S., Scott, D., & Hall, C. M. (2020). Pandemics, tourism and global change: a rapid assessment of COVID-19. *Journal of Sustainable Tourism*, 1–20.

Government of Nepal. (2020). *Health sector emergency response plan.* Ministry of Health and Population, Kathmandu.

Goyal, A. (2020). Post COVID-19: recovering and sustaining India's growth. *Indian Economic Review, 55*(1), 161–181.

Gregorioa, G. B., & Ancog, R. C. (2020). Assessing the impact of the covid-19 pandemic on agricultural production in Southeast Asia: toward transformative change in agricultural food systems. *Asian Journal of Agriculture and Development, 17*(1362-2020-1097), 1–13.

Gruszczynski, L. (2020). The COVID-19 Pandemic and International Trade: Temporary Turbulence or Paradigm Shift? *European Journal of Risk Regulation, 11*(2), 337–342.

Hayakawa, K., & Mukunoki, H. (2021a). The impact of COVID-19 on international trade: Evidence from the first shock. *Journal of the Japanese and International Economies, 60*, 1–12.

Hayakawa, K., & Mukunoki, H. (2021b). The impact of COVID-19 on international trade: Evidence from the first shock. *Journal of the Japanese and International Economies, 60*, 101135. https://doi.org/10.1016/j.jjie.2021.101135

Johns Hopkins University & Medicine. (2021). *COVID-19 Datasets* (

Johns Hopkins University & Medicine. (2022). *COVID-19 Datasets*

Lin, B.-x., & Zhang, Y. Y. (2020). Impact of the COVID-19 pandemic on agricultural exports. *Journal of Integrative Agriculture, 19*(12), 2937–2945.

Nepal Rastra Bank. (2020). *Current Macroeconomic and Financial Situation.* Baluwatar, Nepal.

Nepal Rastra Bank. (2021). Current Macroeconomic and Financial Situation https://www.nrb.org.np/category/current-macroeconomic-situation/?department=red, *accessed on 9/08/2021.*

Nepal Rastra Bank. (2025). *Current Macroeconomic and Financial Situation.* Baluwatar, Kathmandu, Nepal

Paudel, R. C. (2019). Exports Performance of Nepal: What Can Be Done? *Applied Economics and Finance, 6*(5), 92–103.

Paudel, R. C. (2021). Impact of Covid-19 on Nepal's Economy. In R. Shrestha, R. Sapkota, & M. Shrestha (Eds.), *COVID-19 Multidisciplinary Narratives* (pp. 46–65). Institute of Foreign Affairs (IFA).

Ritchie, H., Ortiz-Ospina, E., Beltekian, D., Mathieu, E., Hasell, J., Macdonald, B., Giattino, C., Appel, C., Rodés-Guirao, L., & Roser, M. (2021). *Statistics and Research: Coronavirus (COVID-19) Vaccinations*

Shahrajabian, M. H., Sun, W., & Cheng, Q. (2020). Traditional Herbal Medicine for the Prevention and Treatment of Cold and Flu in the Autumn of 2020, Overlapped With COVID-19. *Natural Product Communications, 15*(8), 1–10.

Singh, R. R. (2020). Coronavirus-lockdown increased internet consumption by 50 percent in Nepal. https://reviews.com.np/article/coronavirus-lockdown-increased-internet-consumption-by-50-percent.

TEPC. (2021). *Nepal trade informaiton portal.*

Trade and export promotion centre. (2021). *Nepal Trade Information Portal*

Vidya, C. T., & Prabheesh, K. P. (2020). Implications of COVID-19 Pandemic on the Global Trade Networks. *Emerging Markets Finance and Trade, 56*(10), 2408–2421. https://doi.org/10.1080/1540496X.2020.1785426

WITS. (2021). *Trade Data (UN Comtrade)*

World Bank. (2021a). Global Economic Prospects, June 2021. In: The World Bank.

World Bank. (2021b). *World Development Indicators.*

CHAPTER 4

Integrated Agriculture and Manufacturing Sectors for Speedy Growth

4.1 Introduction

Once we knew the role of governance quality in export performance in Chap. 3, we now proceed to seek the role of the integrated agriculture and manufacturing sector in accelerating economic growth. Once the governance quality is improved, this improves the country's trade environment. In the meantime, we need to identify the most productive sector so that, in addition to trade, economic growth can be accelerated due to employment and output increase in the country.

Nepal seems to be facing a trap of jobless economic growth that has hovered below four and a half percent on average for two decades. If we look at the longer term, such as from 1960 to 2023, this average growth rate stands at 3.80 percent, which is higher than that of the United Kingdom and the United States, 2.30 percent 3.00 percent, respectively. However, this rate for Nepal's close neighbours, China and India, stands at about 5.20 percent and 7.95 percent, respectively (World Bank, 2025a). These facts indicate two important aspects of the Nepalese economy in general. First, Nepal is lagging compared to its fast-growing neighbours despite its potential to grow faster. Generally, the slow growth rate of Nepal is primarily attributed to its lack of industrial diversification and its dependence on agriculture, which employs a significant portion of the population but contributes less to the GDP. Second, even the growth rate

R. C. Paudel, *Essays on Key Issues of Development in Nepal*, https://doi.org/10.1007/978-981-95-7715-6_4

of the Nepalese economy is a kind of jobless growth as the number of migrating people for jobs has been increasing every year for more than two decades.

Different trade theories, such as the Heckscher-Ohlin model of factor abundance and the Samuelson model of factor endowment, suggest that the country should rely on its abundant factors of production and endowments for international trade to be beneficial, which can help to accelerate economic growth and increase public welfare in the country. If we believe in these trade theories, probably the best way to remodel the development strategy of the country may be to adopt an integrated approach that combines agriculture with manufacturing to break the cycle of jobless, slow growth. Nepal can create more job opportunities and stimulate economic activities by leveraging the agricultural sector, which has abundant resources, and pairing it with the manufacturing sector. This will increase the value addition of both agriculture and manufacturing sectors, boosting productivity and innovation, and leading to increased exports and a more sustainable economic model. For instance, value addition in agriculture through food processing, packaging, and distribution not only enhances the value chain but also opens new markets and revenue streams creating substantial jobs in the national economy. Unfortunately, this has not happened in Nepal, why?

For this, the structural formation of the Nepalese economy remains a complex issue. For example, the Nepalese economy has a heavy reliance on agriculture, which employs about 65 % of the population but contributes less than 30% to the gross domestic product (GDP). This indicates that the sector suffers from low productivity due to various reasons. A few of them to note are outdated farming techniques, lack of access to modern technology, insufficient investment, poor market chain, lack of proper irrigation system, etc. Moreover, the agrarian nature of the economy has limited industrial diversification, making Nepal highly dependent on imports for most of its industrial needs. It means the sector has a kind of disguised unemployment on the one hand, and on the other hand, it lacks proper investment.

Next, the manufacturing sector, on the other hand, remains underdeveloped, contributing just about five percent to the GDP. It has low employment, investment, and value addition. The reasons behind this scenario can be blamed on the lack of infrastructure, energy shortages, an unfavorable business climate, a poor supply chain in the global market, and a poor supply chain linked to agriculture. Furthermore, political instability, bureaucratic inefficiencies, and poor investment climate have deterred both domestic and foreign investments, which are crucial for manufacturing development.

In the past two decades, investment in the services sector has increased substantially but this sector normally cannot employ many unskilled and semi-skilled human resources. This type of structural scenario has created three major difficulties in the economy. First, as we move from agriculture to the service sector without developing the manufacturing sector, the structure of the economy has become fragile. If a solid foundation for manufacturing had been made before moving to the service sector, the scenario would be much better than the current situation. Second, youth flights from the country as not sufficient jobs are created for them in the economy because of this structural mismatch of the economy. Third, the country has become the net importer with an import-export ratio of more than seven consistently for many years. These backgrounds are responsible for slower economic growth than the normal expectation in Nepal. Also, this has resulted in a peculiar form of economic growth that does not translate into job creation, often referred to as "jobless growth."

Therefore, to come out of the trap of jobless slow growth and to accelerate economic growth, Nepal may need to adopt an integrated approach combining agriculture with manufacturing, as countries like Indonesia, Thailand, and Vietnam have demonstrated remarkable progress by adopting this approach. Indonesia's agrarian transformation through industrialization in the 1980s and Thailand's agro-industrial integration have both shown positive impacts on job creation and economic growth. Similarly, Vietnam has leveraged its agricultural strengths by integrating manufacturing processes, thus boosting its export capabilities and overall economic resilience in the recent decade (Rigg, 2004; Yamauchi et al., 2021). Doing this, the synergy created by the integration of these two sectors can lead to substantial job creation, productivity increment, and expansion of economic activities to boost the national output in the country. Also, this will increase value-addition to both agriculture and manufacturing sectors, providing a solid base to the service sector in the future so that those problems discussed above are solved. Notably, most of the advanced economies have adopted this strategy in the past (Munakata, 2007).

Following these backgrounds, Nepal may do better in terms of economic growth, integrating the agriculture and manufacturing sectors, and can draw inspiration from these examples to remodel its economic strategy. As this strategy helps to develop agro-based industries, Nepal can enhance the value chain of its agricultural products, create more jobs, and position the country for greater participation in the global market. Ney synergy created by these sectors' integration can be expected to yield higher productivity, stimulate innovation, and generate sustainable economic growth with the strong resilience of the economy.

Nepal is a least developed landlocked country intending to graduate from least developed country category by 2026. Therefore, studying Nepal's economic growth issues may be an insightful case for the global context because it offers valuable insights into the challenges and opportunities faced by developing economies that are heavily reliant on agriculture but lack industrial diversification. By analyzing Nepal's economic hurdles and potential solutions for development paths, policymakers, economists, and stakeholders worldwide can gain a deeper understanding of how to foster sustainable growth in similar contexts. Furthermore, Nepal's experience can serve as a blueprint for other developing nations aiming to break free from the cycle of jobless growth and achieve more balanced and inclusive economic development.

I believe understanding these dynamics of least developed agrarian economy is essential for creating effective international trade policies, forming strategic economic partnerships, promoting global economic stability, and maintaining peaceful and happy human beings in the world. Because of strong backward-forward linkages and higher rate of value addition with the integration of these two sectors, this synergy matters more to the economies like of Nepal. Therefore, the main objective of this chapter is to investigate whether the integration of agricultural and manufacturing sectors contributes to faster economic growth in Nepal.

This chapter proceeds as follows. Section 4.2 presents a brief literature review followed by some observations of the agriculture and manufacturing sectors along with the growth episode of Nepal in Sect. 4.3. Section 4.4 presents the Research Methodology of the chapter, and Sect. 4.5 presents the results and discussion from the econometric analysis. The final Sect. 4.6, concludes the chapter with a summary and policy recommendations.

4.2 Brief Literature Review

The integration of agriculture and manufacturing sectors has been studied extensively as a pathway to accelerate economic growth in literature, both in developing and developed countries' contexts. Numerous studies highlight the positive impacts of this integration on job creation, productivity, and overall economic development in a number of countries in different regions.

One of the seminal works in this area is Johnston and Mellor (1961), which argues that agricultural development provides the necessary surplus and resources for industrial growth. The authors emphasize that an efficient agricultural sector can produce food at lower costs, release labor for industrial employment, and generate capital for industrial investment so that the integration of these two sectors can leverage the economic growth in a faster pace.

Thailand's experience with agro-industrial integration is detailed in the work of Rigg (2004), which states that Thailand's agro-industrial policy has facilitated the growth of industries such as food processing that have become significant contributors to the country's GDP. Rigg highlights that such integration has not only enhanced the productivity of the agricultural sector but also created numerous employment opportunities, thereby reducing rural poverty and stimulating economic activities.

The synergistic effects of combining agriculture with manufacturing sectors have been demonstrated in various countries. For instance, Pingali (2007) discusses the concept of 'agro-industrialization' where the processing of agricultural products into higher-value goods has led to significant economic transformation in countries like Indonesia and the Philippines. Pingali's work shows that this approach not only increases the value addition in agriculture but also enhances the competitiveness of the manufacturing sector.

Diao et al. (2010) examine the potential of agro-processing industries in driving economic growth in the context of Sub-Saharan Africa. They suggested that agro-processing can significantly contribute to structural transformation of the economy by creating jobs, increasing agricultural productivity, and expanding export markets. They concluded that the policies promoting the integration of agriculture and manufacturing are crucial for achieving long-term economic growth in the region.

Woldemichael et al. (2017) discusses the broader implications of integrating agriculture and manufacturing in African economies and suggests that many countries achieved their economic status by leveraging their agricultural strengths to support industrialization. The integration of these sectors has led to higher productivity, innovation, and sustainable economic models in many countries in the region.

Vu and Nguyen (2021) provide a comprehensive analysis of Vietnam's economic strategy, which successfully integrated agriculture with manufacturing. They show that Vietnam's policy of developing agro-based industries has bolstered its export capabilities, improved rural incomes, and contributed to sustained economic growth. The authors note that Vietnam's focus on agro-industrial linkages has been pivotal in transforming its economy from one heavily reliant on agriculture to a more diversified and resilient one.

There are a number of studies that analyze the impact of the integration of agriculture and manufacturing sectors in the high-income countries' contexts. For example, Gardner (2002) analyzed the role of agricultural policies and their influence on industrial growth in the case of the United States of America using a combination of historical data and econometric models. The main finding of this research work is that government subsidies and technological advancements in agriculture significantly boosted productivity and provided a foundation for the growth of agro-industrial sectors.

Japan's experience with agro-industrial integration is detailed in the work of Hayami and Godo (2005), employing a mixed-method approach and combining quantitative data with qualitative interviews, investigated how Japan's agricultural sector adapted to post-war industrialization and revealed that the efficient use of land and resources, along with government support for agro-based industries, played a crucial role in Japan's rapid economic development. They mention that the synergy between agriculture and manufacturing was pivotal in transforming Japan into a leading global economy. Italy's agro-industrial sector was examined by Cosentino et al. (2020), conducting a detailed analysis of the country's food processing industry and its growth linked with innovative technology.

These representative studies collectively underscore the importance of adopting an integrated approach combining the agriculture and manufacturing sectors to create a synergy of resources, foster economic growth, and leverage the country's economic development pace. The experiences of countries like Indonesia, the Philippines, Thailand, and Vietnam provide valuable lessons for Nepal and other developing nations aiming to break free from the cycle of jobless growth and achieve more balanced and inclusive economic development.

4.3 Some Observations in the Nepalese Contexts

Figure 4.1 reveals several notable fluctuations in the growth of sectoral value-added, GDP, and per capita GDP over the observed periods, that is from 1974 to 2023. The observed fluctuations in these sectors have had significant impacts on the GDP over the years. In the earlier periods (1974–1983), agricultural value-added showed considerable growth, contributing positively to GDP. However, during the 1984–1993 period, there was a noticeable decline in such trends, which could be attributed to natural disasters such as earthquakes, floods, and droughts, and political turmoil including a trade blockade from India, which adversely affected agricultural productivity in addition to inadequate infrastructure and a lack of modern farming techniques.

From 1994 onwards, there was sporadic improvement due to better irrigation projects and the introduction of high-yield crop varieties, yet the growth was not consistent in this period despite the expectations from the policymakers and stakeholders. The fluctuations continued as the sector

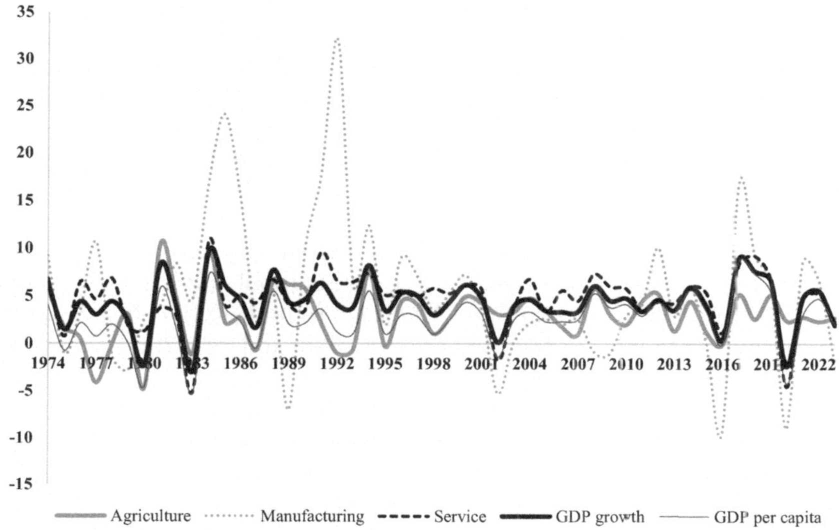

Fig. 4.1 Growth of Sectoral value-added, GDP, and Per capita GDP. (Source: Author's calculation based on data from World Bank (2025a))

faced challenges like climate variability and insufficient investment in agricultural research and development (R&D).

The story of the manufacturing sector's fluctuation seems more sensitive with the records of many ups and downs. This sector experienced significant growth during the 1984–1993 period, helping stabilize GDP growth. This was likely due to the establishment of new manufacturing plants and government policies promoting industrialization. However, in the 2004–2013 period, a decline was observed, possibly due to global economic downturns, abolishment of multi-fiber agreements (MFA), political transition, and increased competition from neighboring countries, which led to reduced industrial output. From 2014 to 2023, the sector showed unstable signs of recovery, attributed to technological advancements and increased foreign investments. Nonetheless, the growth was again interrupted by the COVID-19 pandemic (2021–2023), which caused significant disruptions in the manufacturing supply chain.

The service sector exhibited a steady growth trajectory from 1974 to 2003, becoming a dominant contributor to GDP. The liberalization of the economy and expansion of the tourism and information technology sectors particularly boosted this growth. However, during the 2004–2013 period, the sector faced slower growth, which might be why the earlier-mentioned causes remained responsible.

Post-2014 period, the service sector rebounded and continued to drive GDP growth, with strong performances in finance, real estate, and professional services. The pandemic period (2021–2023) did cause some setbacks due to restrictions on travel and reduced consumer spending, but the sector quickly adapted by shifting to digital platforms and remote services.

The fluctuations in sectoral value-added explain the corresponding ups and downs in GDP. For instance, robust agricultural and manufacturing growth in the early 1980s and late 1990s led to higher GDP. Conversely, the declines in these sectors during the late 1980s and early 2000s resulted in GDP stagnation or decline.

The service sector's consistent growth has been a stabilizing factor, particularly in the latter years. Overall, the interactions between these sectors, influenced by domestic policies and global economic conditions, have shaped the GDP trends illustrated in Fig. 4.1.

Table 4.1 illustrates the percentage growth in sectoral value-added and GDP across various periods, from 1974 to 2023, and the decade average based on data availability. Doing this would help us to understand the

Table 4.1 Sectoral Value-added and GDP Growth (%)

Variables	*1974–1983*	*1984–1993*	*1994–2003*	*2004–2013*	*2014–2023*	*2021–2023*	*Average*
Agriculture	2	3	4	3	3	3	3
Manufacturing	4	12	4	3	3	4	5
Service	3	6	5	5	4	4	5
GDP	3	5	4	4	4	4	4

Source: Author's calculation based on data from World Bank (2025a)

sectoral performance of the different regimes and underscore the critical role of the service sector in stabilizing GDP growth amid fluctuations in agriculture, manufacturing, and service sectors. These sectoral interactions and their responses to domestic policies and global economic conditions have significantly shaped Nepal's GDP trends over the years. In terms of value-added growth, for the overall period, manufacturing and service sectors have dominated agriculture, which is below the growth of the GDP.

During the early period (1974–1993), manufacturing showed significant growth, and it remained at its maximum with a record of 12 percent in the period 1984–1993 followed by the service sector. Also, the GDP growth remained on average at about five percent in the 1984–1993 period. After the 1994–2003 period, both the agriculture and manufacturing sectors have had a visible setback due to political turmoil, followed by transition and instability with policy inconsistency in the country.

The post-2021, post-COVID-19 period saw a slight recovery in the manufacturing sector, with advancements in technology, digital transformation, lightweight products' trade, information technology products and services, and foreign investments playing a vital role. Overall, the manufacturing and service sectors make the major contribution to GDP growth, however, this sector also performs below the expectations of the policymakers and stakeholders.

4.4 Research Methodology

Proper integration of agriculture and manufacturing sectors results from positive changes in various areas and scopes of both sectors, including agricultural productivity (supply side) and processing industries (demand and supply sides). Economic growth is a long-term phenomenon driven by factors such as capital, labor force, and technology. In modern economies, economic growth is complex since numerous diverse factors might contribute in various ways. Therefore, the variables used for modeling economic growth are not unique and can vary significantly.

The original Solow-Swan growth model as discussed in Solow (1956) has been augmented to include the main variables of the interest of the researchers. This chapter uses variables based on growth literature including labour force, capital formation, and sectoral value addition following Nadia et al. (2020). The robustness check of the results is made employing alternative specifications of the model. To know the time series properties of the data, first, the structural break test followed by the unit root test is performed before conducting the econometric estimations.

4.4.1 Model, Variables, and Data

This chapter employs the Solow-Swan growth model that has widely been used in the economic growth literature. For the modeling purpose, I follow the standard literature related with the role of economic sectors' role in economic growth as used in Nadia et al. (2020) but our model mainly differs as we use all economic sectors, such as agriculture, manufacturing and services instead of just agriculture and manufacturing sectors.

Gross domestic product in the natural log form (LGDP), the dependent variable, is employed as the proxy of economic growth. This variable is measured in the United States Dollar (USD). The independent variables are agriculture value added (LAGVAD) measured in USD, gross fixed capital formation (LGCF) measured in USD, and labour force total (LLBF) all in the natural log form as in the Eqn. (4.1) form:

$$LGDP_t = \alpha + \beta_1 LAGVAD_t + \beta_2 LGCF_t + \beta_3 LLBF_t + \epsilon_t \tag{4.1}$$

Where, α is a constant term, $\beta_1 \ldots . \beta_3$ are the coefficients of the variables, ϵ is the error term, t refers to the period, i.e., year, as we are using the annual data from 1990 to 2023. Based on literature, we expect β_1, β_2 and β_3 to be positive.

Then, we test a few alternate specifications of the model, Equation (4.2). The agriculture value added (LAGVAD) is replaced by manufacturing value added (LMFVAD) measured in USD in the natural log form.

$$LGDP_t = \alpha + \beta_1 LMFVAD_t + \beta_2 LGCF_t + \beta_3 LLBF_t + \epsilon_t \tag{4.2}$$

The other economic sector is the service sector, which has been tested in another specification of the model as in Eqn. (4.3), replacing LMFVAD by the service sector value added (LSRVAD) measured in USD in the natural log form.

$$LGDP_t = \alpha + \beta_1 LSRVAD_t + \beta_2 LGCF_t + \beta_3 LLBF_t + \epsilon_t \tag{4.3}$$

Then, for the robustness check and make the estimation more reliable and credible with more robust findings, two alternative specifications are tested as specified in Eqns. (4.4) and (4.5). In Eqn. (4.4), all sectors have been included together to see the much heavier contributor in the growth episode. In Eqn. (4.5), an interaction term of agriculture and manufacturing is included more than in Eqn. (4.4) to see whether the integration is statistically significant in the correct direction.

$$LGDP_t = \alpha + \beta_1 LAGVAD_t + \beta_2 LMFVAD_t + \beta_3 LSRVAD_t + \beta_4 LGCF_t + \beta_5 LLBF_t + \epsilon_t \tag{4.4}$$

$$LGDP_t = \alpha + \beta_1 LAGVAD_t + \beta_2 LMFVAD_t + \beta_3 LSRVAD_t + \beta_4 LGCF_t + \beta_5 LLBF_t + \beta_6 INTAGMF_t + \epsilon_t \tag{4.5}$$

The data used in this empirical analysis for all variables are collected from the world development indicators as given in World Bank (2025b).

4.4.2 *Structural Break Analysis*

Conducting structural break and unit root tests is an essential step on time series data. The reason is that if a structural breakpoint is ignored in the time series analysis, it may lead to a wrong and inferior inference for the policy recommendation. There are several methods for unit root tests with and without structural breaks. Noting the importance of structural break analysis, in this study, the structural break test is conducted. Yes, there are several methods for structural break point/s. Among them, the Chow Test is useful for a single known structural break in a linear regression model, Zivot-Andrews Test is for a single unknown break point in the mean of a time series. It's useful when we suspect a break but don't know when it occurred in the data series. The other method is the Bai-Perron Test suitable for multiple unknown breaks in the mean of a time series. It can identify the number and location of breaks. These three methods do not solve our problem because we do not know the breakpoint, maybe multiple breakpoints. In such a case, the Gregory-Hansen Test may be useful as this tests for a break in the cointegrating relationship between two or more time series and useful for analyzing long-run relationships between variables. This method is specifically designed for cointegrated time series. Therefore I employ the Gregory and Hansen (1996) test.

Here, null hypothesis, H0: no-cointegration at the breakpoint
Alternate hypothesis, H1: there is cointegration at the breakpoint

Table 4.2 shows the results of a structural break using Gregory-Hansen method. The results show that no structural breaks are detected in Eqns. (4.1) and (4.2) by all methods, in the case of Eqn. (4.3) a break year is detected for 2000 by Zt statistics at five percent and one percent level of significance using intercept shift and intercept shift with trend respectively. Here, the lags are chosen by the Bayesian Information Criterion (BIC). Therefore, the interaction term with the year dummy for the year later than 2000 is created. For Eqns. (4.4) and (4.5), we cannot test the break for more than four independent variables, but the chance of a break to occur is almost nil in our case as all of these variables are included in Eqns. (4.1), (4.2) and (4.3). Next, for those Eqns. (4.1) and (4.2), we need to

Table 4.2 Structural break analysis, Gregory-Hansen cointegration test

	ADF		Z_t		Z_a	
	Statistics	*Break Year*	*Statistics*	*Break Year*	*Statistics*	*Break Year*
Equation (4.1)						
Intercept shift	−3.19	2015	−3.58	2015	−21.19	2015
Intercept shift with a trend	−4.65	2013	−4.73	2005	−28.28	2005
Intercept shift with slope	−5.72	2001	−4.95	2003	−32.38	2003
Equation (4.2)						
Intercept shift	−3.67	2007	−4.90	1994	−19.79	1994
Intercept shift with a trend	−4.24	2007	−4.86	2014	−22.56	2014
Intercept shift with slope	−5.31	2005	−5.34	1999	−31.43	1999
Equation (4.3)						
Intercept shift	−4.85	2001	−5.30**	2000	−27.98	2000
Intercept shift with a trend	−5.52	2000	−6.09***	2000	−31.32	2000
Intercept shift with slope	−5.13	2008	−5.53	2008	−28.46	2008

Note: (1) **indicates the variables are significant at a 5 % level of significance

(2) The results detect year 1999 has a structural break as indicated by *ADF* and *Zt* results at 5% level of significance

test the unit root for the variables to detect whether I(0) or I(1). Identifying the variables' integration order will help us to choose the cointegration method.

4.4.3 *Unit Root Tests*

Our next step to conduct the empirical analysis is to test the stationarity of the time series data. If the structural breaks were detected, it would mean the variables have unit root automatically. One important point to note here is that the variables may be non-stationary even without a structural break. Therefore, we need to confirm whether each series is integrated and has a unit root using Dickey-Fuller test (DF), augmented Dickey-Fuller (ADF) test, and the Phillips and Perron (PP) test.

We follow the standard technique and procedure for the unit root tests. The test results are achieved assuming the presence of a unit root (non-stationary variable) in the null hypothesis (H0) and no unit root (stationary variable) in the alternative hypothesis (Ha). For this, a decision is made based on the calculated statistic and McKinnon's critical value; that is, if the calculated statistic is higher than McKinnon's critical value, then H0 is not rejected, and the considered variable is non-stationary (has a unit root). To make the test systematic and reliable, we observed level and then first differences, including the intercept and time trend, because this is the most flexible specification of the test, as illustrated in Eqn. (4.6).

$$\Delta Z_t = \alpha_1 + \alpha_{2t} + \gamma Z_{t-1} + \sum_{j=1}^{k} \beta_j \Delta Z_{t-j} + \varepsilon_t \tag{4.6}$$

In the equation, Δ represents the first difference operator, Z denotes the variable of interest, $\alpha\!-\!1$ is the intercept, t signifies time, ΔZ are the augmented terms, k is the appropriate lag length of the augmented terms, and ε represents the white noise error term. The ADF test essentially examines the significance of the coefficient γ in this equation. The DF test is conducted without the augmented term. To determine the lag length k, we begin with a maximum lag of 4 and reduce it to the appropriate lag by reviewing the Schwarz Criterion (SC).

The unit root test results for all dependent and independent variables are presented in Table 4.3. Following the standard practice, we employ the DF, ADF and PP tests. The results suggest that only LGDP, LAGVAD,

Table 4.3 Unit root test results of the variables

At levels						
	Test with constant			*Test with constant & trend*		
Variables	DF	ADF	PP	DF	ADF	PP
LGDP	−0.35	0.35	0.32	−1.85	−2.31	−2.33
LAGVAD	0.03	0.26	0.12	−2.15	−2.75	−2.56
LMFVAD	0.56	0.47	−1.78	−2.64	−4.55***	−2.98
LSRVAD	−0.08	−0.03	0.02	−2.07	−2.29	−2.19
LGCF	0.36	−0.48	−0.48	−1.54	−1.49	−1.63
LLBF	−0.41	−3.60**	−3.48**	−1.38	−1.12	−2.31
Critical value @ 5%	*−1.95*	*−2.943*	*−2.943*	*−3.190*	*−3.536*	*−3.537*
At first difference						
	Test with constant			*Test with constant & trend*		
Variables	DF	ADF	PP	DF	ADF	PP
LGDP	−4.96***	−4.89***	−4.89***	−4.99***	−4.89***	−4.89***
LAGVAD	−3.92***	−4.10***	−4.10***	−4.16***	−4.04***	−4.04***
LMFVAD	−4.81***	−5.58***	−5.53***	−5.08***	−5.68***	−5.58***
LSRVAD	−6.05***	−6.51***	−6.49***	−6.34***	−4.85***	−6.45***
LGCF	−4.88***	−5.08***	−5.10***	−4.75	−4.99***	−5.01***
LLBF	−1.79*	−2.75*	−1.58	−3.75**	−3.71**	−2.33
Critical value @ 5%	*−1.95*	*−2.943*	*−2.943*	*−3.191*	*−3.548*	*−3.540*

Note: ** indicates the statistics are significant at a 5% level of significance

LMFVAD, LSRVAD and LGCF are found to be I (1). The results indicate that the variables such as LGDP, LAGVAD, LMFVAD, LSRVAD, and LGCF are found to be integrated of order one, I(1), meaning they are non-stationary at levels but become stationary after first differencing. For the variable LLBF, the results are not straight forward as the other variables' case. The test without trend is statistically significant at the level indicating the variable is I(0). Looking at the data length (1990–2023) of the data sample and labour force growth rate has a population growth rate of less than two percent, we assume the trend is not important, so we conclude this variable is I (0).

4.4.4 *Econometrics*

The structural break test detected no breakpoint except for Eqn. (4.3). Therefore, the next step is to check the stationarity of the variables using different methods and a combination of varying order of cointegration is detected in our data set. This means the set of variables in our model is mixed, such as I(0) and I(1). To proceed further, Equations (4.1), (4.2), (4.3), (4.4), and (4.5) are analyzed using a co-integration test based on the autoregressive distributed lag (ARDL) approach, which gives the long-run and short-run relationship among the dependent and independent variables irrelevance of the order of their integration (Paudel and Jayanthakumaran, 2009; Pesaran et al., 2001). The appropriate lag selection criteria, Schwartz-Bayesian Criteria (SBC), has been applied looking at the length of the data in the cointegration analysis.

The ARDL version of Eqn. (4.1) is presented in Eqn. (4.7):

$$\begin{aligned}\Delta LGDP_t &= \alpha + \beta_1\, LGDP_{t-1} + \beta_2 LAGVAD_{t-1} + \beta_3 LGCF_{t-1} \\ &\quad + \beta_4 LLBF_{t-1} + \sum_{i=1}^{34} \gamma_i \Delta LGDP_{t-i} + \sum_{i=1}^{34} \delta_i \Delta LAGVAD_{t-i} \\ &\quad + \sum_{i=1}^{34} \theta_i \Delta LGCF_{t-i} + \sum_{i=1}^{34} \varphi_i \Delta LLBF_{t-i} + v_t\end{aligned} \tag{4.7}$$

Here, Eqn. (4.7) captures the dynamic impact in the form of Autoregressive Distributed Lag Model. In the model,Δstands for the first-order differential variable. In the equation, α is intercept, β_1, β_2, β_3, β_4 *and* β_5 are the coefficients of first-order variables. Similarly, γ_i, δ_i, θ_i, *and* φ_i are the parameters of the error correction model, and v_t is the vector of random error.

In a similar fashion, Eqns. (4.2) and (4.3) are developed into Eqns. (4.8) and (4.9), where LAGVAD is replaced by LMFVAD and LSRVAD respectively.

$$\begin{aligned}\Delta LGDP_t &= \alpha + \beta_1\, LGDP_{t-1} + \beta_2 LMFVAD_{t-1} + \beta_3 LGCF_{t-1} \\ &\quad + \beta_4 LLBF_{t-1} + \sum_{i=1}^{34} \gamma_i \Delta LGDP_{t-i} + \sum_{i=1}^{34} \delta_i \Delta LMFVAD_{t-i} \\ &\quad + \sum_{i=1}^{34} \theta_i \Delta LGCF_{t-i} + \sum_{i=1}^{34} \varphi_i \Delta LLBF_{t-i} + v_t\end{aligned} \tag{4.8}$$

$$\begin{aligned}\Delta LGDP_t &= \alpha + \beta_1 LGDP_{t-1} + \beta_2 LSRVAD_{t-1} + \beta_3 LGCF_{t-1} \\ &+ \beta_4 LLBF_{t-1} + \sum_{i=1}^{34} \gamma_i \Delta LGDP_{t-i} + \sum_{i=1}^{34} \delta_i \Delta LSRVAD_{t-i} \\ &+ \sum_{i=1}^{34} \theta_i \Delta LGCF_{t-i} + \sum_{i=1}^{34} \varphi_i \Delta LLBF_{t-i} + v_t\end{aligned} \tag{4.9}$$

Next, for the robustness checks, two more equations are developed and tested similarly—an ARDL version of Eqns. (4.4) and (4.5).

4.5 Results and Discussions

Table 4.4 presents the ARDL bound test results to suggest whether the long-run relationship exists among the variables of the model. The results column of the table shows that the results for Eqn. (4.1) do not show the long-run relationship, while for Eqns. (4.4) and (4.5) are inconclusive. Notably, in all these equations, the agriculture value added (LAGVAD) is included. If there is no long-run relationship, we depend on the short-run coefficients. If the test results are inconclusive or a long-run relationship, we estimate the long-run relationship and see the coefficients. The long-run coefficients are presented in Tables 4.5 and 4.6, and the short-run coefficients are reported in Table 4.7, respectively.

Table 4.5 presents the long-run coefficients for the model analyzed using the ARDL approach, which shows the estimated association between the dependent and independent variables over the long term. The analysis

Table 4.4 ARDL Bound test results

Equations	*F-statistics*	*Lower bound critical value 5%*	*Upper bound critical value 5%*	*Results*
(4.1)	0.77	3.23	4.35	No LR relationship
(4.2)	9.19	3.23	4.35	LR relationship
(4.3)	7.86	2.45	3.61	LR relationship
(4.4)	2.97	2.62	3.79	Inconclusive
(4.5)	3.03	2.45	3.61	Inconclusive

Note: LR = Long-run. If F-statistics greater than upper bound critical value at 5% level of significance, there is long run relationship among the variables of the model, if F-statistics in between lower and upper bound critical value, that relationship is inconclusive, if F-statistics is lower than the lower bound critical value, we conclude there is no long-run relationship between the variables of the model

Table 4.5 ARDL Long-run Relationship Results

Dependent Variable GDP-Log	*(1)*	*(2)*	*(3)*
Agriculture value added (LAGVAD-log)	0.362***		
	(0.061)		
Manufacturing value added (LMFVAD-log)		0.762***	
		(0.168)	
Service value added (LSRVAD-log)			1.237
			(0.785)
Gross fixed capital formation (LGCF-log)	0.474***	0.315***	−0.342
	(0.031)	(0.068)	(0.339)
Labour force (LLBF-log)	1.116***	0.484	−0.228
	(0.128)	(0.308)	(1.842)
Year *x* Service			−0.223
			(0.636)
Year *x* LGCF			0.312
			(0.329)
Year *x* LLBF			−0.126
			(0.902)
Number of observations	*30*	*30*	*30*
R-squared	*0.97*	*0.96*	*0.96*
Root MSE	*0.01*	*0.02*	*0.01*
Log Likelihood	*90.34*	*82.91*	*85.86*
ARDL Lags	*(1,1,1,4)*	*(1,3,1,4)*	*(1,1,1,4)*

Note: ***, **, and * indicate that the statistics are significant at 1%, 5%, and 10% level of significance. The figures in the parenthesis are the standard error

indicates that certain key variables have statistically significant impacts on the dependent variable, holding other variables constant in the model. The results suggest four important points about the given growth story of Nepal.

First, the agriculture and manufacturing sectors have a strong association with economic growth. It indicates that a one percent increase in agriculture value added causes an increase in economic growth by 0.36 percent, holding other variables in the model constant. Similarly, this figure stands bigger, almost double with the same significance level, in the case of the manufacturing sector value added.

Second, the contribution of service sector value added is not statistically significant as in the case of the agriculture and manufacturing sector; however, the direction of this sector seems positive on the role of economic growth. Third, the role of gross capital formation seems stronger in the

Table 4.6 ARDL long-run relationship -robustness check

Dependent variable GDP-Log	*(4)*	*(5)*
Agriculture value added (LAGVAD-log)	0.283***	−0.803
	(0.062)	(0.594)
Manufacturing value added (LMFVAD-log)	0.246*	−0.852
	(0.141)	(0.647)
Service value added (LSRVAD-log)	0.138*	0.126***
	(0.078)	(0.046)
Gross fixed capital formation (LGCF-log)	0.349***	0.290***
	(0.060)	(0.039)
Labour force (LLBF-log)	0.316	0.439**
	(0.338)	(0.213)
LAGVAD *x* LMFVAD		0.053**
		(0.025)
Number of observations	*30*	*30*
R-squared	*0.99*	*0.99*
Root MSE	*0.01*	*0.01*
Log Likelihood	*113.72*	*117.92*
ARDL Lags	*(1,1,3,1,1,4)*	*(1,1,3,1,1,4,1)*

Note: ***, **, and * indicate that the statistics are significant at 1%, 5%, and 10% level of significance. The figures in the parenthesis are the standard error.

equation with agriculture than in the manufacturing sector as indicated by the coefficients. The capital formation in the service sector has a negative but not statistically significant result. It indicates that the agriculture and manufacturing sectors are yielding better results in terms of enhancing economic growth. This result is consistent with the literature on the developing countries context. Fourth, as indicated by the results, the agriculture sector is the most significant in terms of labour productivity, followed by the manufacturing sector.

For the robustness check and further investigation on whether the integration of agriculture and manufacturing sectors causes accelerated economic growth, I conduct the econometric tests in the ARDL form of Eqns. (4.4) and (4.5), of which the results are presented in Table 4.6. Column (4) represents the model in which all three sectors are put together to know the comparative perspective on the role of the individual sectors in economic growth. Column (5) confirms the role of the integration of agriculture and manufacturing sector in economic growth. The results underscore the significant role both sectors play in driving economic growth in Nepal.

Table 4.7 ECM results for the ARDL model

Variable Details	*(1)*	*(2)*	*(3)*	*(4)*	*(5)*
LAGVAD(-1)	0.17			0.23**	1.18**
	(0.11)			(0.09)	(0.60)
LMFVAD(-1)		−0.11		0.01	1.08
		(0.16)		(0.09)	(0.66)
LMFVAD(-2)		0.03		−0.01	0.03
		(0.07)		(0.03)	(0.04)
LMFVAD(-3)		0.11*		−0.03	0.01
		(0.05)		(0.03)	(0.04)
LSRVAD(-1)			0.04	0.1	0.01
			(0.11)	(0.06)	(0.07)
LGCF (-1)	0.08	0.29***	0.33***	−0.00	−0.02
	(0.10)	(0.09)	(0.09)	(0.08)	(0.07)
LLBF(-1)	−1.01	−3.15***	0.55	−0.79	−1.33*
	(0.67)	(1.01)	(0.98)	(0.51)	(0.62)
LLBF(-2)	0.05	4.04***	0.47	0.46	0.65
	(0.91)	(1.33)	(1.23)	(0.69)	(0.67)
LLBF(-3)	1.56	1.87	1.42	1.01	1.39
	(0.85)	(1.59)	(1.11)	(0.77)	(0.82)
LLBF(-4)	0.44*	−4.76**	−0.18	−0.27)	−2.03
	(0.95)	(1.98)	(1.26)	(0.99)	(1.39)
LAGVAD *x* LMFVAD (-1)					−0.05
					(0.03)
ECM(-1)	−0.71***	−0.75***	−0.50***	−0.65**	−1.08***
	(0.21)	(0.19)	(0.16)	(0.25)	(0.32)

Note: ***, **, and * indicate that the statistics are significant at 1%, 5%, and 10% level of significance. The figures in the parenthesis are the standard error

First, there is an important role of agriculture, manufacturing, and service sectors in accelerating economic growth and their rank seems agriculture, manufacturing and service sector as indicated by their coefficients and standard error.

The second important point, the main concern of this chapter, is the integration of agriculture and manufacturing sectors, which shows a robust positive impact on economic growth. The coefficients indicate that a one percent increase in the combined value added to these sectors results in a substantial boost to GDP, underscoring their critical importance relative to other sectors. The result shows that a one percent increase in the integration of the agriculture and manufacturing sector causes to increase in the economic growth rate by an average of 0.05 percent value additional, holding other variables in the model constant as indicated by the results of the column (5).

The third important point from the results is that the integration of the two sectors increases labour productivity and enhances economic growth. This is probably the best way to break the chain of youth flights from the country in the present scenario. Integration creates synergy and by there more employment, additional value addition, better productivity of capital, labour, and other production forces to increase the national output.

Overall, Table 4.6 complements the findings in Table 4.5, providing a comprehensive view of how the integration of agriculture and manufacturing sectors can drive sustained economic growth in Nepal. The robust checks confirm these sectors' pivotal role in enhancing economic performance, consistent with the broader literature on developing economies.

Similarly, Table 4.7 presents the results of the Error Correction Model (ECM) for the short-run coefficients of the ARDL model. In all three specifications, ECM (−1) is statistically significant with an expected negative sign indicating the disequilibrium that occurred in the previous period is corrected in the present period following a short-run shock in a quicker pace. For the monotonic transformation and adjustment process, we expect these values to be smaller than one, which is an exception in the case of Eqn. (4.5) as stated in Column (5) of the same table, which in this case indicates an oscillation nature of transformation in the adjustment process in the short run. We did not find that impressive impact of the variables in the short run. The agriculture value added variable has a positive impact on all specifications but appears to be significant on a few occasions, indicating that the agriculture value added is an important backbone of the Nepalese economy even in the short-run.

The high values of the R-squared show that the overall goodness of fit of the model is high. The diagnostic test results show that the model passes the tests for serial correlation, functional form, normality, and heteroscedasticity. Further, the stability test results (CUSUM squared) are plotted against the critical bounds of a five percent level of significance (Figs. 4.2, 4.3, 4.4, 4.5, and 4.6). Among these figures, the CUSUM squared value for Fig. 4.2 seems stable within 10 percent, Figs. 4.3, 4.4, and 4.6 are within the range of a five percent level of significance indicating that the model is structurally stable, while this value for Fig. 4.5 seems unstable even at the significance level of 10 percent.

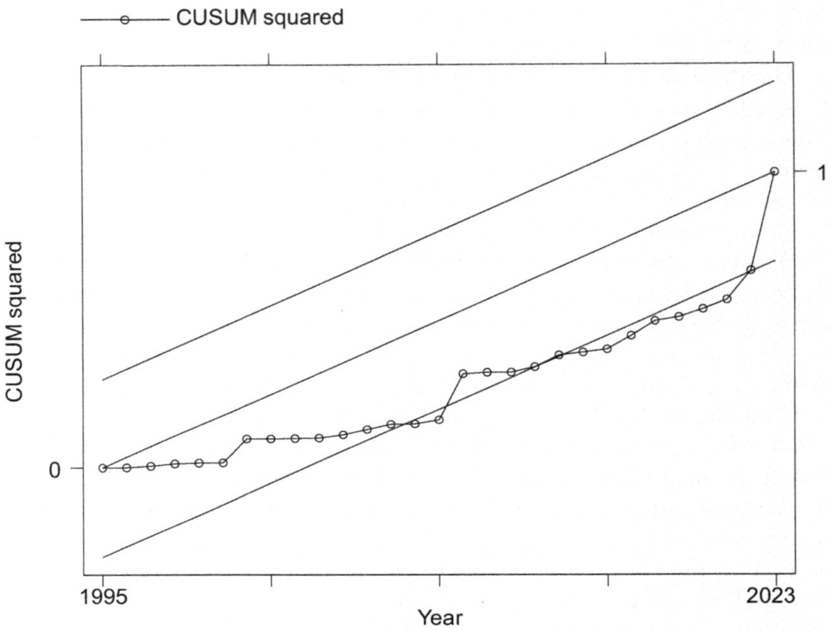

Fig. 4.2 CUSUM squared test for Eqn. (4.1)

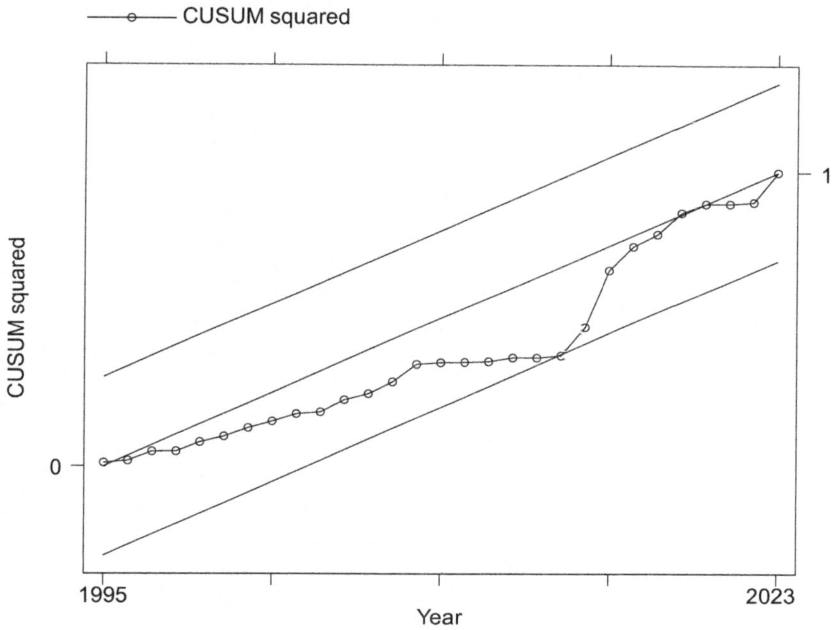

Fig. 4.3 CUSUM squared test for Eqn. (4.2)

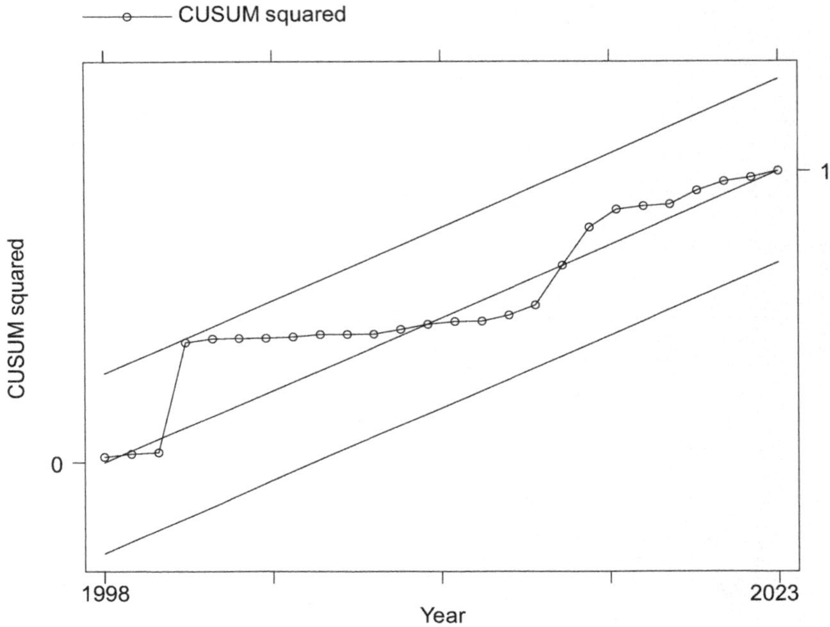

Fig. 4.4 CUSUM squared test for Eqn. (4.3)

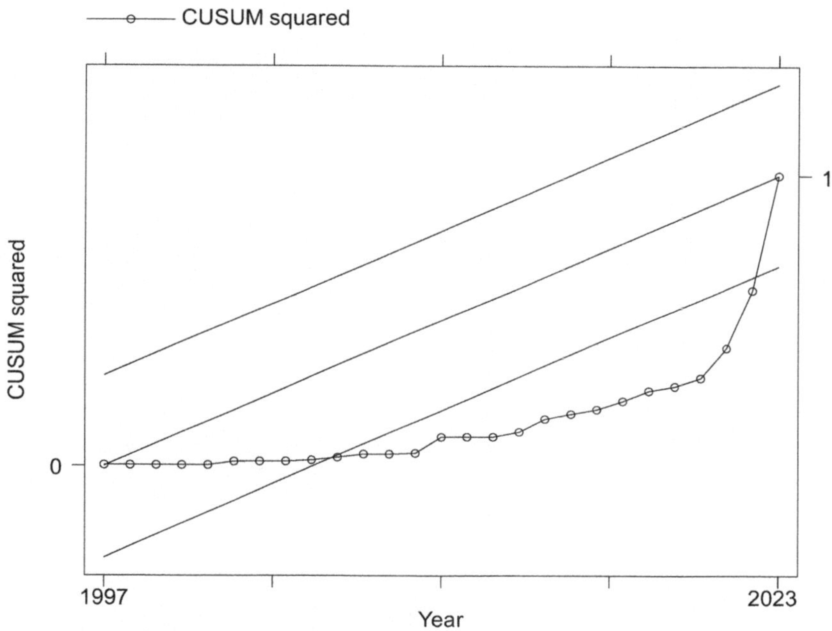

Fig. 4.5 CUSUM squared test for Eqn. (4.4)

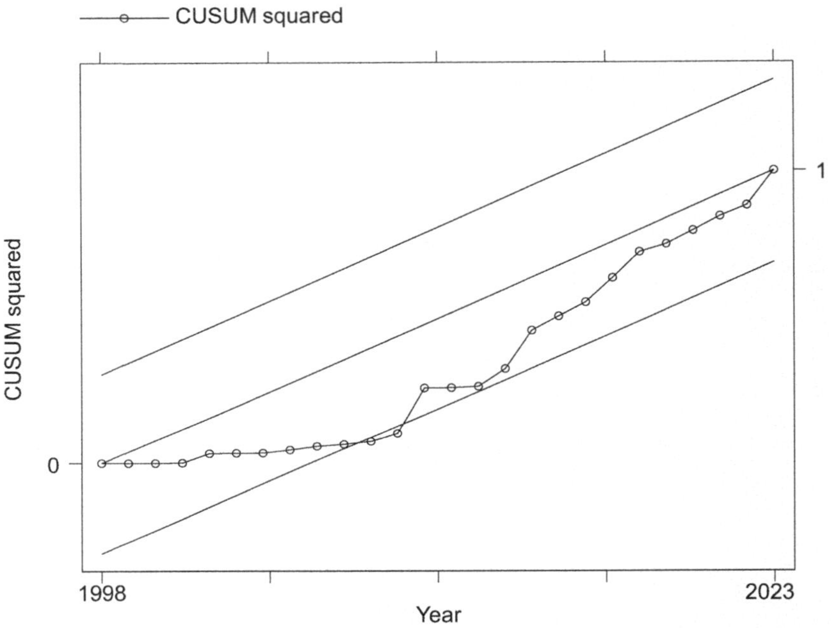

Fig. 4.6 CUSUM squared test for Eqn. (4.5)

4.6 Conclusions

This chapter is focused on investigating whether the integrated agriculture and manufacturing sectors help to accelerate much sought-after economic growth in Nepal. In doing so, this chapter documents the brief trends and structure of sectoral value added along with the economic growth episodes in Nepal. It is revealed from the literature review that the impact of the integration of agriculture and manufacturing sectors on economic growth has not been analyzed systematically yet in the context of Nepal, which is the major objective of this chapter.

To achieve the objective of this chapter, the impact of the integration of agriculture and manufacturing sectors is analyzed using the ARDL approach of cointegration with structural break analysis employing comprehensive data from 1990 to 2023. After conducting the structural break tests, we conduct unit root tests in case the structural breaks are not detected. Then, the bound test statistics are calculated to detect whether the long-run relationship in the model exists. Then, the different specifications of the models are estimated to detect the long-run and short-run relationship among the dependent and independent variables in the model.

In addition to the relationship examined between the sectoral value added and economic growth, it is essential to consider the synergy between integrated agriculture and manufacturing sectors as a driver for accelerated economic growth. By fostering closer ties between these sectors, Nepal can utilize its agricultural resources for manufacturing processes, creating a value chain that improves productivity, and economic resilience, and provides jobs for semi-skilled and unskilled labour in the country. Also, agriculture, being a predominant sector in Nepal, provides raw materials that can be effectively utilized by the manufacturing sector to produce high-value goods. This integration can lead to improved efficiency, innovation, and competitiveness—critical factors for economic development. Policies that support this integration can facilitate technology transfer, skill development, and infrastructure improvements, further strengthening the economic fabric of the nation.

The primary findings indicate a significant role of the agriculture, manufacturing, and service sectors in accelerating economic growth in Nepal, with agriculture being the most impactful. The integration of agriculture and manufacturing shows a robust positive impact on economic growth, with a one percent increase in their combined value adding significantly to enhance GDP. This integration can boost labor productivity and curb youth emigration by creating new jobs and enhancing capital and labor productivity within the country. The results demonstrate that the integration of these sectors is pivotal for sustained economic growth, as evidenced by the robust statistical results from the long-run model.

Moreover, the Error Correction Model (ECM) results reveal the short-run dynamics of the ARDL model, showing that short-run shocks are corrected moderately quickly. While the short-run impact of the variables is not as impressive, the agriculture sector still plays a crucial role. The positive impact of agricultural value added, although occasionally significant, underscores its importance to the Nepalese economy even in the short term. The findings suggest that policies aimed at integrating these sectors can drive economic resilience and growth, aligning with broader developmental goals for Nepal.

Based on the findings, a major policy recommendation would be to promote the integration of agriculture and manufacturing sectors by providing incentives for collaborative projects, investing in infrastructure to support these industries, and implementing training programs to enhance the skills of the workforce, and several potential financing options from the banking sector in such activities. These measures will help to create a synergistic environment that fosters economic growth and resilience in the Nepalese economy.

References

Cosentino, A., Paoloni, P., Iannone, B., & Temperini, V. (2020). Tradition, innovation and relationships: Emergent profiles from agro-food Italian industry. *British Food Journal, 123*(1), 279–299.

Diao, X., Hazell, P., & Thurlow, J. (2010). The role of agriculture in African development. *World Development, 38*(10), 1375–1383.

Gardner, B. (2002). *American Agriculture in the Twentieth Century: How It Flourished and What It Cost.* Harvard University Press.

Gregory, A. W., & Hansen, B. E. (1996). Residual-based tests for cointegration in models with regime shifts. *Journal of Econometrics, 70*, 99–126.

Hayami, Y., & Godo, Y. (2005). *Development economics: From the poverty to the wealth of nations.* Oxford University Press.

Johnston, B. F., & Mellor, J. W. (1961). The role of agriculture in economic development. *The American Economic Review, 51*(4), 566–593.

Munakata, N. (2007). *Transforming East Asia: The evolution of regional economic integration.* Rowman & Littlefield.

Nadia, Ali, S. W., & Pasha, R. (2020). Relationship among Agriculture and Manufacturing Value Added and Economic Growth in Pakistan. *Contemporary Social Sciences*, 1–13.

Paudel, R. C., & Jayanthakumaran, K. (2009). Financial Liberalization and Performance in Sri Lanka: The ARDL Approach. *South Asia Economic Journal, 10*(1), 127–156.

Pesaran, M. H., Shin, Y., & Smith, R. J. (2001). Bounds testing approaches to the analysis of level relationships. *Journal of Applied Econometrics, 16*, 289–326. https://doi.org/10.1002/jae.616

Pingali, P. (2007). Agricultural growth and economic development: a view through the globalization lens. *Agricultural Economics, 37*, 1–12.

Rigg, J. (2004). *Southeast Asia: The human landscape of modernization and development.* Routledge.

Solow, R. M. (1956). A Contribution to the Theory of Economic Growth. *The Quarterly Journal of Economics, 70*(1), 65–94. https://doi.org/10.2307/1884513

Vu, L. H., & Nguyen, L. Q. D. (2021). Agricultural productivity growth in vietnam in reform and post-reform period. *Cogent Economics & Finance, 9*(1), 1972524.

Woldemichael, A., Salami, A., Mukasa, A., Simpasa, A., & Shimeles, A. (2017). Transforming Africa's agriculture through agro-industrialization. *Africa Economic Brief, 8*(7), 1–12.

World Bank. (2025a). World Development Indicators. https://data.worldbank.org/ (accessed 25 January 2025).

World Bank. (2025b). *World Development Indicators*

Yamauchi, F., Huang, J., & Otsuka, K. (2021). Changing farm size and agricultural development in East Asia. *Agricultural development: New perspectives in a changing world*, 79–110.

CHAPTER 5

Revenue Efficiency in Nepal: The Key Determinants

5.1 Introduction

The accelerated growth based on extended economic activities contributes to more revenue collection and creates a broader base of revenue in the country. As we discussed the sectoral contribution to economic growth in Chap. 4, we aim to investigate the revenue efficiency in Nepal. Here, an issue is clear that growth and revenue efficiency have a two-way causality. Therefore, this chapter is focused on the determinants of revenue efficiency.

As we know that the government's revenue plays a key role in the quality of welfare and economic activities within a country. Revenue is of paramount importance to a nation's economy and the overall quality of life of its citizens. It serves as the lifeline for a country, funding essential services, infrastructure projects, and welfare activities that support the well-being and prosperity of the population. Efficient revenue collection and effective spending play a crucial role in determining the scope and quality of public services such as healthcare, education, and social security. These services, in turn, foster a healthier, more educated, and more secure society, which is fundamental for sustainable development and economic growth.

Moreover, revenue efficiency directly impacts a country's fiscal health and stability. When a government maximizes its tax capacity and uses the collected funds wisely, it can reduce deficits and avoid excessive borrowing, thereby maintaining fiscal discipline. Efficient revenue systems also

R. C. Paudel, *Essays on Key Issues of Development in Nepal*,
https://doi.org/10.1007/978-981-95-7715-6_5

ensure fair taxation, reducing inequality and boosting social cohesion. By addressing structural and economic variables that influence tax capacity, governments can identify areas for improvement and implement policies that enhance revenue efficiency. This creates a virtuous cycle, where increased revenue leads to better public services and infrastructure, which in turn stimulates economic activity and generates even more revenue.

In recent years, there have been many concerns about the revenue efficiency in Nepal as the targets are not met, however, the amount has increased. It seems that the revenue efficiency has not improved or even deteriorated in terms of meeting policymakers' expectations over recent years. In this background, the main objective of this chapter is to present an in-depth analysis of revenue efficiency and find the key determinants of revenue efficiency in Nepal.

The entire revenue sector of Nepal has evolved significantly over the past few decades, responding to both internal demands and external pressures for modernization of the economy, but this is not enough to meet the expectations of the stakeholders. This chapter highlights the key trends, challenges, opportunities, and the key determinants of revenue efficiency in Nepal.

In this background, the main objective of this chapter is to present an in-depth analysis of revenue efficiency and identify the key determinants of revenue efficiency in the country. The current revenue collection challenges in Nepal are multifaceted, such as inadequate infrastructure, lack of skilled personnel, outdated technology, poor performance of the manufacturing sector, low integration of agriculture and manufacturing sector, and so on. These challenges have hindered the efficiency of the revenue collection process and have led to a revenue shortage. The literature suggests that the economic variables such as per-capita gross domestic product (GDP) and the relative size of the agriculture sector and its integration with the manufacturing sector may have a significant impact on revenue efficiency. While a higher per-capita GDP has a positive effect on revenue collection, a larger agriculture sector without its integration with the manufacturing sector may have an adverse effect, and vice versa, as that integration contributes to increasing economic activities and more value addition in the economy.

This chapter proceeds as follows. Section 5.2 presents revenue trends and patterns to document the status of revenue and some other macroeconomic variables. Section 5.3 presents a brief literature review. Section 5.4 presents the Research Methodology of the chapter, and Sect. 5.5 is about the results and discussion from the econometric analysis. The final Sect. 5.6, concludes the chapter with a summary and policy recommendations.

5.2 Revenue Trends and Patterns

This has been a tradition of higher tax revenue compared to non-tax revenue in Nepal. In recent decades, especially since 2002, the gap between tax and non-tax revenue has widened further with negligible fluctuations.

In this context, Fig. 5.1 showcases the comparative status of tax revenue versus non-tax revenue in Nepal over the period from 1975 to 2023, measuring their share of total revenue. It highlights a clear and consistent trend wherein tax revenue has significantly surpassed non-tax revenue. This disparity has grown wider since 2002, with tax revenue displaying a steady increase, while non-tax revenue has remained relatively stagnant, experiencing only minimal fluctuations. This shows that tax revenue is the primary source of government income.

The increasing gap between tax and non-tax revenue suggests a few underlying facts. The first is, it indicates the government's focus on tax collection mechanisms and policies aimed at broadening the tax base and improving compliance. This tax is also largely from the import side. The second is, the stagnation of non-tax revenue could point to limited growth in other sources of government income, such as fees, fines, and state-owned enterprise profits, which in general indicate the poor level of economic activities in the nation. These trends are crucial for formulating strategies to diversify revenue sources and ensure sustainable fiscal growth, thereby addressing some of the challenges discussed in subsequent sections of this chapter and other chapters. The fitted lines show a slight increasing trend of tax revenue and a slight declining trend of the non-tax revenue, thus increasing the gap in Nepal for the selected period.

If so, the next interest may be in how the tax structures and their trends are realized over the period. For this purpose, Fig. 5.2 delves deeper into the trends and the structure of tax revenue (income tax, customs duties, excise duties, and value-added tax in Nepal), measured in billions of Rupees. This figure shows the evolution of tax revenue over time and provides insight into the government's focus on enhancing tax compliance and broadening the tax base. The sharp increase in the tax has been found since 2008/2009 continuously, with a visible exception in 2020 due to COVID-19. The VAT has overtaken the taxes to become the largest contributor to revenue since 2017 for the second time, and the gap has

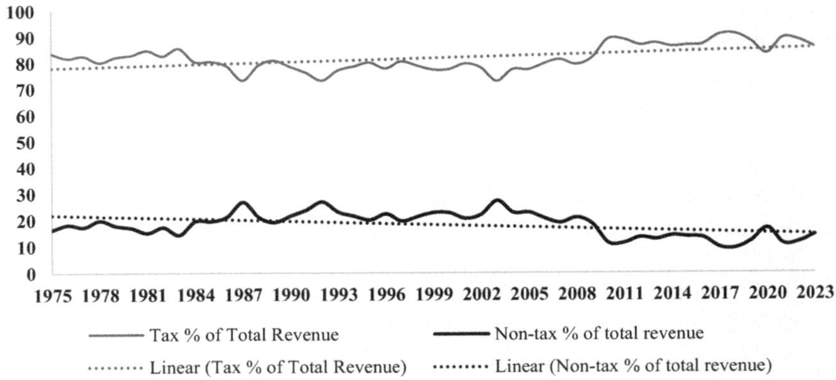

Fig. 5.1 Tax and Non-tax revenue in Nepal. (Sources: Ministry of Finance (2024) and Nepal Rastra Bank (2025))

Fig. 5.2 Trends and structure of tax revenue in Nepal, Rupees (Billion). (Sources: Ministry of Finance (2024))

widened thereafter. This clearly shows that the revenue growth is one of the major supports for Nepal's economy to remain the status as of now. The federal republic system has experienced a substantial growth of revenue.

The growth of income tax seems more consistent than other taxes in the country, while the excise duties seem to be lower, indicating the lower contribution from the consumption of luxury goods and commodities.

Also, it is well noted that the gap between customs duties and excise duties has been widening since the COVID-19 pandemic.

Once we know the tax structure and trend of Nepal, it may be a good idea to have a general idea of how Nepal's tax performance is recorded compared to other countries. For this purpose, I select three other major economies of South Asia, namely Bangladesh, India, and Sri Lanka (other South Asian economies are excluded due to data issues). Figure 5.3 shows the tax as a percentage of the respective GDP of these countries from 1990 to 2021. This period is limited by the data availability of these countries.

Over the period, we observe varying trends among the countries. Nepal's tax revenue as a percentage of GDP shows a steady increase, indicating enhanced tax compliance and broader tax bases compared to its neighbors. Bangladesh and Sri Lanka also exhibit rising trends, though not as pronounced as Nepal's. India's case demonstrates a more fluctuating pattern, reflecting changes in tax policies and economic conditions, and growth is more stagnant compared to that of Nepal's case. Sri Lanka's case seems to be declining over the period, indicating that Nepal's case is collecting the highest percentage of GDP taxes among South Asian countries. This comparative analysis provides a broader context for evaluating Nepal's fiscal health and the effectiveness of its revenue-collection strategies.

Similarly, Fig. 5.4 demonstrates the share of tax revenue derived from income, profits, and capital gains as a percentage of total revenue over the given period measured as a percentage of their respective GDP. It highlights the emphasis placed on taxing income and profits, which reflects the government's strategy to capture earnings from individuals and businesses in the respective countries.

The figure also demonstrates that India and Bangladesh collect a higher percentage of total revenue from the tax on income, profit, and capital gains. This tax is more progressive as it is levied directly on the individual and institutional income. Nepal and Sri Lanka have less than 30 percent of revenue from this tax, while India has recorded within the range of 40 to 50 percent in the recent decade.

Figure 5.5 illustrates the tax revenue derived from goods and services as a percentage of total revenue and it provides a complementary perspective to the insights gained from Fig. 5.4. While Fig. 5.4 focuses on the taxes collected from income, profits, and capital gains (more direct tax),

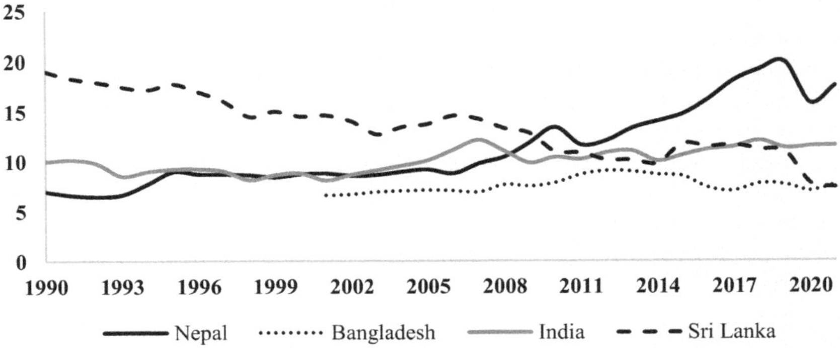

Fig. 5.3 Tax as a percent of GDP in South Asian major economies. (Source: World Bank (2025a))

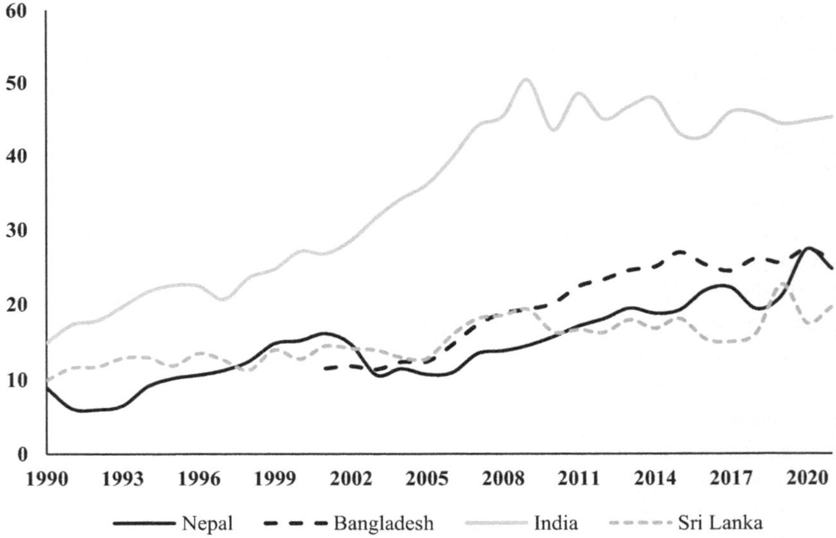

Fig. 5.4 Tax on income, profits and capital gains (% of Revenue). (Source: World Bank (2025a))

Fig. 5.5 shifts the attention to consumption-based taxes (indirect tax), which are generally less progressive but easier to administer.

From these two figures, it is evident that countries with a lower percentage of revenue from income and profit taxes, like Nepal and Sri Lanka, tend to rely more heavily on taxes from goods and services. This reliance indicates a broader tax base but may have a regressive impact, as consumption taxes disproportionately burden lower-income individuals. In contrast, India and Bangladesh, which derive a significant portion of their revenue from income and profit taxes, display a more progressive taxation approach, though they also face challenges in capturing complex income streams. Moreover, the comparative analysis of these figures underscores the strategic differences in tax policy among South Asian economies.

Figure 5.6 illustrates a basis for a comparative analysis of revenue, exports, and imports as percentages of GDP for Nepal. It is evident that both imports and revenue as percentages of GDP show increasing trends, suggesting that revenue is largely dependent on imports, in contrast to exports as a percentage of GDP, which have a declining trend with few exceptions in the latter half of the 1990s. The figure also captures the economic impact of the COVID-19 pandemic, illustrating a decline in both revenue and imports post-2020 with some fluctuations.

The global health crisis disrupted international trade and economic activities, leading to a reduction in Nepal's import volumes and, subsequently, its revenue. However, the figure also indicates a rise in exports during the same period, driven by increased global demand for specific products such as information technology, medical supplies, herbs, sanitary items, and food products like soups and noodles. These trends underscore the adaptive nature of Nepal's export sector in responding to global market demands, even amidst challenging circumstances. Overall, Fig. 5.6 provides valuable insights into the dynamic interplay between Nepal's revenue, imports, and exports over time.

Figure 5.7 presents an insightful comparison of revenue against the value added by different economic sectors in Nepal, specifically Service, Agriculture, and Manufacturing, as a percentage of GDP. This highlights the relative contributions of these three economic sectors to the nation's economic output and underscores the pivotal role of revenue in bolstering the country's fiscal framework. Historically, the service sector has shown a significant and consistently increasing share in value added to GDP, reflecting Nepal's gradual transition toward a more service-oriented economy. This sector's rise indicates growing importance in areas such as tourism,

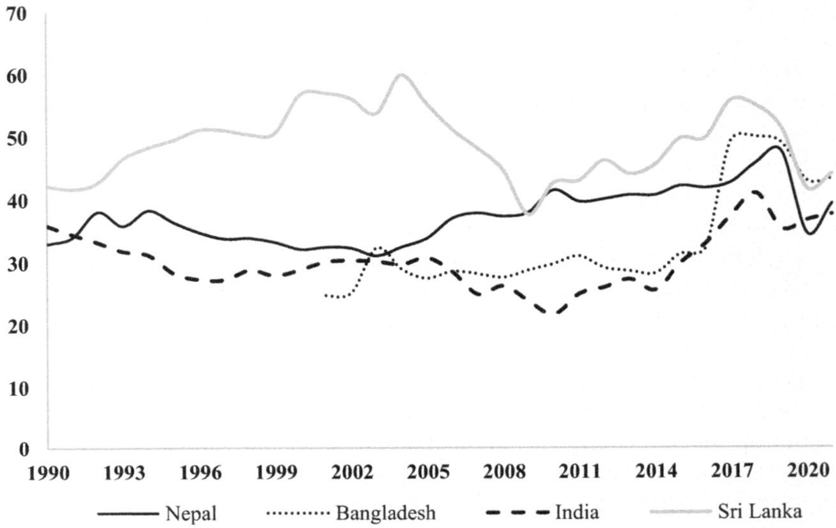

Fig. 5.5 Tax on goods and services (% of revenue). (Source: World Bank (2025a))

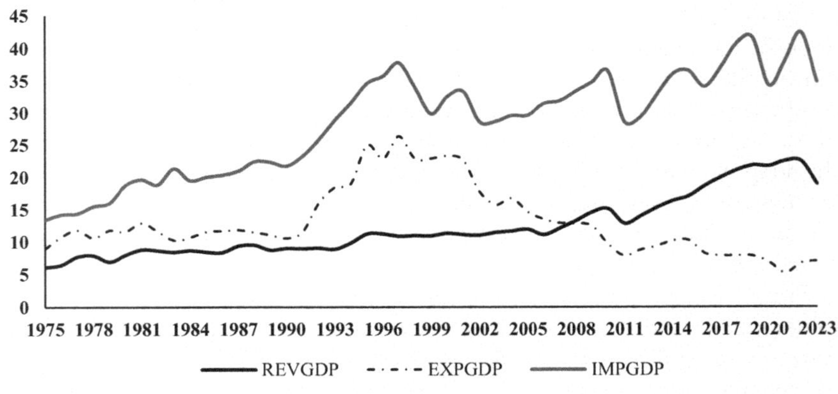

Fig. 5.6 Revenues, Exports, and Imports of Nepal (GDP %). (Source: Ministry of Finance (2024), World Bank (2025a, 2025b)

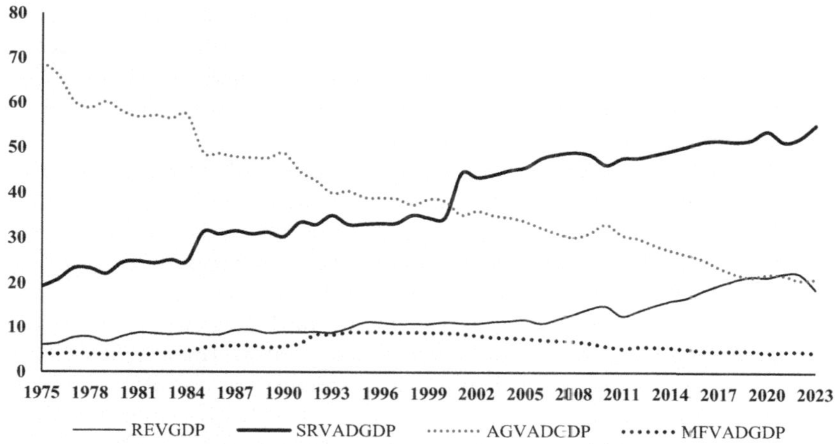

Fig. 5.7 Revenue and Sectoral value added (GDP %). (Source: Ministry of Finance (2024), World Bank (2025a, 2025b))

information technology, and financial services, which have become key for economic growth and revenue generation at this stage, however, this situation is blamed to be jobless growth in the country.

Conversely, the Agriculture and Manufacturing sectors display more varied trends, with Agriculture still holding a substantial but gradually declining share of GDP value added. This decrease can be attributed to the structural transformation of the economy, where there is a shift from traditional agriculture to more diversified and sophisticated industrial or service practices. The Manufacturing sector, while smaller in comparison, has also shown notable contributions, particularly in areas such as textiles, food processing, and pharmaceuticals. Figure 5.7 effectively captures these dynamics, illustrating the interplay between revenue and sectoral value added, and offering a comprehensive view of how different sectors contribute to Nepal's economic stability and growth. Probably, early 1990s was the best period for the manufacturing sector.

Figure 5.8 outlines the intricate relationship between revenue contributions and exports from the Agriculture and Manufacturing sectors within Nepal, expressed as a percentage of GDP. This figure serves as a pivotal analytical tool to comprehend the structural dynamics underpinning Nepal's fiscal landscape. The juxtaposition of revenue against sector-specific exports highlights the nuanced interplay between domestic economic activities and external trade dependencies, and it underscores the critical role of these sectors in bolstering national revenue streams, offering a granular perspective on the economic contributions derived from agricultural and manufacturing exports.

Figure 5.8 also reveals a multifaceted narrative of Nepal's economic evolution, particularly focusing on the post-liberalization period. The fluctuations observed in the revenue generated from agricultural exports reflect the sector's responsiveness to global market conditions and domestic policy shifts. Meanwhile, the manufacturing exports, although comparatively smaller, exhibit a significant upward trajectory, indicating progressive industrialization and diversification within the country's economic framework. This figure implicitly suggests a transitional phase wherein manufacturing gains momentum, potentially offsetting the traditional reliance on agriculture as a primary revenue source.

In addition, Figure 5.8 provides a comprehensive overview of the economic valorization attributed to agricultural and manufacturing exports, which are instrumental in shaping Nepal's GDP composition. Despite the declining manufacturing exports and almost stagnancy of agricultural exports, the revenue has increased, exposing the fact that it is from the import side rather than the export side.

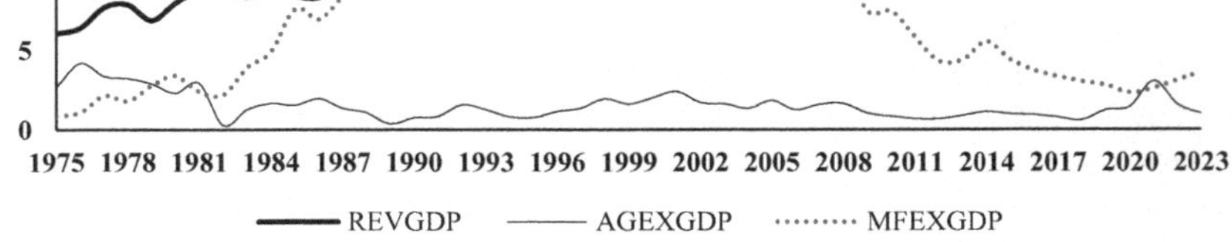

Fig. 5.8 Revenue and agriculture and manufacturing exports (GDP %). (Source: Ministry of Finance (2024), World Bank (2025a, 2025b)

5.3 A Brief Literature Review

In the context of revenue efficiency in a macroeconomic perspective, we mainly focus on the federal government's capacity to collect and mobilise revenue in the country. A standard approach to evaluate revenue efficiency is to look at the growth rate of revenue or to look at revenue as a percentage of GDP, or even to look at the elasticity of natural logarithm of revenue value in the regression. In terms of potential determinants of revenue efficiency, several variables are examined, and their magnitude and direction have been detected in the literature (Morrissey et al., 2016; Profeta and Scabrosetti, 2010). The research framework for the revenue efficiency analysis also differs in the literature. Regression analysis using various methods and frontier analysis are important techniques.

5.3.1 Theoretical Foundation

In the theoretical perspectives of government revenue, three main aspects are analysed in the literature. First, government revenue contributes to maintaining fiscal regulation in the country, primarily through imposing progressive taxes and others. Second, a country with a more efficient revenue system can sustain a higher level of social welfare, enhancing people's living standards. Third, government revenue plays a role in economic growth, and the efficiency of a country's revenue can be influenced by the per capita income of its citizens.

Government Revenue and Fiscal Regulation

Chugunov et al. (2020) suggested that effective fiscal regulation is ensured only by a synergy of a country's fiscal, regulatory, and incentive functions to accelerate economic growth. They argue that increasing the share of direct taxes in the general government revenue structure to implement the prudential and coherent fiscal policy with the strategic goals of the countries' social and economic development will be an option to maintain a good fiscal regulation in a country.

Khan (2024) analyzed the structure of government revenue and its implications in the economic activities and by which its impact on social benefits in the country.

Government Revenue and Social Welfare

Dash and Raja (2014) used a total of four revenue measures related to tax collection and internal debt, and four different sets of hypotheses were developed by linking the political determinants with each of the revenue measures. This study found that the government-specific political determinants are significant and robust determinants of revenue collections of the Indian states, and these are somehow related to the level of social welfare status of the states, too.

Dang et al. (2015), using data for the period 2006 to 2015 in Plateau State, found that revenue generation as a whole has an impact on social service delivery and that the revenue generated and allocated to health and education sectors were not adequately utilized about total revenue generated and suggest to focus on the utilization of revenue on social services capital expenditure to improve the quality of the living standard of the people.

Government Revenue and Economic Growth

Hinrichs (1965), summarizing past studies in the context and theoretical rationale with an empirical analysis in a panel data set for 60 countries to find the determinants of revenue collection, suggested that trade openness (imports as a share of GNP) is a superior indicator over per capita income. However, the author acknowledged that many previous articles found that per capita income is one of the major determinants of government revenue.

Weiss (1969) emphasized that the increased revenue can contribute positively to economic development and other well-being activities in a country, and some extent, it safeguards the inflationary pressure.

Jegede (2014), using the data from Nigeria for the period from 1980 to 2008, suggested that the federal government should revise its macroeconomic policies to improve efficiency and productivity of recourses allocation in the economy and recommended to reexamine its non-oil revenue by way of increasing tax rate and introducing new taxes in such a way that it does not distort the working of the economy.

Roşoiu (2015) examined the impact of the government revenues and government expenditures on the economic growth in Romania using a quarterly data set for the period from 1998q1 to 2014q1 and employing the Granger causality test through cointegrated vector autoregression (VAR) methods. The results of this study confirm that both government revenue and expenditure impact economic growth in Romania.

5.3.2 *Empirical Foundation*

Hwang (2002) investigated the impact of corruption on the revenue collection of the government using cross-national evidence and found that several corruption indices are positively and significantly associated with the taxes on international trade over current government revenue, and corruption is negatively and significantly related to the domestic tax revenue as well as the total amount of government revenue over GDP.

Narayan and Narayan (2006) investigated the causality between government revenue and government expenditure within a multivariate framework for 12 developing countries and found that the tax-and-spend hypothesis remained valid for Mauritius, El Salvador, Haiti, Chile and Venezuela while for Haiti, there is evidence for the spend-and-tax hypothesis, and for Peru, South Africa, Guatemala, Uruguay and Ecuador there is evidence of neutrality. It indicates that public expenditure can also work as a source of revenue.

Morrissey et al. (2016), using the data from developing countries, found that there is a negative relationship between manufacturing exports and revenue in lower-income countries, while the situation for upper-middle-income countries is different.

Lin and Jia (2019) investigated the relationship between direct tax on labor income, government revenue, and economic performance from the perspective of the Laffer curve by applying the Computable General Equilibrium (CGE) modelling technique and found that the top of China's Laffer curve is about 40% indicating that the government should consider changes in the entire taxation system and not just changes in direct taxes while increasing direct tax rate and suggested that tax cuts will have positive implications for the economy and government revenue.

Hussain et al. (2022) analyzed the relationship between corruption, governance, and government revenue using panel data from 2005 to 2020 of ninety-six countries collected from the corruption perception index (CPI), World Development Indicator (WDI), and worldwide Governance Indicators (WGI). The estimations were conducted using the fixed effect estimation method and found that corruption significantly and negatively affects government revenue, while governance significantly and positively impacts government revenue. This study suggested that the government needs to improve the governance quality to enhance the tax revenue and control the corruption level in the economy.

5.3.3 Nepalese Context

Very few articles in the context of Nepal relating with the different issues of revenue have been published in domestic or similar outlets but very few are directly related with the determinants of revenue or related with the revenue efficiency in Nepal.

Dahal (1983), using time series data of Nepal from fiscal year 1967/1965 to 1980/1981, found that per capita GDP as the primary variable to determine the revenue performance while other variables, such as trade openness had not such statistically significant however, the import and money supply had a positive association with the revenue.

Ghimire (2019), using the data from fiscal year 2002/2003 to 2016/2017, assessed the contribution of tax on government revenue and GDP employing correlation and multiple regression analysis. This study suggests that GDP and government revenue have been strongly related to direct and indirect tax revenues of Nepal.

Bhoosal and Byanjankar (2022), using Nepalese data from 1975 to 2021 for macroeconomic variables such as GDP per capita, imports, CPI, exchange rate, and foreign aid, found that GDP per capita and imports are the major determinants of government revenue in the short run while for the long run GDP per capita, imports, and exchange rate are important determinants of government revenue.

Adhikari and Poudel (2025), using data from 2003/2004 to 2022/2023, found a strong correlation between total revenue and taxes. They suggest broadening the revenue base with sources other than taxes to improve the revenue capacity.

These representative studies collectively underscore the importance of revenue efficiency; however, a proper analysis of revenue efficiency has not been made yet in the context of Nepal. This scenario motivates us to go further, analyzing the revenue efficiency of Nepal as aimed in this chapter.

5.4 Research Methodology

The research gap of this chapter indicates that the determinants of revenue and enhancing revenue efficiency are important issues in the context of Nepal. The methodology of this chapter is designed to seek the answer to questions, such as how to improve revenue efficiency and what can contribute substantially to garner more revenue. This process also provides a general idea about where things went wrong in the revenue efficiency of

Nepal. These are probably the most important issues for the economic development of Nepal at present, as the revenue growth rate has declined visibly in recent years.

5.4.1 *Research Design*

This chapter employs descriptive and quantitative analytical frameworks for a systematic analysis. A desk review of the literature in national and international contexts and methodological studies has been made with a standard academic critical approach, following research ethics and norms.

5.4.2 *Descriptive Framework*

This chapter has incorporated a desk review and some figures based on the most relevant data sets to see the trends and patterns of the relevant variables that are potential determinants of revenue. Also, these variables have been discussed in the comparative perspectives of some South Asian countries, as discussed earlier

5.4.3 *Quantitative Framework*

The Model and Variables
To identify the determinants of revenue and revenue efficiency, I follow Morrissey et al. (2016) for model guidance of revenue performance. In terms of the methodology, Djokoto (2012) is followed, that is, using the stochastic frontier analysis approach. First, the export and import as a percentage of GDP and per capita GDP in the natural log form is estimated as stated in Eqn. (5.1)

$$REVGDP_t = \alpha_t + \beta_1 EXPGDP_t + \beta_2 IMPGDP_t + \beta_3 LGDPPC_t + \varepsilon_t \tag{5.1}$$

where, the dependent variable is the revenue proxied by the revenue as a percentage of GDP (REVGDP). The independent variables are export as a percentage of GDP (EXPGDP), import as a percentage of GDP (IMPGDP), and a natural log of per capita GDP (LGDPPC). The first term on the right-hand side of the model is constant, subscript t represents the time (year in our case, as we use the annual data). In addition, β_1 to β_3

are the parameters of the regressors, and the final term is the error term. Based on the literature, we expect the coefficient β_1 to β_3 to be positive.

Once we know the general direction and magnitude of the association of the variables as indicated in Eqn. (5.1), we want to know the disaggregated form of export's role in the revenue collection. As we know in the Nepalese case, most of the revenue is based on imports and the exports are not reported as imports. Knowing this background, we disaggregate the export further into agriculture exports (AGEXP) and manufacturing exports (MFEXP), and they are measured as a percentage of GDP, respectively, as shown in Eqns. (5.2), (5.3), and (5.4). Doing this will help to identify the most important sector for overall revenue collection in the country. We estimate Eqn. (5.4) to identify the heavier variables of exports, such as either agriculture exports or manufacturing exports, putting them together.

$$REVGDP_t = \alpha_t + \beta_1 AGEXPGDP_t + \beta_2 IMPGDP_t + \beta_3 LGDPPC_t + \varepsilon_t \quad (5.2)$$

$$REVGDP_t = \alpha_t + \beta_1 MFEXPGDP_t + \beta_2 IMPGDP_t + \beta_3 LGDPPC_t + \varepsilon_t \quad (5.3)$$

$$\begin{aligned} REVGDP_t = \alpha_t + \beta_1 AGEXPGDP_t + \beta_2 MFEXPGDP_t + \beta_3 IMPGDP_t \\ + \beta_4 LGDPPC_t + \varepsilon_t \end{aligned} \quad (5.4)$$

Data and Sources

This study uses the annual data from 1975 to 2023 for Nepal. The data for all variables used for the empirical analysis are collected and constructed, where not readily available, from Ministry of Finance (2024), World Bank (2025a), and World Bank (2025b). All the variables except LGDPPC are measured as a percentage of GDP, and the LGDPPC is the natural log of per capita GDP measured in the United States Dollar (USD). The data consistency is maintained while cleaning up for the empirical analysis.

Econometrics

Here, our data are time series to measure the variables, therefore, the first step is to check the stationarity or time-series properties of these data. For this purpose, we conduct Dicky Fuller (DF), Augmented Dicky Fuller (ADF), and Philips and Peron (PP) tests to detect whether the variables are cointegrated with vector one or otherwise. The results of these tests are reported in Table 5.1. We conducted the test at the level with a constant only, and then with a constant and a trend first. Then, tests are

Table 5.1 Unit root test results of the variables

Variables	*Level with intercept*			*Level with intercept & trend*		
	DF	**ADF**	**PP**	**DF**	**ADF**	**PP**
REVGDP	0.31	−0.58	−0.58	−1.83	−1.83	−1.95
EXPGDP	−1.05	−1.07	−1.28	−1.19	−1.41	−1.52
IMPGDP	−0.82	−1.91	−1.84	−2.82	−2.82	−2.86
LGDPPC	2.35**	1.16	1.11	−1.15	−1.56	−1.61
AGEXGDP	−2.61***	−3.22**	−3.06**	−3.48**	−3.49*	−3.49*
MFEXGDP	−0.98	−1.29	−1.29	−1.01	−1.34	−1.34
Critical value: 1%	**−2.61**	**−3.61**	**−3.61**	−3.77	**−4.21**	**−4.21**
5%	**−1.94**	**−2.93**	**−2.94**	**−3.19**	**−3.53**	**−3.53**
10%	**−1.61**	**−2.61**	**−2.61**	**−2.89**	**−3.20**	**−3.20**
Variables	*First difference with intercept*			*First difference with intercept & trend*		
	DF	**ADF**	**PP**	**DF**	**ADF**	**PP**
REVGDP	−4.49***	−4.59***	−4.41***	−4.27***	−4.44***	−4.23***
EXPGDP	−3.01***	−6.67***	−6.71***	−6.75***	−6.79***	−6.80***
IMPGDP	−6.97***	−7.18***	−6.73***	−6.56***	−7.25***	−6.88***
LGDPPC	−1.54	−6.03***	−6.01***	−5.51***	−6.07***	−6.04***
MFEXGDP	−5.44***	−5.39***	−5.33***	−5.71***	−5.65***	−5.55***
Critical value: 1%	**−2.63**	**−3.61**	**−3.61**	−3.77	−4.21	−4.21
5%	**−1.94**	**−2.93**	**−2.94**	−3.19	−3.53	−3.53
10%	**−1.61**	**−2.61**	**−2.61**	−2.89	−3.20	−3.20

Notes: ***, **, and * indicate the values are significant at 1%, 5%, and 10% significance levels, respectively. The standard errors are in parentheses

conducted at the first difference level following the same approach. Here, the variables listed in the lower panel of the table, such as REVGDP, EXPGDP, IMPGDP, LGDPPC, and MFEXGDP, are identified as I(1) by the majority rule. Only the variable named AGEXGDP is detected as I(0) as it is significant at the level in all methods, however, the significance level is and varies over the test methods. At the bottom rows of the lower and upper panels of the table, the critical values at 1%, 5%, and 10% levels of significance are given.

Therefore, in conclusion, as we have a mixed set of variables with I(0) and I(1), we need to make them stationary to run the econometrics for the efficiency analysis using the Stochastic Frontier Analysis (SFA) method. Therefore, a new data set is prepared, taking the first difference value for I(1) variables and the level value for I(0) variables. One of the fundamental conditions to employ stochastic frontier analysis (SFA) is that the data should be stationary. For that purpose, the I(1) variables are transformed considering the first difference, and these variables have become stationary data. Then, the data are qualified to employ the SFA method for the revenue technical analysis.

The SFA is a method to identify the technical efficiency analysis using the input and output variables. In our model, the input variables are independent variables that directly impact the revenue growth and, apparently, the revenue volume. The output variable in this case is the dependent variable, the revenue variable. The econometrics of this chapter is guided by the concept of SFA and the method to explain the technical efficiency, which are explained in Greene (1990), Shaik and Miljkovic (2011), Djokoto (2012), and Kumbhakar et al. (2020).

5.5 Results and Discussions

5.5.1 Qualitative Analysis

In Sect. 5.2, we analyzed a few data and facts comparing the trends and patterns of different series of revenue and their sources in Nepal and in comparative perspectives. In a total of eight figures, using the long series of data for tax and non-tax revenue, the structures of disaggregated revenue sources of Nepal are displayed. Also, Nepal's data are compared with major neighboring countries- Bangladesh, India, and Sri Lanka for revenue analysis.

From the qualitative or even we can say the descriptive analysis, four important messages can be noted. First, tax revenue is the major dominant source of revenue, and it has substantially increased since 2002. Second, as of now, Nepal's tax revenue as a percentage of GDP is the highest among these countries. However, the taxes on income, profits, and capital gains are almost a similar percentage of revenue for Bangladesh and are almost equally comparable with Sri Lanka for recent years. Notably, India's share of this tax as a percentage of total revenue is much higher among the selected countries. This refers to the portion of direct tax in total revenue in Nepal has room to improve in the revenue administration in Nepal, which is the third key finding in the context.

Fourth, Nepal's revenue is directly dominated by taxes on imports. The export-based tax revenue is not visible in the revenue administration at this stage. Agriculture exports are more visible in the data than manufacturing exports.

5.5.2 Quantitative Analysis

In Sect. 5.4.3, after analyzing the time series properties of the data, these are smoothed as suggested before conducting the empirical analysis employing the stochastic frontier analysis (SFA). In this process, first, we conduct the econometric estimation for our benchmark model as specified in Eqn. (5.1). Then, for the robust estimation and deeper analysis of the relevant regressors, we test the alternative specifications of the model as of Eqns. (5.2), (5.3), and (5.4). The econometric estimations' results are reported in columns (1), (2), (3), and (4) of Table 5.2.

The estimated results for Eqn. (5.1) of the model are presented in column (1) of Table 5.1. The result indicates that imports solely determine the revenue, and the exports have not contributed to the revenue collection, rather have a negative impact. The results suggest that a one percent increase in imports to GDP ratio cause to increase revenue to GDP ratio by 0.17 percent, on average, holding other variables in the model constant. It implies that if imports are increased by USD 100, this causes to increase revenue by USD 17. This seems natural because we do not generally charge duties or taxes on exports; we have a mechanism to provide cash incentives to promote exports. However, if exports were boosted, it would help to generate revenue via more employment generation and the value addition process, which has not happened substantially in the country yet.

This finding from econometric estimation is consistent with our figures in Sect. 5.2. Against our expectations, the per capita income also shows a negative, but statistically not significant, coefficient, indicating a negative association with revenue. This means that as the per capita GDP increases, the revenue declines. This may be due to the governance issue and as we see the low rate of direct tax revenue in the same section of this chapter.

Now, let's move to the results of Column (2) of the same table, where the EXGDP is replaced by agriculture export to GDP (AGEXPGDP). The results from this column seem consistent with the results of Column (1), as we can see that the major determinant of revenue efficiency is IMPGDP, with almost a similar coefficient as in Column (1) and the same level of statistical significance and sign. The coefficient of the new variable AGEXPGDP is not meaningfully different from that of the coefficient of

Table 5.2 Estimates of Stochastic frontier analysis

Variables	*(1)*	*(2)*	*(3)*	*(4)*
Export % of GDP-EXPGDP	−0.05			
	(0.064)			
Import % of GDP - IMPGDP	0.17***	0.14***	0.15***	0.15***
	(0.047)	(0.038)	(0.039)	(0.039)
Per capita GDP in log - LGDPPC	−1.1.89	−1.73	−2.01	−2.05
	(1.411)	(1.354)	(1.323)	(1.337)
Agriculture exports % GDP - AGEXPGDP		−0.06		−0.02
		(0.122)		(0.124)
Manufacturing exports % GDP - MFEXPGDP			−0.10*	−0.09*
			(0.061)	(0.06)
Lambda	2.51***	2.89***	2.74***	2.75***
	(0.372)	(0.273)	(0.277)	(0.275)
Sigma (u)	1.03***	1.08***	1.04***	1.04***
	(0.244)	(0.193)	(0.194)	(0.193)
Number of Observations	*48*	*48*	*48*	*48*
Log Likelihood	*−52.71*	*−52.93*	*−51.64*	*−51.62*
Prob Chi-squared	*0.002*	*0.002*	*0.001*	*0.002*

Note: ***, **, and * indicate that the statistics are significant at 1%, 5%, and 10% significance levels, respectively. The figures in the parentheses are the standard errors. Dependent variable: Revenue as a percentage of GDP (REVGDP)

EXPGDP, such as EXPGDP had a coefficient of −0.05 compared with −0.06 of AGEXPGDP, having a slightly bigger standard error, but both coefficients are statistically not significant.

Then, we want to see how the association manufacturing exports (MFEXPGDP) is with REVGDP. Therefore, this variable is included in Column (3) of the same table. The results reveal one important point, that it hurts revenue at a 10 percent level of significance. This is probably due to the net loss in revenue from export incentives produced by the manufacturing sector. The coefficient for this variable is consistent in the same direction and magnitude with the same level of significance in Column (4), in which a full set of variables is included to test the aggregate impact of all variables in the model.

The results in Column (4) show that our results from columns (1), (2), and (3) are consistent, as we can see all variables' coefficients are similar in all columns. The direction, as determined by the sign of the coefficients, is similar in columns, and the magnitude, as determined by the value of the coefficients, is not meaningfully different between the columns. Therefore, the results suggest that Nepal's revenue is determined by imports, while the exports (both agricultural exports and manufacturing exports) hurt revenue. The role of per capita GDP in improving revenue efficiency is found to be negative but not statistically significant. It indicates the room to improve the policy perspective for revenue collection, for example, some measures of direct tax, rather than indirect tax, to focus on enhancing revenue efficiency in the country.

Now let's move to see some statistics (variance parameters) mentioned in the lower segment of the same table. Both the statistics for Lambda and Sigma (u) are statistically significant at a one percent level of significance, reflecting the scenario to Greene (1990). The trend is not statistically significant; therefore, it indicates no technical efficiency gain during this period for revenue efficiency. These statistics are statistically significant consistently in all estimations, as indicated by the results of all columns of the table.

Table 5.3 presents the statistics for the technical efficiency analysis estimates of Nepal's revenue efficiency. A total of 48 years has been used in the estimation, out of which five years have an efficiency of 5% to 25%, indicating that there is a huge gap between the potential revenue and collected revenue in these years (see Table 5.4 for details of efficiency by year). In total of 16 years, the revenue efficiency stands in the range of above 25% to below 50%. This indicates that out of 48 years, 21 years' revenue efficiency is found below 50%. A total of 20 years have had the revenue efficiency realized between 50% to 75%, and only for seven years this figure stands above 75%. Notably, in one year, the revenue efficiency is found above 80%, which is the year 2016, and the efficiency is about 87%.

5.6 Conclusions

5.6.1 Summary

The main objective of this chapter is to analyze the overall revenue efficiency of Nepal's government using the data from 1975 to 2023 and to find the major determinants of revenue. In the process of doing so, the chapter adopted two paths. First, to analyze the trends and patterns of revenue and other relevant variables from national and regional perspectives. Then, following the literature, appropriate methods and techniques are followed, knowing the time series properties of the variables used in econometric estimations. To identify the determinants of revenue and to

Table 5.3 Summary of the technical efficiency estimates in Nepal's revenue

Range	*Frequency years*	*Percent*	*Cumulative Percent*
0.05–0.25	5	10.42	10.42
0.25–0.50	16	33.30	43.75
0.50–0.75	20	41.67	85.42
0.75–0.80	6	12.50	97.92
0.80–1.00	1	02.08	100
Mean of 47 observations: 0.52		Standard deviation: 0.20	

Source: Author's calculations based on efficiency analysis data

Table 5.4 Estimates of Technical Efficiency (TE) of revenue collection

Year	*TE*	*Year*	*TE*	*Year*	*TE*
1976	0.44	1992	0.29	2008	0.78
1977	0.77	1993	0.27	2009	0.75
1978	0.46	1994	0.65	2010	0.59
1979	0.21	1995	0.79	2011	0.27
1980	0.63	1996	0.32	2012	0.74
1981	0.73	1997	0.28	2013	0.68
1982	0.40	1998	0.59	2014	0.61
1983	0.21	1999	0.64	2015	0.66
1984	0.64	2000	0.44	2016	0.87
1985	0.31	2001	0.33	2017	0.75
1986	0.41	2002	0.57	2018	0.65
1987	0.72	2003	0.54	2019	0.62
1988	0.45	2004	0.52	2020	0.73
1989	0.21	2005	0.54	2021	0.48
1990	0.53	2006	0.17	2022	0.26
1991	0.35	2007	0.76	2023	0.06

Source: Author's calculations based on efficiency analysis data

know the technical efficiency of revenue collection, the stochastic production frontier analysis (SFA) method is employed, and the results are reported accordingly in the relevant section.

5.6.2 *Findings*

The results from the qualitative framework suggest a few important points. First, Nepal's revenue consists of around 90 percent from tax sources, which are largely based on import-based taxes, such as customs, excise duties, then value added tax (VAT), and a low portion of direct taxes, such as income taxes, taxes on profits and capital gains. Also, it is well noted that Nepal's direct tax is almost half compared to that of India's direct tax in terms of total revenue; that is, 27 percent of Nepal's revenue comes from direct tax, but this stands at about 47 percent in the case of India. However, Bangladesh and Sri Lanka have even lower rates than Nepal's rates. On the other hand, Nepal's tax-to-GDP ratio is the highest among these four countries.

The results from the quantitative analysis suggest a few important points. First, imports solely determine the revenue, and the exports have not contributed to the revenue collection, rather have a negative impact. The results for exports (both agricultural exports and manufacturing exports) show a negative impact on revenue. The role of per capita GDP in improving revenue efficiency is found to be negative but not statistically significant.

In the case of revenue efficiency for the entire selected period, no technical efficiency gain is realized. Out of the 48 years used in the estimation, only in one year, the revenue efficiency is found above 80%, which is the year 2016, and the efficiency is about 87%. Keeping these facts in mind, a suitable revenue policy should be designed and planned. The base of the revenue is to be expanded, and governance, logistics, and required infrastructure to make digital revenue administration should be in priority.

References

Adhikari, H. P., & Poudel, S. P. (2025). The relation of direct and indirect taxes on government revenue collection of Nepal. *Nepalese Journal of Management Research, 5*(1), 1–6. https://doi.org/10.3126/njmgtres.v5i1.75865

Bhoosal, Y. L., & Byanjankar, R. (2022). An Empirical Study on the Determinants of Government Revenue in Nepal. *NRB Economic Review, 34*(2), 30–49.

Chugunov, I., Vatulov, A., & Markuts, Y. (2020). General government revenue in the system of fiscal regulation. *Investment Management & Financial Innovations, 17*(1), 134–142.

Dahal, M. (1983). Determinants of Government Revenue Share-A case Study of Nepal. *Economic Journal of Nepal, 6*(4), 23–38.

Dang, D. Y., Bako, E., & Lalu, I. D. (2015). Impact of revenue generation and utilization on social service delivery in Plateau State: 2006–2015. *Tax Academy Research Journal, 1*(1), 29–48.

Dash, B. B., & Raja, A. V. (2014). Do political determinants affect revenue collection? Evidence from the Indian states. *International Review of Economics, 61*, 253–278.

Djokoto, J. G. (2012). Technical efficiency of agriculture in Ghana: a time series stochastic frontier estimation approach. *Journal of Agricultural Science, 4*(1), 154.

Ghimire, P. (2019). Role of tax towards government revenue of Nepal. *International Journal of Business and Economics Research, 8*(3), 85–96.

Greene, W. H. (1990). A gamma-distributed stochastic frontier model. *Journal of Econometrics, 46*(1–2), 141–163.

Hinrichs, H. H. (1965). Determinants of Government Revenue Shares Among Less-Developed Countries. *The Economic Journal, 75*(299), 546–556. https://doi.org/10.2307/2228952

Hussain, T., Maitlo, S., Raza-ul-Mustafa, A., & Mujahid, H. (2022). Corruption, governance, and government revenue. *Journal of History and Social Sciences, 13*(2), 122–133.

Hwang, J. (2002). A note on the relationship between corruption and government revenue. *Journal of Economic Development, 27*(2), 161–176.

Jegede, C. A. (2014). Econometric analysis of the effectiveness of public revenue in economic growth in developing countries: An examination of Nigerian economy. *International Journal of Economics and Finance, 6*(8), 187–196.

Khan, A. (2024). An Overview of Government Revenues: Sources, Measures, and Alternatives. In *Fundamentals of Public Budgeting and Finance* (pp. 117–164). Springer International Publishing. https://doi.org/10.1007/978-3-031-53674-8_4

Kumbhakar, S. C., Parmeter, C. F., & Zelenyuk, V. (2020). Stochastic frontier analysis: Foundations and advances I. *Handbook of production economics*, 1–40.

Lin, B., & Jia, Z. (2019). Tax rate, government revenue and economic performance: A perspective of Laffer curve. *China Economic Review, 56*, 101307.

Ministry of Finance. (2024). *Economic Survey.* Ministry of Finance, Government of Nepal, Kathmandu

Morrissey, O., Von Haldenwang, C., Von Schiller, A., Ivanyna, M., & Bordon, I. (2016). Tax revenue performance and vulnerability in developing countries. *The Journal of Development Studies, 52*(12), 1689–1703.

Narayan, P. K., & Narayan, S. (2006). Government revenue and government expenditure nexus: evidence from developing countries. *Applied Economics, 38*(3), 285–291. https://doi.org/10.1080/00036840500369209

Nepal Rastra Bank. (2025). *Current Macroeconomic and Financial Situation.* Baluwatar, Kathmandu, Nepal

Profeta, P., & Scabrosetti, S. (2010). *The political economy of taxation: Lessons from developing countries.* Edward Elgar Publishing.

Roşoiu, I. (2015). The impact of the government revenues and expenditures on the economic growth. *Procedia Economics and Finance*, *32*, 526–533.
Shaik, S., & Miljkovic, D. (2011). The impact of trade openness on technical efficiency in US agriculture. *Journal of International Agricultural Trade and Development*, *7*(2), 131.
Weiss, S. J. (1969). Factors affecting the government revenue share in less developed countries. *Social and Economic Studies*, 348–364.
World Bank. (2025a). *World Development Indicators.*
World Bank. (2025b). *World Integrated Trade Solution, WITS database.*

CHAPTER 6

Democracy, Governance Quality, and Economic Development

6.1 Introduction

The role of quality governance in the economic development of a country is widely discussed in the literature [*see* Fayissa and Nsiah (2013) for details] and we also discussed that the role of the quality of governance is positive to boost much-needed exports and accelerate economic growth in the earlier chapters, then, we think about how to improve the quality of governance. Therefore, an immediate question arises: what makes the quality of governance better? Burns (2000) and Sharma (2007) suggested that true democracy, with the exercise of fundamental rights of human beings, such as democratically elected leadership to govern the nation, voice and accountability, a proper community representation and participation system, use of modern information technology, strengthening of property rights, and the rule of law, contributes to the quality of governance. Here, the concern is that not democracy, but a quality democracy can only contribute to enhancing the quality of governance. The quality of democracy encompasses many components of governance, including, but not limited to, voting rights, accepting multiplicity and diversity, the right to private property and personal income, a fully maintained rule of law, business contract enforcement, an efficient judicial system, and well-practiced democratic exercises to elect leadership.

Nepal is in its transition phase for both political and economic systems. First, let's discuss the political transition. In the political system, Nepal,

R. C. Paudel, *Essays on Key Issues of Development in Nepal*,
https://doi.org/10.1007/978-981-95-7715-6_6

during the last six decades or more, the country has gone through seven political paradigm shifts, from the Rana Regime to the Federal Republic in different years. In about every decade, Nepal's political system has been unstable. In this background, Kaur (2018) explained how Nepal is in transition politically. As of now, since 2008, Nepal has practiced a federal republic system, but it has not taken the full phase shape yet. Still, the situation seems to be as discussed in Strasheim and Bogati (2016), which suggested that how the republic federalism was introduced in the country has become a driver of new violence in the country. Many political activities, including the results of the 2022 national election with the rise of the Rastriya Prajatantra Party demanding the restoration of monarchy system in the country, indicate the country is still in the political transition phase.

Second, in the arena of economic systems during the same period, Nepal went through various economic regimes, such as from a fully controlled to an open economy, now practicing a mixed (hybrid) economic system. Nepal can be said a transitional country in terms of its economic system because of three reasons. Firstly, Nepal is graduating from the least developed countries (LDCs) category in 2026, it has resulted in various economic policies, particularly the trade, aid, and investment policies, which will remain in transition for a few years. Secondly, Nepal's current constitution aims to establish a socialist economy through the elected governments. The problem here is that a solid majority of a political party seems impossible due to the adopted election system, which has a combination of the first-past-the-post voting system (165 members elected directly from the constituency) and 110 elected through the proportional electoral system in which the members' seat is distributed among the parties (Constituent Assembly Secretariat, 2015). The political powers believe the hardcore socialist economy to open economy are active and strong. This situation has resulted in many unstable governments making democracy a fragile democracy in the country. Thirdly, Nepal seems to be a strategically important country because of its geographical location and geopolitics scenario, as a result, the country has received promising connectivity offers from China, India, and the United States (Vater, 2020). Their political ideology and economic system seem to have a direct or indirect impact on the Nepalese economy. As these countries' role in the international arena changes over time, Nepal's economy seems to have been directly affected as discussed in Paudel and Le Billon (2020). These backgrounds make Nepal a transitional country.

Therefore, how democracy has impacted the quality of governance in the case of the transitional country is an interesting research question as the number of transitional countries in the world is changing over the time and time because of many reasons, such as the change in political and economic paradigms in many respects. Also, Nepal is a unique country for such study because of its unique geographical situation (landlockedness where the trade of goods and commodities has additional costs) requiring a more important role of governance to compensate such additional trade costs.

The major findings from this paper are the focus of the nation should be assuring democracy, either in the form of local democracy or civil society participation, to enhance the quality of governance in the country. Also, it suggests that Nepal should focus to develop a more systematic channel or way of civil society participation so that the quality of governance would be improved.

This paper is structured as follows. Some casual observations on Nepal's democracy and governance along with the relevant variables are presented in Sect. 6.2. A brief literature review is presented in Sect. 6.3. Research methodology is discussed in Sect. 6.4 followed by results and discussion in Sect. 6.5 before concluding with some recommendations in Sect. 6.6.

6.2 Democracy and Governance in Nepal: Some Casual Observations

6.2.1 *Modern History and Economic System of Nepal*

In ancient history, Nepal was ruled by different dynasties. For example, Dahal (2017) states Gopal dynasty, Mahispalas, Kirants, Lichhavies and Mallas dynasties were the major ones to rule the country until the eighteenth century. In modern history, the Shah dynasty from 1769 to 1847 (as the executive head of the state from the dynasty) and the Rana dynasty from 1847 to 1951 (as the executive head of the state for 104 years) are two dynasties in modern shape of Nepal. King Prithvi Narayan Shah (1723–1775) of the Shah dynasty united Nepal in 1769, largely as the current geographic shape of the country, as the Hindu Kingdom. Shah dynasty lead the country, as both the executive and ceremonial head of the country in a different period, until 2008 when the country was declared as a republic country abolishing the monarch system. This shows Shah dynasty remained as the head of the country in different forms from 1769 to 2008 (a total of 239 years).

Until 1951, the foundation of the economy was largely for self-sustainability. The economy was fully closed (in terms of formal international market access) for the public. The Rana regime is historically known as the tough autocratic regime that suppressed but did not abolish the monarch system. Because of the Rana regime's autocratic governing system, a foundation for democracy was laid (Dahal, 2017). The main reasons for the democratic movement in the Rana regime were the autocratic governing system; internal clash within the dynasty because of their internal categorisation, such as A, B and C classes, and political awareness among the people because of the movement in India for independence as discussed in Brown (2003).

Modern political and economic history begins with the establishment of democracy, and the abolishment of the Rana regime, in 1951. A new constitution was promulgated in 1951, which laid the foundation for democracy and the first election was held in 1959. Later just after one and half years, King Mahendra dissolved the elected parliament and took all the powers into his hands in 1960 (Ministry of Foreign Affairs, 2023). Then, the party-less Panchayat system ruled the country for about 30 years until 1990, when democracy was restored. The Panchayat system adopted a mixed economy with major features of a closed economy.

After the restoration of democracy in 1990, the country adopted an open economic policy, and Nepal became of the earlier entrants in the reform era in the region. Nepal adopted liberalization, deregulation, and decontrol policy in the economic system. Mostly, the privatization of public property remained one of the most critical issues in this period but in a way, the economy was picking up momentum. In 1996, Nepal entered a direct conflict era because of the armed struggle initiated by the then Nepal Communist Party (Maoist), which raised the issues of inequality, rampant corruption, mass poverty and unfair cast and social system in the country. In this context, Deraniyagala (2005), indicating the decade-long insurgency and examining the links between economic reform and conflict in Nepal, suggested that deprivation and conflict are the outcomes of an uneven process of development and negative distributional effect that led to the social and economic exclusion of a large segment of the population. Because of this background, the country remained very fragile and was heading towards a failure state as discussed in Kernot (2006), and Radha Krishna Khadka (2020).

Figure 6.1 shows a brief snapshot of the democratic movements, local governance as replicated by the local elections and the unstable nature of governments over the last seventy years in the country. Even in modern political and economic history, the focus on local governance was a practice only in a few decades however there is a notable time of direct democracy at the national level. Even at the central level, the governments have been changed very frequently, parties have been divided while leading the governments, these indicate a kind of bad governance and the country is unstable because of the lack of policy inconsistency for a long time now as discussed in Gurung (2011). Changing the Prime minister so frequently has resulted in political instability and has become a major cause of policy implementation failure and policy inconsistency on many occasions. It has embraced the nation-building process weakening the governance system in the country.

6.2.2 Democracy and Governance

Khan and Islam (2014) and Knight (2018) have highlighted the link between democracy and governance. Khan and Islam (2014) stated that if democracy is not practised well, even the elected government and the governing system lose the trust of the people an example of Bangladesh. In addition, Knight (2018) suggested that democracy validates the quality of governance, but the condition is that democracy should govern inclusively and humanely following the norms of human rights and rule of law. In this background, Fig. 6.2 shows the trends of civil society participation, local democracy, and governance in Nepal. Civil society participation and local democracy data are indexed between zero and one, while governance data are indexed ranging from −2.5 to +2.5. For the governance data, the average of control of corruption, government effectiveness and rule of law is taken as an index.

The data in Fig. 6.2 shows that civil society participation has not much improved during the entire period, and stands at about 0.6, with few exceptions such as a bit increased from 2007 to 2009 and a slight decline from 2019 onward. The trend for local democracy, overall, has an increasing trend but a huge fall from 2003 to 2016 as the country could not hold local elections for about one and half a decade.

In the context of governance, overall, Nepal's index has always remained negative, and it is between −0.34 to −0.88 with a slightly declining trend. The index declined sharply from the mid-1990s to the mid of the first

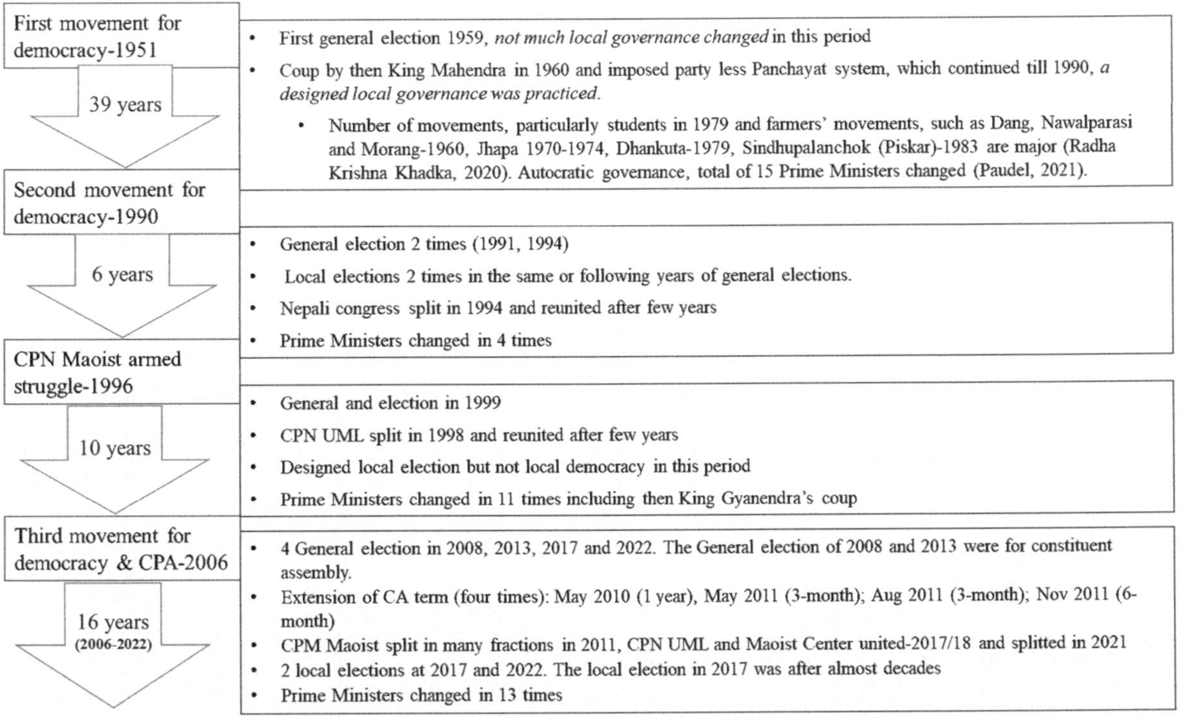

Fig. 6.1 Democratic process and political changes in a snapshot. (Source: Adopted from Gurung (2011) covering the updated data to 2023)

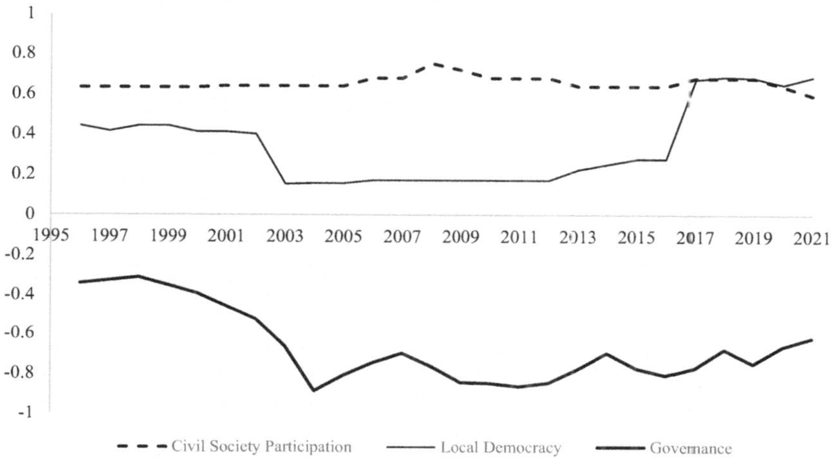

Fig. 6.2 Democracy and governance indices of Nepal, 1996–2021. (Source: Data from International IDEA (2022) for the democracy and civil society participation index series and World Bank (2023) for the governance index series)

decade of the century. Then, it fluctuated a bit to reach −0.62, indicating a bit improved situation since 2019.

6.2.3 *Per capita GDP, Trade Openness and Education*

Al-Marhubi (2004) stated that per capita GDP growth (level of economic development), trade openness, and democracy are the major determinants of governance. In this context, Fig. 6.3 shows the per capita GDP growth rate (measured in percent) and trade openness (measured in the percent of GDP). In most of the year, both variables have a similar structure in the fluctuations. The per capita GDP growth rate seems to hover below seven percent with few exceptions of being negative growth on three occasions (2002, 2016 and 2020). The average growth rate for this selected period is just three percent. The trend of trade openness seems slightly declining during the selected period, with some fluctuation between 36 percent (in 2011) to 64 percent (in 1997). Garcia-Sanchez et al. (2013) highlighted that the education status of a country has a direct and significant impact on the quality of governance. Figure 6.4 shows the rate of enrolment in

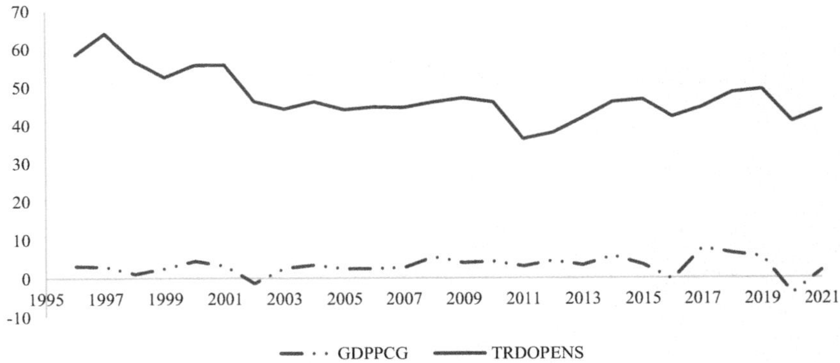

Fig. 6.3 GDP per capita growth (GDPPCG) and trade openness (TRDOPENS), 1996–2021, percent. (Source: Data from World Bank (2025))

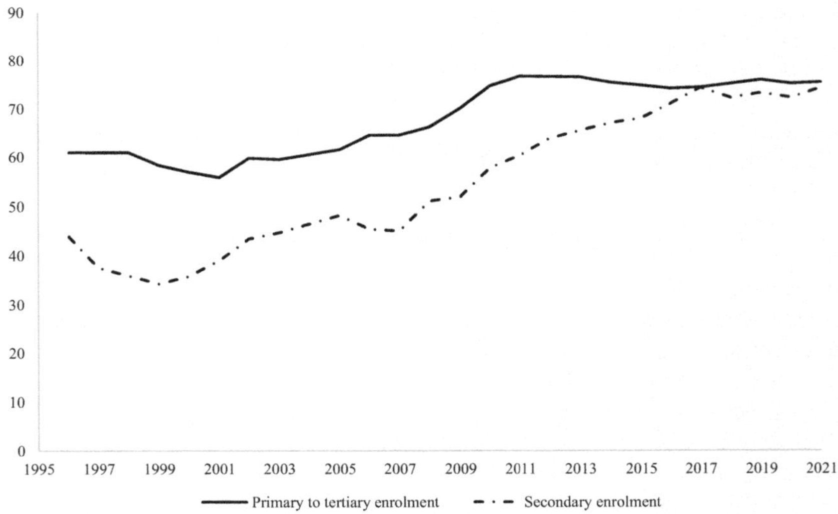

Fig. 6.4 Primary to tertiary and secondary level enrolment, 1996–2021, percent. (Source: Data from World Bank (2025))

primary to tertiary level and secondary level, both of which have a gradual increasing trend.

6.3 A Brief Literature Review

6.3.1 *Theoretical Foundation*

The major stream of literature on governance emphasises democratic procedures as the most influential factor of governance. Klijn and Skelcher (2007) emphasise that representative democracy enables greater participation in the policy process and effective implementation of the programs that contribute to enhancing the quality of governance. Chhotray and Stoker (2009) suggest that governance theory refers to the ways of practising the collective decision-making process. This statement indicates that democracy has a strong link to the governance of a society. Elstub and Escobar (2019) highlight the role of democratic innovations in the governance system.

6.3.2 *Empirical Context*

Somerville (2005) highlighted the key issues of governance and democracy and methods to change the governance. It provides various theories and evidence so that governance can be more conducive to human liberation. Here, the article has distinguished between governance and meta-governance, and it is afterwards linked with democracy. Qualitative data sources are used in this paper.

Tarvedi (2019) discusses the democracy that is authorized through the election which helps to make it fair and free. Here the paper uses Principal Component analysis to determine indicators for governance to understand the level of democracy needed to employ governance. It uses panel data analysis from the period of 1996–2012 covering 100 countries. It uses a basic linear regression method to measure the impact of democracy in governance. This paper concludes that political freedom and civil society rights have a nonlinear relationship with governance. Governance is assisted by electoral democracy and democracy is a foundation to strengthen levels of governance.

Adnan Karatas (2021) verified the relationship between governance and democracy through empirical analysis using quantitative data for 214 countries covering the period from 2009 to 2018 to measure the quality of governance. For the analysis of data, regression analysis is conducted, and correlations are calculated. It concludes that there is a high correlation between governance and democracy.

6.3.3 *Nepalese Context*

Khadka (1993), using a descriptive analysis method, stated that the history of the political system of Nepal, like many other countries, went through the absolute constitutional monarchy after the upsurge of the party-less panchayat regime in 1990. Nepal is now focusing on the consolidation of democracy and conducting general elections. The major challenges highlighted in the paper are parliamentary opposition, inefficient bureaucracy, and conflicts between the parties.

Dahal (2002) links good governance and decentralization in the Nepalese context using qualitative measures and states that democracy and governance available to all places without proper decentralization have a core role, indicating the importance of a quality democracy. The paper focuses on the role of diverse and heterogeneous environments and decentralization to expand the peoples' participation, development, resource mobilization, conflict resolutions and community building. This paper concludes with the remark of decentralization, self-governance and democracy are conditions necessary to emancipate quality livelihoods among diverse people.

Webster (2011), using a qualitative analysis method, raises concerns with methods of fundamental restructuring in case of the failed state of democracy and governance in Nepal linking the political challenges and restructuring to address the formal issue of breakdown due to demand for greater autonomy by regional and ethnic communities. Current frustration leads to reorganization for an effective and efficient state. This paper concludes with the need of drafting a new constitution for overcoming the challenges of political opposition, reform in governance and federal system reform.

Dahal (2017) discusses the long history of the democratic movement in Nepal and the establishment of Nepal as the Federal Democratic Republic after the mass movement in 2006. After the democratic movement by Nepal Praja Parishad, many other parties were established that facilitates movements and revolutions. This paper also highlights the close relationship between democracy and good governance. Various dimensions of good governance are studied in detail and also facilitate democracy. Democratic movements' role in democracy and good governance is analyzed in this paper using a descriptive-analytical method to understand democratic movement and good governance. It concludes that good governance in Nepal has been made possible with democratic movement and it is increasingly being prioritized in the Constitution of Nepal.

Rai (2021) precisely discusses existing practices of inclusive government practices and the challenges of inclusive democracy in Nepal. This paper is based on qualitative data and uses a descriptive method to analyze the data obtained from secondary sources. The paper concludes on challenges faced in the pathway of inclusive governance and democracy.

6.3.4 The Research Gap

After a brief review of the literature, we can conclude that the role of democracy is important to form the shape and improve the quality of governance. If so, how is the role of democracy in the context of Nepal's governance quality is a matter to be studied in a systematic way, which has not been made yet. Therefore, this paper aims to make a systematic econometric analysis to identify whether democracy has contributed to improving the quality of governance in Nepal.

6.4 Research Methodology

6.4.1 Research Design

This paper adopts two approaches to achieving its objectives. First, to explain the trends of governance and democracy with other relevant variables, we use figures as in Sect. 6.2 of this paper. Second, to know the impact of democracy, we conduct a time series econometric analysis after knowing the property of the time series data as discussed in the rest of this section.

6.4.2 The Model and Variables

The issue of governance is a complex matter as several factors might contribute to its determinants. This paper adopts the approaches developed by Al-Marhubi (2004), Klijn and Skelcher (2007), Khan and Islam (2014) and Knight (2018) which have been augmented to include the main variables of the interest of the researchers and contexts. The key message from the model is that economic status, trade openness, democratic factors, and education factors are the major determinants of the quality of governance. Considering these facts, Eqn. (6.1) is estimated as the benchmark model. The robustness check of the results is made by employing alternative specifications of the model as specified in Eqns. (6.2), (6.3) and (6.4). Also, the approach of variable alteration is adopted while estimating the model.

$$GOVE_t = \alpha + \beta_1 LDEMOC_t + \beta_2 GDPPCG_t + \beta_3 OPENNESS_t + \beta_4 EDUC_t + \epsilon_t \tag{6.1}$$

$$GOVE_t = \alpha + \beta_1 LDEMOC_t + \beta_2 OPENNESS_t + \beta_3 EDUC_t + \epsilon_t \tag{6.2}$$

$$GOVE_t = \alpha + \beta_1 CIVPART_t + \beta_2 GDPPCG_t + \beta_3 OPENNESS_t + \beta_4 EDUC_t + \epsilon_t \tag{6.3}$$

$$GOVE_t = \alpha + \beta_1 CIVPART_t + \beta_3 OPENNESS_t + \beta_3 EDUC_t + \epsilon_t \tag{6.4}$$

Where α is a constant term, $\beta_1 \ldots \beta_4$ are the coefficients of the independent variables, ϵ is the error term, and the subscript t refers to the period-year as we are using the annual data from 1996 to 2021. Based on the literature, we expect β_1, β_2, β_3 and $\beta_4$to be positive.

In the model, GOVE refers to the governance index, the dependent variable, which varies between −2.5 to 2.5. Because of potential collinearity issues, we take the average of Control of Corruption and Government Effectiveness from the Kaufmann Indicator of Governance available in the World Bank Database namely the Global Governance Database. The data for 1997, 1999, and 2001 are extrapolated taking the average of the earlier and following years.

The other variables LDEMOC (local democracy index), CIVPART (civil society participation index), GDPPCG (GDP per capita growth rate in percent), OPENNESS (trade openness measured in rate percent of GDP), EDUC (education proxied by primary to tertiary enrolment rate in percent) are the independent variables. Here, democracy is measured by two different indices: local democracy and civil society participation, which are used in the estimation following standard procedures. These two variables are the main variables of interest in the estimation and their roles in governance are expected to be positive and statistically significant.

Before starting the econometric estimation, as this paper uses a time series analysis method based on Nepal's data, we conduct the unit root tests employing Dickey-Fuller (DF), augmented Dickey-Fuller (ADF), Phillips and Perron (PP) and Kwiatkowski–Phillips–Schmidt–Shin (KPSS) methods using the model in Eqn. (6.5) and the results are presented in Tables 6.1 and 6.2. These test results are achieved assuming the presence of a unit root (non-stationary variable) in the null hypothesis (H0) and no unit root (stationary variable) in the alternative hypothesis (Ha) of Eqn. (6.5).

$$\Delta Z_t = \alpha_1 + \alpha_{2t} + \gamma Z_{t-1} + \sum_{j=1}^{k} \beta_j \Delta Z_{t-j} + \varepsilon_t \tag{6.5}$$

Where, Δ is the first difference operator, Z is the variable of interest, α_1 is the intercept, t is the time, ΔZ is the augmented terms, k is the appropriate lag length of the augmented terms and ε is the white noise error term. The ADF test is essentially the test of the significance of the coefficient γ in the above equation. The DF test is performed without the augmented term. To select the lag length k, we start with a maximum lag of 4 and compare it to the appropriate lag by examining the Schwarz Criterion (SC).

The unit root test results suggest that we have both I(0) and I(1) variables, such as GDPPCG detected as I(0) and the rest in the baseline model as I(1) by the majority of the methods. We largely consider the DF, ADF, and PP results as they are consistent in all methods. In some cases, the results suggested by KPSS are slightly different, but they do not force to alter the results. Similarly, other specifications also would have a mixed set of I(0) and I(1) variables as seen in Tables 6.1 and 6.2. If the variables in Table 6.1 are significant, noted as I(0) and if they are not significant, then tested with the first difference and results are presented in Table 6.2, and are declared as I(1) as they are estimated in the first difference.

6.4.3 *Data Sources*

We use the data from two major sources. First, we collect the data for the democracy and civil society participation index from International IDEA (2022) and for the governance index series from World Bank (2023). Also, for GDP per capita growth, trade openness, and education data from World Bank (2025).

Table 6.1 Unit root test results at the level

	With Constant				*With Constant & Trend*			
	DF	*ADF*	*PP*	*KPSS*	*DF*	*ADF*	*PP*	*KPSS*
GOVE	−1.27	−1.80	−1.82	0.43*	−1.04	−0.78	−0.85	0.18**
LDEMOC	−0.78	−0.64	−0.70	0.24	−1.20	−1.09	−1.07	0.18**
CIVPART	−1.69	−1.68	−1.82	0.16	−1.68	−1.31	−1.46	0.15**
GDPPCG	−4.72***	−4.62***	−4.62***	0.16	−4.76***	−4.71***	−4.60***	0.12*
OPENNES	−1.76	−2.22	−2.14	0.49**	−2.44	−2.37	−2.14	0.19**
EDUC	−0.76	−0.50	−0.69	0.64**	−1.35	−1.38	−1.74	0.10

Notes: *, ** and *** indicate the variables are significant at 10 %, 5% and 1% levels of significance

Table 6.2 Unit root test results at first difference

	With Constant				*With Constant & Trend*			
	DF	*ADF*	*PP*	*KPSS*	*DF*	*ADF*	*PP*	*KPSS*
GOVE	−3.65**	−3.63**	−3.61**	0.38*	−4.20***	−4.1194**	−4.4597***	0.0733
LDEMOC	−4.66***	−4.59***	−4.59***	0.36*	−5.25***	−5.0335***	−5.1193***	0.0780
CIVPART	−4.19***	−4.12***	−4.12***	0.20	−4.51***	−4.2954**	−4.2954**	0.0677
OPENNES	−4.41***	−5.67***	−5.53***	0.50**	−5.77***	−6.1047***	−10.838***	0.3735***
EDUC	−3.16***	−3.12**	−3.10**	0.13	−3.18*	−3.0482	−3.0284	0.1389*

Notes: *, ** and *** indicate the variables are significant at 10 %, 5% and 1% levels of significance

6.4.4 Econometrics

As stated earlier, we detect the time series properties by identifying the mixed set of variables I(0) and I(1). Now, the standard procedure is to conduct the cointegration test to find out the coefficients to explain the relationship between the dependent and independent variables. As we have the time series data with different orders of integration, the variables included in Eqns. (6.1), (6.2), (6.3) and (6.4) will be analyzed using a co-integration test based on autoregressive distributed lag (ARDL) approach to identify the long-run and short-run relationship among the dependent and independent variables irrelevance of the order of their integration (Pesaran et al., 2001). In such as case, the advantage of using ARDL is that this fits well with the combination of I(0) and I(1) variables and predicts both long-run and short-run cointegration. As the model regressed with the lag of dependent variables, it adopts a dynamic modelling approach that captures the lag effects too.

Therefore, Eqns. (6.1), (6.2), (6.3) and (6.4) will be modified as in Eqns. (6.6), (6.7), (6.8) and (6.9) to represent the ARDL version of the specifications.

$$\begin{aligned}\Delta GOVE_t = {} & \alpha + \beta_1 GOVE_{t-1} + \beta_2 LDEMOC_{t-1} + \beta_3 GDPPCG_{t-1} \\ & + \beta_4 OPENNESS_{t-1} + \beta_5 EDUC_{t-1} + \sum_{i=1}^{26} \gamma_i \Delta GOVE_{t-i} \\ & + \sum_{i=1}^{26} \delta_i \Delta LDEMOC_{t-i} + \sum_{i=1}^{26} \theta_i \Delta GDPPCG_{t-i} \\ & + \sum_{i=1}^{26} \varphi_i \Delta OPENNESS_{t-i} + \sum_{i=1}^{26} \lambda_i \Delta EDUC_{t-i} + v_t\end{aligned} \tag{6.6}$$

$$\begin{aligned}\Delta GOVE_t = {} & \alpha + \beta_1 GOVE_{t-1} + \beta_2 LDEMOC_{t-1} + \beta_3 OPENNESS_{t-1} \\ & + \beta_4 EDUC_{t-1} + \sum_{i=1}^{26} \gamma_i \Delta GOVE_{t-i} + \sum_{i=1}^{26} \delta_i \Delta LDEMOC_{t-i} \\ & + \sum_{i=1}^{26} \varphi_i \Delta OPENNESS_{t-i} + \sum_{i=1}^{26} \lambda_i \Delta EDUC_{t-i} + v_t\end{aligned} \tag{6.7}$$

$$\Delta GOVE_t = \alpha + \beta_1 GOVE_{t-1} + \beta_2 CIVPART_{t-1} + \beta_3 GDPPCG_{t-1} + \beta_4 OPENNESS_{t-1} + \beta_5 EDUC_{t-1} + \sum_{i=1}^{26} \gamma_i \Delta GOVE_{t-i} + \sum_{i=1}^{26} \delta_i \Delta CIVPART_{t-i} + \sum_{i=1}^{26} \theta_i \Delta GDPPCG_{t-i} + \sum_{i=1}^{26} \varphi_i \Delta OPENNESS_{t-i} + \sum_{i=1}^{26} \lambda_i \Delta EDUC_{t-i} + v_t \quad (6.8)$$

$$\Delta GOVE_t = \alpha + \beta_1 GOVE_{t-1} + \beta_2 CIVPART_{t-1} + \beta_3 OPENNESS_{t-1} + \beta_4 EDUC_{t-1} + \sum_{i=1}^{26} \gamma_i \Delta GOVE_{t-i} + \sum_{i=1}^{26} \delta_i \Delta CIVPART_{t-i} + \sum_{i=1}^{26} \varphi_i \Delta OPENNESS_{t-i} + \sum_{i=1}^{26} \lambda_i \Delta EDUC_{t-i} + v_t \quad (6.9)$$

Here, Eqns. (6.6), (6.7), (6.8) and (6.9) show the dynamic impact in the form of the Auto-Regressive Distributed Lag Model of Eqns. (6.1), (6.2), (6.3) and (6.4) respectively. In the model, Δ stands for the first-order lagged variable, α is the intercept, β_1, β_2, β_3, β_4 *and* β_5 are the coefficients of first-order variables. Similarly, γ_i, δ_i, θ_i, φ_i and λ_i are the parameters of the error correction model, and v_t is a vector of random error.

6.5 Results and Discussion

In the process of conducting the econometric estimation, first, the baseline model as specified in Eqn. (6.1) is tested and the results are presented in Column (1) of Table 6.3. In the second estimation, we remove the income variable from the estimation to see if the variable deletion bias is there in the estimation, and the results are given in column (2) of the same table. Then, in the next step, we use the civil society participation index in the benchmark model replacing the local democracy variable and the results are presented in column (3) of the same table. Finally, the same treatment is given to local democracy in the second estimation, and the results are presented in column 4 of Table 6.4.

At the first step of ARDL estimation, we want to know the bound test statistics, which are presented in Table 6.3. The statistics show that the calculated *F*-statistics are above the upper bound of critical values, indicating that there exists long run relationship for specifications (1), (2), and

Table 6.3 Bound test results of all specifications of the model

	Equation (6.1)	*Equation (6.2)*	*Equation (6.3)*	*Equation (6.4)*
	ARDL(2,2,2,2,1)	*ARDL(3,3,3,2,3)*	*ARDL(3,3,3,2,3)*	*ARDL(2,0,0,0,0)*
Calculated *F*-statistics	**10.05**	**7.53**	**15.79**	**6.09**
Lower bound @ 5%	4.40	5.02	4.47	5.02
Upper bound @ 5%	5.87	6.39	6.01	6.39
Results	LRR exists	LRR exists	LRR exists	Inconclusive

Note: Critical *F*-statistics are measured for upper and lower bound at a 5 percent level of significance, LRR refers to the long-run relationship and Inconclusive means ambiguity status of whether LRR exists or not

(3) of the model, as the calculated *F*-statistics are above the upper bound of the critical values. However, this could not remain valid in the case of Eqn. (6.4) as the calculated *F*-statistic is just 6.09, which is between the lower and upper bounds of the critical values, indicating an ambiguous status of whether there exists the long-run relationship.

Now, the next step is to estimate the long-run relationship and short-run relationship between the dependent variable with the independent variables. Table 6.4 presents the long-run relationship results for the model. Similarly, Table 6.5 presents the results for the ECM model in those different specifications of the model. Combinedly, these tables show the long-run and short-run coefficients of the ARDL model with different lags as shown in the tables for the given model. Schwartz-Bayesian Criteria (SBC) is selected due to the relatively small size of the series; however, we cover 26 years, from 1996 to 2021, in this study.

The estimated results in column (1) of Table 6.4 show that local democracy (LDEMOC) does have a strong long-run relationship with the quality of governance with a coefficient of 0.60 and statistically significant at the five percent level of significance. This indicates that a one percent increase in the local democracy index causes to increase in the governance index by on average 0.60 percent holding other variables in the model constant. Yes, this indicates a big impact of local democracy in governance as seen in Fig. 6.2. The next important variable in the model seems to be education, which states that a one percent increase in primary to tertiary level enrolment cause to increase in the quality of governance index by 0.014 percent on average other things remain the same. The coefficient

Table 6.4 Long-run coefficients of the ARDL model

Dependent variable: Governance-index (GOVE)	*(1)*	*(2)*	*(3)*	*(4)*
Local democracy-index (LDEMOC)	0.60***	0.72***		
	(0.175)	(0.065)		
Civil society participation-index (CIVPART)			1.19**	1.49*
			(0.415)	(0.820)
Per capita income growth-rate (GDPPCG)	−0.04**		0.06**	
	(0.014)		(0.013)	
Trade openness-rate (OPENNESS)	−0.001	−0.00	−0.007	0.013**
	(0.009)	(0.003)	(0.004)	(0.005)
Education enrolment-rate (EDUC)	0.014**	0.13***	−0.03***	−0.005
	(0.005)	(0.003)	(0.003)	(0.005)
Number of observations	24	23	23	23
R-squared	0.98	0.97	0.94	0.94
ARDL lag selection	(2,2,2,2,1)	(3,3.0,3)	(3,3,3,2,3)	(2,2,3,3)
Time trend	Yes	Yes	Yes	Yes

Notes: ***, **, and * indicate the values are significant at 1%, 5%, and 10% levels of significance, respectively. The standard errors are in parentheses

for per capita GDP growth is negative at a 1 percent level of significance. This situation explains that growing income has not been reflected to improve the quality of governance. However, this nature is not consistent while we control the civil society participation variable, where growing income has a positive impact on governance.

Column (2) of the same table shows the results for an alternative specification of the model, where per capita GDP has been dropped to determine if the bias of the variables exists in the estimation. The coefficient for local democracy has maintained consistency in sign and significance; rather, the magnitude has increased to 0.72, indicating the positive impact on governance. The results for the education variable also remain consistent as in column (1) of the table.

In columns (3) and (4) of the same table, we replace the local democracy variable with civil society participation. The results for civil society participation show that the coefficients are greater than those of local democracy but statistically significant at a 5 percent level of significance. The per capita GDP growth rate variable turns out to be positive, and the education variable turns out to be negative, unlike in column (1). However, both local democracy and civil society participation variables are statistically significant consistently throughout the estimations as specified in columns (1), (2), (3), and (4) of the same table.

Table 6.5 presents the short-run results for all specifications of the model. In all four specifications, the results for ECM (-1) are statistically

Table 6.5 Short-run ECM coefficients of ARDL model

Dependent variable: change in Governance-index (dGOVE)	*(1)*	*(2)*	*(3)*	*(4)*
dGOVE1	0.19	0.84***	2.22***	1.116***
	(0.127)	(0.172)	(0.307)	(0.295)
dGOVE2		0.33**	0.65**	
		(0.15)	(0.297)	
dLDEMOC	0.45***	0.302***		
	(0.102)	(0.108)		
dLDEMOC1	0.44***	−0.359**		
	(0.104)	(0.160)		
LDEMOC(-2)		−0.557***		
		(0.135)		
dCIVPART			−4.96***	−0.59
			(0.991)	(0.647)
dCIVPART1			−4.585***	−1.65*
			(1.026)	(0.909)
dCIVPART2			2.05***	
			(0.621)	
dGDPPCG	−0.02***		0.06***	0.001
	(0.005)		(0.015)	(0.009)
dGDPPCG1	−0.01**		−0.009	
	(0.004)		(0.016)	
dGDPPCG2			−0.02*	
			(0.008)	
dOPENNESS	0.008*	−0.00	−0.05***	−0.008
	(0.004)	(0.001)	(0.011)	(0.007)
dOPENNESS1	−0.00		−0.045***	−0.019***
	(0.004)		(0.007)	(0.005)
dOPENNESS2				−0.010*
				(0.014)
dEDUC	−0.01	0.005	−0.08***	−0.036**
	(0.005)	(0.006)	(0.012)	(0.014)
dEDUC1		−0.011	−0.101***	−0.038**
		(0.007)	(0.015)	(0.014)
dEDUC2		−0.023***	−0.07***	
		(0.007)	(0.012)	
ecm(-1)	−0.71***	−2.34***	−2.34***	−01.47***
	(0.165)	(0.327)	(0.327)	(0.328)

Notes: ***, ** and * indicate the values are significant at 1%, 5% and 10% levels of significance, respectively. The standard errors are in parentheses

significant with an expected negative sign indicating the disequilibrium that occurred in the previous period is corrected in the present period following a short-run shock at a relatively slow pace as the coefficients are higher. As seen in the results of all columns (1) to (4), the immediate past growth rate of the governance index and democracy index have a strong positive impact on the governance index in the short run, while some of the other variables have a negative impact if the variables are measured in further lagged form.

Now let's consider the stability test of the model. In the test, as reported in the results tables, the moderately high value of R-square (ranged from 0.94 to 0.98) in the different specifications shows that the overall goodness of fit of the model is high, that is on average all specification-above 90 percent of the variation observed in the target variable is explained by the model. The diagnostic test results show that the model passes the tests for serial correlation, functional form, normality, and heteroscedasticity. Further, the stability test results (CUSUM and CUSUMSQ) plotted against the critical bounds of a 5 percent level of significance are within the range, indicating that the model is structurally stable (Figures in Appendix A1, A2, A3 and A4).

6.6 Conclusions and Policy Recommendations

6.6.1 Conclusions

This chapter's main objective is to examine the role of democracy in improving the quality of governance. For this purpose, a thorough analysis of governance and democracy, including local democracy and civil society participation, has been made in this paper using an advanced econometric methodology based on time-series data.

The results suggest that both the proxies of democracy, such as local democracy and civil society participation have a strong positive association with the quality of governance in the long run. Also, it shows that, in the short run, democracy and civil society participation may have both positive and negative associations with governance but in the long run it will pay off to improve the quality of the governance.

The major determinants of governance in this context seem to be democracy, either in the form of local democracy or civil society participation, and education. The education policy should work hard to get the results as supported by literature, making more vocational and technical education from the base level, so that it will contribute to improving the quality of governance in the country. In the meantime, the per capita income growth needs to be tied to improving the quality of governance.

6.6.2 *Policy Recommendations*

It seems that improving the quality of democracy, either improving the local democracy or improving civil society participation, is equivalent to improving the quality of governance in the country. It means that democracy is a fundamental condition for improving the quality of governance. Therefore, it might be a good way to promote democratic exercise by promoting civil society rights to participate, and it would be a meaningful contribution to further improve the quality of governance. Therefore, a strong recommendation from this study is to invest more in the education sector and more rational expenditure in promoting democratic and civil society rights to improve the quality of democracy and by there improve the quality of governance in Nepal. Education and income growth need to be tied up further to improve the quality of governance to a new height.

Appendix A

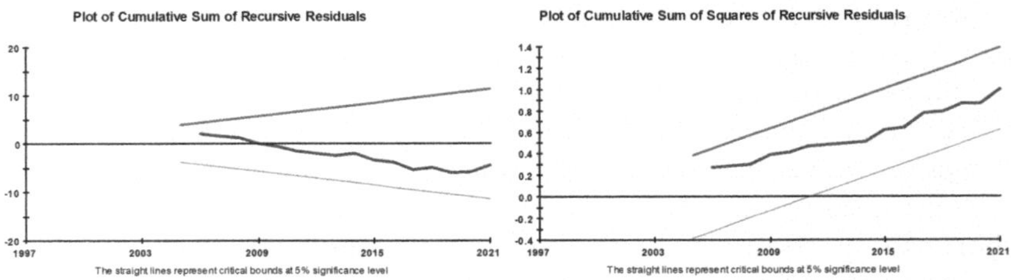

Fig. A1 Plot of CUSUM and CUSUMQ plots for model specification (1)

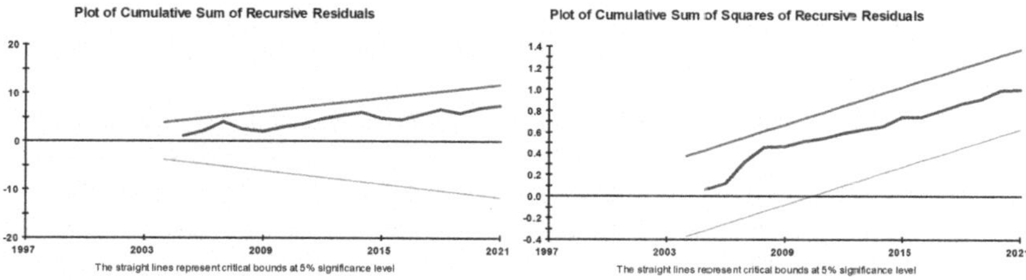

Fig. A2 Plot of CUSUM and CUSUMQ plots for model specification (2)

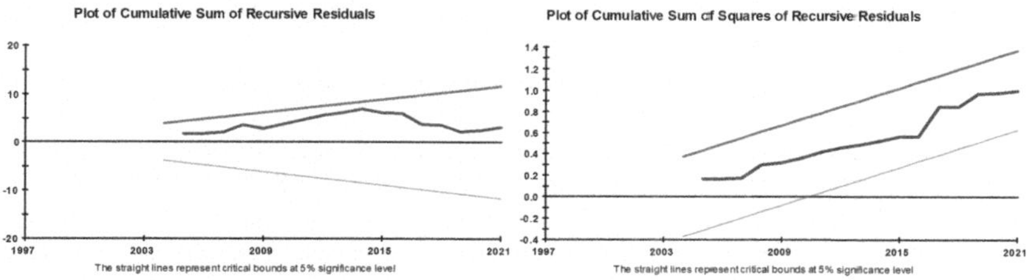

Fig. A3 Plot of CUSUM and CUSUMQ plots for model specification (3)

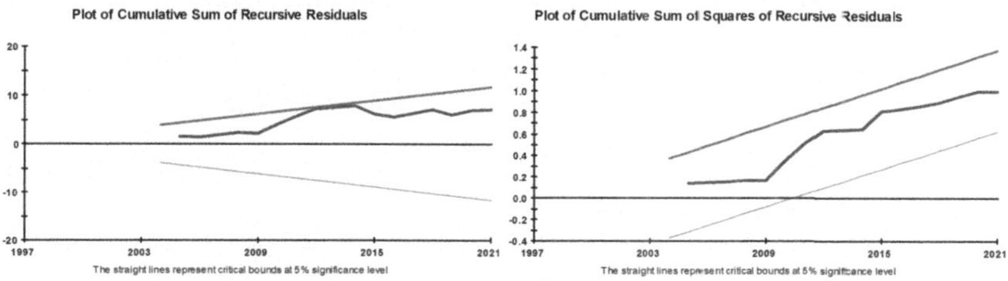

Fig. A4 Plot of CUSUM and CUSUMQ plots for model specification (4)

References

Adnan Karatas, A. (2021). Evaluation of the relationship of democracy and governance: An emperical analysis. *Hrvatska i komparativna javna uprava: casopis za teoriju i praksu javne uprave*, *21*(4), 623–651.

Al-Marhubi, F. (2004). The determinants of governance: A cross-country analysis. *Contemporary Economic Policy*, *22*(3), 394–406.

Brown, T. L. (2003). *The challenge to democracy in Nepal.* Routledge.

Burns, D. (2000). Can local democracy survive governance? *Urban studies, 37*(5–6), 963–973.

Chhotray, V., & Stoker, G. (2009). *Governance: From theory to practice.* Springer.

Constituent Assembly Secretariat. (2015). *Constitution of Nepal 2015.* Constituent Assembly Secretariat, Government of Nepal, Singha Durbar, Kathmandu, Nepal.

Dahal, G. (2017). Democratic Practices and good governance in Nepal. *Journal of Political Science, 17*, 18–35.

Dahal, D. R., Uprety, H.C., & Friedrich- Ebert-Stiftung. (2002). Goog governance and decentralization in Nepal

Deraniyagala, S. (2005). The Political Economy of Civil Conflict in Nepal. *Oxford Development Studies, 33*(1), 47–62. https://doi.org/10.1080/13600810500099659

Elstub, S., & Escobar, O. (2019). *Handbook of democratic innovation and governance.* Edward Elgar Publishing.

Fayissa, B., & Nsiah, C. (2013). The impact of governance on economic growth in Africa. *The Journal of Developing Areas, 47*(1), 91–108.

Garcia-Sanchez, I. M., Cuadrado-Ballesteros, B., & Frias-Aceituno, J. (2013). Determinants of Government Effectiveness. *International Journal of Public Administration, 36*(8), 567–577. https://doi.org/10.1080/01900692.2013.772630

Gurung, N. (2011). *Local democracy in the political transition of Nepal.*

International IDEA. (2022). *The Global State of Democracy Indices*

Kaur, H. (2018). Transition of Nepal from Monarchy to Democracy. *IOSR Journal of Humanities and Social Science (IOSR-JHSS), 23*(2), 22–27.

Kernot, S. (2006). Nepal: A development challenge. *South Asia: Journal of South Asian Studies, 29*(2), 293–307.

Khadka, N. (1993). Democracy and development in Nepal: Prospects and Challenges. *Pacific Affairs, 44*(1), 44.

Khan, M. M., & Islam, M. S. (2014). Democracy and good governance in Bangladesh: are they compatible? *Millennial Asia, 5*(1), 23–40.

Klijn, E.-H., & Skelcher, C. (2007). Democracy and Governance Networks: Compatible or Not ? *Public Administration, 85*(3), 587–608. https://doi.org/10.1111/j.1467-9299.2007.00662.x

Knight, W. A. (2018). Democracy and Good Governance. In T. G. Weiss & S. Daws (Eds.), *The Oxford Handbook on the United Nations* (pp. 734–749). Oxford University Press. https://doi.org/10.1093/oxfordhb/9780198803164.013.40

Ministry of Foreign Affairs. (2023). *History of Nepal.* Ministry of Foreign Affairs, Government of Nepal, Singha Durbar, Kathmandu

Paudel, D., & Le Billon, P. (2020). Geo-logics of power: Disaster capitalism, Himalayan materialities, and the geopolitical economy of reconstruction in post-earthquake Nepal. *Geopolitics, 25*(4), 838–866.

Pesaran, M. H., Shin, Y., & Smith, R. J. (2001). Bounds testing approaches to the analysis of level relationships. *Journal of Applied Econometrics, 16*, 289–326. https://doi.org/10.1002/jae.616

Radha Krishna Khadka. (2020). History of land rights movement in Nepal. *Onlinekhabar.*

Rai, P. K. (2021). Governance, Democracy and Inclusion in the Perspective of Nepal. *Asian Journal of International Affairs 1, 1*, 89–98.

Sharma, S. D. (2007). Democracy, good governance, and economic development. *Taiwan journal of democracy, 3*(1), 29–62.

Somerville, P. (2005). Community, governance and democracy. *Policy & Politics, 33*(1), 117–144.

Strasheim, J., & Bogati, S. (2016). *Nepal's quest for federalism: a driver of new violence.* GIGA German Institute of Global and Area Studies, Hamburg.

Tarvedi, Y., Saha, S., & Campbell, N. (2019). Governance, democracy and development. *Economic Analysis and Policy, 63*, 220–233.

Vater, J. J. (2020). *The great game in Nepal: a Himalayan state's search for higher ground.*

Webster, N. (2011). Nepal: Governance and democracy in a frail state *Trysts with Democracy:Political Practice in South Asia; Madsen, ST, Nielsen, KB, Skoda, U.,Eds*, 195–213.

World Bank. (2023). *Worldwide Governance Indicators*

World Bank. (2025). World Development Indicators. https://data.worldbank.org/ (accessed 25 January 2025).

CHAPTER 7

Export Efficiency from the Perspective of Fiscal Policy in Nepal

7.1 Introduction

By now, we know from the earlier chapter that exports need to be boosted to minimise or eliminate the trade deficit (Chap. 2), for which governance quality needs to be improved as suggested in Chap. 3. Then, because of improved quality of governance and export performance, create synergy effect is created in economic growth, but at the same time, resources need to be properly allocated, knowing the role of economic sectors in economic growth as discussed in Chap. 4. Economic growth needs heavy investment in different sectors and quality infrastructure, which is not possible with the sizable revenue collection. Therefore, in Chap. 5, revenue efficiency is analysed. Again, the role of the quality of governance seems to be important for every aspect of the macroeconomic indicators. Therefore, determinants of the quality of governance are analysed in Chap. 6. To manage the entire economy, fiscal policy, also known as the political economy of the country, plays a key role in economic growth and boosting exports, and reducing trade deficits. In this background, Chap. 7 analyses the export efficiency from the perspective of fiscal policy in the country.

Export efficiency is a crucial issue for Nepal, as the country faces a challenge from expanding trade deficits, which may have direct impacts on the major fiscal policy issues. A noteworthy point to note is that Nepal's export performance has been a serious concern for a long time, as it has not met

R. C. Paudel, *Essays on Key Issues of Development in Nepal*,
https://doi.org/10.1007/978-981-95-7715-6_7

the expectations of the policymakers and other stakeholders despite various policies, strategies, plans, and program initiatives aiming to promote exports. Nepal entered the era of globalization and reform quite earlier than many neighbours in the region, in line with which, Nepal documented many trade policies in different years, such as the Trade Policy 2015, and developed many strategies to boost export performance in recent decades. Some important documents to list are the Diagnostic Trade Integration Studies 2004, Nepal Trade Integration Strategy-2010, and Nepal Trade Integration Strategy-2016. Different five-year plans also have a similar focus on trade and export performance issues for about four decades now, and there are many studies and policy briefs covering many aspects of export performance.

In this background, this chapter provides brief evidence on how sensitive fiscal policy instruments are to influencing export efficiency in the country. Generally, fiscal policy is an effective tool to implement governments' overall strategies on national issues and boost economic activities in the country. Rodrik (1995) highlighted aims of fiscal policies about international trade, of which the potential outcome depends not only policy but also on the implementation of that policy, rightly, with a quality of governance. Arestis (2012) stated that the fiscal policy is not only a major branch of macroeconomics, but also a major part of political economics, which reflects economic strength under the existing political system of a country. Paudel and Verma (2016) suggested that the fiscal policy should have a clear direction to promote both private and public investment to boost economic activities, which are directly related to export efficiency, to enhance economic growth. Enhancing export efficiency leads to employment generation, economic expansion, and ultimately helps to improve the living standards of people, both in the short and long run.

There are a few studies focused on the export performance of Nepal, but none of them are about the technical efficiency of Nepal's exports. Most importantly, those studies are focused on finding the determinants of export performance based on time series or panel data analysis using a mixed set of variables (Paudel, 2019; Paudel et al., 2020a, 2020b; Paudel and Bhusal, 2021; Paudel and Burke, 2015). These studies have explained, based on their analysis, the determinants of export performance and the association of many macroeconomic variables with exports.

In addition, this chapter aims to analyze export efficiency and export potentials with Nepal's partners, making methodological differences, and focusing on the general disaggregation of fiscal policy variables along with gravity variables. Export efficiency is particularly important in the Nepalese context as the gap between imports and exports is widening every year. A proper analysis of export efficiency will help us to find out the shortcomings and focus on enhancing such efficiency, and it will help us to review the export policy of the country at the same time. Therefore, doing so in this chapter will be a significant contribution to the literature, particularly in the context that the debate over whether fiscal policy plays any role in improving the export efficiency of Nepal remains a doubtful and unsolved issue.

To achieve the objective of this chapter, first, I document the fiscal policy variables and export trends and patterns to show how these variables have emerged over the selected period. It helps for a descriptive analysis of the context using the relevant data. Then, I investigate the role of selected fiscal variables to find out the major determinants as well as the technical efficiency of the exports using the gravity modelling technique based on the stochastic frontier analysis approach in Nepal's export data. Then, export potentials with Nepal's trading partners are identified. The main finding from this chapter suggests that Nepal should focus on improving the quality of governance as the first priority. Because, unless the regulatory quality is improved and linked with fiscal policy, export efficiency will remain low. In other words, only the fiscal policy tools directly linked with governance quality can contribute to export efficiency significantly. Also, Nepal has more export potentials with China about 85% followed by Saudi Arabia 76%, Brazil 74%, and Israel about 74%. Notably, Nepal has a potential trade more than 50% with total of 25 trading partners.

This chapter proceeds as follows. Export and fiscal policy variables' trends and patterns are discussed in Sect. 7.2 before briefly reviewing the literature on the field in Sect. 7.3. Section 7.4 covers the research methodology of this chapter. Section 7.5 is about the estimated results and discussion with their economic interpretation, and Sect. 7.6 concludes with some policy inferences.

7.2 Exports and Fiscal Policy Variables: Some Observations

This section highlights the trend of exports and major fiscal variables for the longest possible period. Nepal has a Gulliver effect in most of the monetary variables from India, as discussed in Paudel and Thapa-Parajuli (2018), particularly for the two important variables: inflation and exchange rates. Therefore, they need a separate analysis and have not been included in this analysis. Also, our focus in this chapter is on fiscal policy perspectives; accordingly, the trends of the said variables are discussed.

7.2.1 GDP and Export Growth

To examine the visible relationship between national output and exports, the trends in the growth of gross domestic product (GDP) and exports serve as important indicators. It is noted that GDP is commonly regarded as a proxy for economic growth in the growth literature. Also, the export growth rate is an important parameter to know the export efficiency. Then, an issue comes to mind about how these two variables have emerged over the period. For this purpose, Figure 7.1 shows the trends of the growth rates of GDP and exports for the period from the fiscal year 1974/1975 to 2022/2023. The figure shows that the GDP growth rate has not contributed to export growth, as the export growth rate has fluctuated like a random walk.

7.2.2 Foreign Aid and Exports

Foreign aid is another crucial variable in the context of export efficiency, and this has been widely discussed in the literature (Morrissey, 1993). Foreign aid has been considered as one of the major fiscal variables in developing countries for about half a century now. Nepal has also been receiving foreign aid for more than five decades in different forms. Figure 7.2 shows the exports and foreign aid as a share of GDP measured in percentage, to indicate how efficiently the foreign aid has been utilised to improve exports' efficiency, which is one of the major concerns of policymakers in the country at present. The data shows that foreign aid has remained below five percent of Nepal's GDP throughout the period and has a normal fluctuation between half a percent to three and a half percent. In recent years, say for this decade, the share of aid is declining.

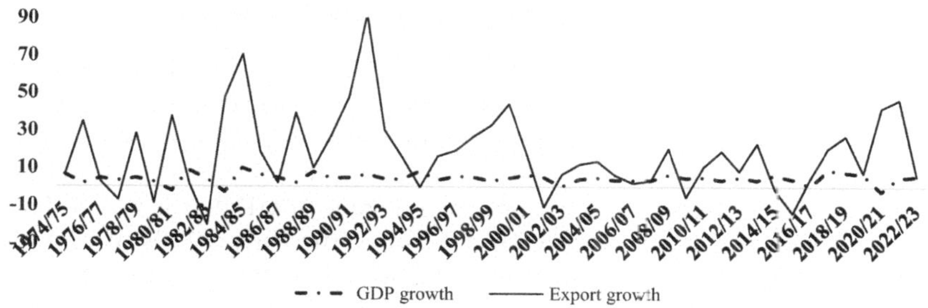

Fig. 7.1 GDP and export growth rate (%). (Source: Author's presentation based on data from Nepal Rastra Bank (2025))

Fig. 7.2 Exports and foreign aid (% of GDP). (Source: Author's presentation based on data from Nepal Rastra Bank (2025))

The share of exports does not seem encouraging, and in fact, it has declined more sharply during the last decades despite various efforts from the government side. The figure shows that this share increased impressively with some fluctuation from 1988/1989 to 1999/2000, maintaining the peak in 1999/2000 with a record of about 13 per cent of GDP. Then, it has gradually declined to two and a half per cent in 2019/2020 and has seen a slight increase since then. Again, a not-so-visible direct relationship is found between these two economic variables.

7.2.3 *Domestic Debt, Foreign Debt and Revenue*

In the context of government finance, which is a major part of fiscal policy, the government collects money in the form of domestic debt, foreign debt and different types of revenues to spend in different headings and to meet the budgetary requirements of the country. Figure 7.3 shows the trend of these sources in Nepal compared to the per cent of GDP. It is noted that Nepal is heavily relying on foreign debt since the early 1980s when the foreign debt had overshot revenue and domestic debts and then started declining since 2006/2007. The volume of foreign debt increased to about 54 per cent in the early 2000s when the country was suffering from political turmoil, then started declining gradually until 2016/2017 to about 16 per cent with some fluctuations in different fiscal years. Since 2016/2017, it started to increase again and now it is above 20 per cent of GDP. The fastest growth of foreign debt was noticed in the mid-1980s.

The domestic debt to GDP share stands below 15 per cent throughout the selected period, with some fluctuation. This has increased visibly above around 20 percent since then. In the revenue side, since the fiscal year 2007/2008, the share of revenue has exceeded both domestic and foreign debts. For the last fiscal year, the revenue to GDP share remains above 22 per cent. For recent fiscal years, all three variables are hovering around 20 percent.

Fig. 7.3 Domestic debt, foreign debt, and revenue (% of GDP). (Source: Author's presentation based on data from Nepal Rastra Bank (2025))

7.2.4 Exports and Government Expenditure

Next, we are interested in knowing the relationship between capital expenditure and current expenditure with exports. Capital expenditure and current expenditure are two broad categories of government expenditures. Generally, the higher the capital expenditure refers to the higher the degree to which development tasks are completed. Capital expenditure is the proxy of development expenditure, while recurrent expenditure is an administrative expenditure, which is assumed not to directly contribute to the developmental activities in the country. Therefore, the policymakers and stakeholders prefer a higher amount of capital expenditure compared to recurrent expenditure. If we stand on the same point, capital expenditure is more desirable in the country.

Figure 7.4 displays the trend of the capital and recurrent expenditure of Nepal for the selected period, along with exports, all measured in terms of GDP percentage. As shown in the figure, the share of capital expenditure was higher than the share of recurrent expenditure until the late 1990s; since then, it has declined in comparison to recurrent expenditure. In the last decade, the gap between these two expenditures has widened due to a faster increase in recurrent expenditure. In the latter two decades, the gap between the lead of current expenditure and capital expenditure is widened visibly.

7.3 Brief Literature Review

A brief literature review helps to find the research gap and to set the research objectives. Therefore, this section offers a brief review of the literature. For this purpose, review is made based on theme and chronological approaches. I noticed a few research studies have investigated the connection between fiscal policy and exports based on panel or timeseries data. In this process, gravity model based fixed or random effect estimations are widely used. Also, country specific timeseries analysis is dominant in the different countries' contexts. The literature indicates that the relationship of the set of fiscal variables and export efficiency has not been explored much, although the link between exports and one or two fiscal variables has been widely studied.

Nepal's exports efficiency concerning the set of fiscal policy variables, public revenue, expenditure, foreign aid, and debts- domestic and foreign appear to be an unexamined area of research to date. This chapter aims to

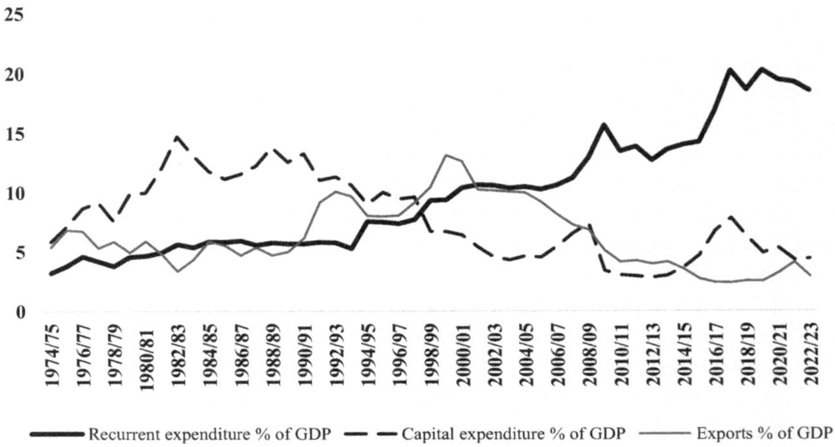

Fig. 7.4 Exports and government expenditures (% of GDP). (Source: Author's presentation based on data from Nepal Rastra Bank (2025))

explore the ideas on the relationship between fiscal policy and export efficiency by reviewing the relevant literature related to the theoretical framework, international context, and national context, briefly focusing on the major fiscal policy variables.

7.3.1 Public Revenue, Expenditure, Aids, Debts, and Exports

Morlin (2022), using a descriptive analysis method, suggested that the fiscal policy variables, including export performance, can support the stability conditions for economic growth in an open economy because of the role of those policy variables, indirectly clarifying that the fiscal rule can contribute via export boom to economic growth.

Epaphra (2016), using time series data from Tanzania for the period from 1966 to 2015, examined the factors affecting the export performance of the country. According to this paper, per capita GDP, trade reform policy, and exchange rate are the major determinants of exports efficiency. Tagkalakis (2015), using post-2000 period data for Greece, found that the reduction in government spending reduces demand, which may have a direct impact on export performance of the country. Dao (2014) stated that the positive relationship between the GDP and export performance can be more tied as a result of public expenditure focusing on filling the investment gap.

Ilegbinosa et al. (2012), using time-series data from Nigeria from 1986 to 2010, investigated the impact of macroeconomic variables on non-oil export performance, and finds that exchange rate, government capital expenditure, and government recurrent expenditure are positively related to non-oil exports. Jongwanich (2010), using a panel database for eight East and Southeast Asian countries from 1993 to 2008, examined the determinants of exports and suggested that foreign capital, export strategies based on parts and components trade, and world demand side factors are important determinants of export efficiency.

Gupta (2007), using panel data from different developing countries, found that foreign aid, debt, and the share of direct and indirect taxes have a direct impact on exports, but the directions of the impact are not unique and different. In a similar fashion, Emran (2005) suggested that a reduction in the export tax promotes export performance, but the strategy should be to reduce the export tax and offset the increase in production tax to keep the producers' prices unchanged. It means that direct tax revenue has a negative association with the export performance of a country.

Roper and Love (2002) investigated the role of innovations on export performance in the UK and German manufacturing plants and find that the spending on innovation makes a positive contribution to the export capacity of both countries' manufacturing plants. This refers to the fact that government expenditure plays a role in exports.

7.3.2 Investment and Exports

Paudel et al. (2020b), using annual time-series data of Nepal, showed a strong association between energy consumption and export performance, indicating the importance of investment for exports. In terms of fiscal variables, even the current expenditure contributes to increasing the productivity of human resources as well as the source of energy for the firms, having a positive impact on export performance.

FDI and exports, investment and exports, and tax and exports have been well explained in the literature as the major determinants of export performance. Conconi et al. (2016) found that most of the firms serve the market via export to the host countries at the initial stage, and later they invest as FDI. Dao (2014) suggested that a country's GDP positively influences export performance, and this contribution can be further enhanced by foreign aid or investment.

Kahrl and Roland-Holst (2008) indicate that the export sectors are significant consumers of energy in China, and energy investments can improve the export performance in various ways. Girma et al. (2005) investigated the impact of foreign direct investment on exports using firm-level data and found a positive contribution of FDI to exports. Similarly, Rob and Vettas (2003) explored the idea that FDI results in increased exports in a country, either by enhancing exports through the utilization of resources or by creating productive capacity and lowering the marginal costs of existing firms in the country.

Even in the country-specific case of China, Zhang and Song (2001), using panel data set from the provincial level of China from 1986 to 1997, stated that exports and inward FDI into China have substantially increased due to the open-door policy adopted by the Chinese government. This role of the investment seems to be consistent in the very early period in the advanced economies, while this was not the case in developing countries, as discussed in Lipsey and Weiss (1981).

7.3.3 Governance and Exports

The role of quality of governance also plays a crucial role in maintaining a good business environment, which can promote export performance or enhance export efficiency. A few studies are linked to the quality of governance and exports' association in the literature. Kaushal (2022) employed a stochastic frontier version of the gravity model in Indian data to study the impact of regional trade agreements and regulatory quality of governance for the period from 2008 to 2018, and found that better institutions and regulatory quality of importing nations are important determinants of export efficiency of India. Nguyen and Wu (2020), using the data from Vietnam for the period from 1996 to 2014, the study examined the association between bilateral governance quality of importing and exporting countries and export efficiency of Vietnam as an exporter to find the positive association of those variables.

Dehshiri et al. (2013) analyzed major governance indicators' impact on exports of oil-exporting countries, and found that voice and accountability, political stability, efficiency, governmental effectiveness, and financial burden of regulation have a strong association with export efficiency.

This brief literature survey suggests the importance of major fiscal variables in export performance. The export efficiency and potential export of Nepal have not been systematically analyzed yet. This chapter aims to fill this vacuum in the trade literature of Nepal.

7.4 Research Methodology

This chapter follows a panel of secondary data-based quantitative research approach. The estimation is made by employing the stochastic frontier version of the gravity modelling technique in various specifications for a robustness check. The model consists of the main variables of interest, major fiscal policy variables, along with other control variables as discussed in the next subsection.

7.4.1 The Model and Variables

The gravity model was first introduced in economics by Walter Isard in 1954 in a journal article [see Isard (1954)]. This model is as stated in Eqn. (7.1):

$$F_{ij} = G.\left(M_i M_j\right) / D_{ij} \tag{7.1}$$

Where in this equation, F refers to trade flows between country *i* to *j*, G is a constant that represents an intercept in the equation, M is the economic dimension of the importing and exporting countries, and D is the distance between the two trading countries. If this is a linear equation, the model can be transformed into the log form and indicates that economic dimensions may have different relationships.

The gravity model has been widely used in the applied trade economics literature and the relevant economic dimensions have been clearly explained in Tinbergen (1962), which states the gravity model for trade flows analysis in the form of Eqn. (7.2).

$$\text{Trade}_{ij,t} = \alpha + \beta_1 GDP_{i,t}.GDP_{j,t} + \beta_2 POP_{i,t}.POP_{j,t} + \beta_3 Dist_{ij,t} + \epsilon_t \tag{7.2}$$

where, in addition to the details of Eqn. (7.1), the multiplication of trading partners' GDP and population clearly defines the market dimension, capturing the market size. The last term is an error term. Among the notations: *i* refers to the exporting country, *j* is the importing country, and *t* refers to the time of the transaction (year in case of annual data). The coefficient of the distance (Dist) is negative, as more distance means more costs that restrict or lower the trade flows.

The stochastic frontier version of the gravity model of Eqn. (7.2) is developed as in Eqn. (7.3), following Kalirajan and Paudel (2015) and Kaushal (2022).

$$\text{Trade}_{\text{ij,t}} = \alpha + \beta_1 GDP_{i,t}.GDP_{j,t} + \beta_2 POP_{i,t}.POP_{j,t} + \beta_3 Dist_{ij,t} + V_{it} - U_{it} \tag{7.3}$$

Where, V_{it} is the conventional error term assumed to be ***iid*** with mean 0 and variance σv^2 and U_{it} refers to the one-sided error term with observation-specific mean and "variance of its pre-truncated distribution.

To achieve the objective of this chapter, Eqn. (7.4) is estimated to employ the said methodology. Here, better to note that the supply-side constraints are more crucial than the demand-side constraints in the case of Nepal's export efficiency; therefore, the focus of this study is to analyze the supply-side factors that are related to the fiscal policy variables to impact export efficiency.

$$LEXPORT_{ij,t} = \beta_1 + \beta_2 LNEPGDP_{i,t} + \beta_3 LNEPPOP_{i,t} + \beta_4 LPARGDP_{j,t} + \beta_5 LPARPOP_{j,t} + \beta_6 LDIST_{ij,t} + \beta_6 CONTIG_{ij,t} + V_{it} - U_{it} \tag{7.4}$$

where LEXPORTS refers to annual mirror exports to each partner country measured in the United States Dollar (USD) in the natural log form. The first notation on the right-hand side, β_1, is an intercept. Nepal's GDP (LENPGDP) and partners' GDP (LPARGDP) are also measured in USD terms and transformed into the natural log form. Similarly, Nepal's population (LNEPPOP) and partners' population (LPARPOP) are measured in number and converted into natural log form. The distance between Nepal's most dense city and partners' most dense city (LDIST) is measured in kilometers and converted into natural log.

Then, in the next step, fiscal policy variables are included in the model. In Eqn. (7.5), we add Nepal's current expenditure (LNEPCUREXP) and Nepal's capital expenditure (LNEPCAPEXP). Both variables are converted into USD using the official exchange rate and transformed into natural log form.

$$\begin{aligned} LEXPORT_{ij,t} = {} & \beta_1 + \beta_2 LNEPGDP_{i,t} + \beta_3 LNEPPOP_{i,t} + \beta_4 LPARGDP_{j,t} \\ & + \beta_5 LPARPOP_{j,t} + \beta_6 LDIST_{ij,t} + \beta_6 CONTIG_{ij,t} \\ & + \beta_7 LNNEPCUREXP_{i,t} + \beta_8 LNEPCAPEXP_{i,t} + V_{it} - U_{it} \end{aligned} \quad (7.5)$$

Our next interest is whether Nepal's revenue (LNEPREVENUE) and foreign aid (LNEPAID) variables have contributed to export efficiency. For this purpose, Eqn. (7.6) is developed including these two variables in the benchmark model as stated in Eqn. (7.4). Both variables are measured in USD and transformed to natural log form.

$$\begin{aligned} LEXPORT_{ij,t} = {} & \beta_1 + \beta_2 LNEPGDP_{i,t} + \beta_3 LNEPPOP_{i,t} + \beta_4 LPARGDP_{j,t} \\ & + \beta_5 LPARPOP_{j,t} + \beta_6 LDIST_{ij,t} + \beta_6 CONTIG_{ij,t} \\ & + \beta_7 LNEPAID_{i,t} + \beta_8 LNEPREVENUE_{i,t} + V_{it} - U_{it} \end{aligned} \quad (7.6)$$

Further, Nepal's foreign debt (LNEPFDEBT) and domestic debt (LNEPDOMDEBT) are added in Eqn. (7.4) and presented in the form of Eqn. (7.7). These two variables also are measured in USD and transformed into natural log form consistently with other variables.

$$\begin{aligned} LEXPORT_{ij,t} = {} & \beta_1 + \beta_2 LNEPGDP_{i,t} + \beta_3 LNEPPOP_{i,t} + \beta_4 LPARGDP_{j,t} \\ & + \beta_5 LPARPOP_{j,t} + \beta_6 LDIST_{ij,t} + \beta_6 CONTIG_{ij,t} \\ & + \beta_7 LNNEPFDEBT_{i,t} + \beta_8 LNEPDOMDEBT_{i,t} + V_{it} - U_{it} \end{aligned} \quad (7.7)$$

In the next step, we want to see whether the quality of governance interacted with these fiscal policy variables makes a significant contribution in export efficiency of Nepal. Particularly, it is said in the absence of regulatory quality (part of governance) is a powerful tool to improve the business environment in the country. Therefore, regulatory quality of Nepal (NEPREGQ) is added with interaction with LNEPCAPEXP, LNNEPCUREXP, LNNEPFDEBT, and LNEPDOMDEBT and presented in Eqns. (7.8), (7.9), (7.10), and (7.11). Here the respective interaction terms are introduced in these equations, such as CAPEXPxNEPREGQ, CUREXPxNEPREGQ, NEPFDEBTxNEPREGQ, and NEPDOMDEBTxNEPREGQ respectively.

$$LEXPORT_{ij,t} = \beta_1 + \beta_2 LNEPGDP_{i,t} + \beta_3 LNEPPOP_{i,t} + \beta_4 LPARGDP_{j,t} + \beta_5 LPARPOP_{j,t} + \beta_6 LDIST_{ij,t} + \beta_6 CONTIG_{ij,t} + \beta_7 LNEPCAPEXP_{i,t} + \beta_8 NEPREGQ_{i,t} + \beta_9 CAPEXPxNEPREGQ_{i,t} + V_{it} - U_{it} \quad (7.8)$$

$$LEXPORT_{ij,t} = \beta_1 + \beta_2 LNEPGDP_{i,t} + \beta_3 LNEPPOP_{i,t} + \beta_4 LPARGDP_{j,t} + \beta_5 LPARPOP_{j,t} + \beta_6 LDIST_{ij,t} + \beta_6 CONTIG_{ij,t} + \beta_7 LNNEPCUREXP_{i,t} + \beta_8 NEPREGQ_{i,t} + \beta_9 CUREXPxNEPREGQ_{i,t} + V_{it} - U_{it} \quad (7.9)$$

$$LEXPORT_{ij,t} = \beta_1 + \beta_2 LNEPGDP_{i,t} + \beta_3 LNEPPOP_{i,t} + \beta_4 LPARGDP_{j,t} + \beta_5 LPARPOP_{j,t} + \beta_6 LDIST_{ij,t} + \beta_6 CONTIG_{ij,t} + \beta_7 LNNEPFDEBT_{i,t} + \beta_8 NEPREGQ_{i,t} + \beta_9 NEPFDEBTxNEPREGQ_{i,t} + V_{it} - U_{it} \quad (7.10)$$

$$LEXPORT_{ij,t} = \beta_1 + \beta_2 LNEPGDP_{i,t} + \beta_3 LNEPPOP_{i,t} + \beta_4 LPARGDP_{j,t} + \beta_5 LPARPOP_{j,t} + \beta_6 LDIST_{ij,t} + \beta_6 CONTIG_{ij,t} + \beta_7 LNEPDOMDEBT_{i,t} + \beta_8 NEPREGQ_{i,t} + \beta_9 NEPDOMDEBTxNEPREGQ_{i,t} + V_{it} - U_{it} \quad (7.11)$$

The expected signs for other than β_6 are expected to be positive if they contribute to export efficiency, otherwise negative. The distance is associated with the trade costs, resulting in lower export efficiency. Similarly, the revenue may have a negative impact as the taxes deter the exports; in such a case, the coefficient, β_8 in Eqn. (7.6) would be negative.

7.4.2 Data and Their Sources

This study covers the mirror exports of Nepal to all those countries (Nepal's trading partners), which have imported at least USD100000 in a year. These data are normally covered for the period from 1988 to 2023. This is an unbalanced panel dataset for export data using SITC revision 3. During this period, Nepal exported to 191 countries out of which 115 countries have Nepal's exports more than USD100000.

The exports data are collected from World Bank (2025b). The data for Nepal's and partners' GDP and Population, official exchange rate, and regulatory quality are collected from World Bank (2025a). The data for domestic and foreign debt, government revenue, current and capital expenditure, and foreign aid are collected from Nepal Rastra Bank (2025). The gravity data for the distance between the most dense cities of the partner countries were collected from CEPII (2025).

7.4.3 *Econometrics*

In the next step, our path is to examine the determinants of export efficiency using the model's equations. Many previous studies have estimated the gravity equations using either pooled ordinary least squares (POLS) estimation, fixed effect (FE) estimation, or random effects (RE) estimation (Paudel and Cooray, 2018). Very few studies have used production frontier analysis (SFA) approach of the gravity model. In this chapter, the main variables of interest are all the fiscal variables used in the model. We follow the SFA in unbalanced panel data. We start by estimating the benchmark model as of Eqn. (7.4) and include the additional variables as explained earlier and reaching up to Eqn. (7.11).

7.5 Results and Discussion

In this section, we focus on the discussion of the econometric results. Then, the major findings from the study and robustness check of the estimated results are interpreted in line with economic sense.

7.5.1 *Results Interpretation*

Table 7.1 presents the results of econometric estimation using the gravity modelling technique employing the stochastic frontier analysis (SFA) approach. All the Eqns. (7.4), (7.5), (7.6), and (7.7) are examined from different perspectives. As the fiscal policy variables remained statistically insignificant, regulatory quality, as the proxy for governance quality, is used, and this has been interacted with major fiscal policy variables, which have been presented in Table 7.2 for Eqns. (7.8), (7.9), (7.10), and (7.11).

The results from Table 7.1 column (4) show that among the gravity variables, all variables except Nepal's GDP and partners' population have a statistically significant association with export efficiency, as the direction is as expected. It suggests that Nepal's population and partners' GDP are the major contributors to Nepal's export performance. Nepal's major trade with India and China is reflected in the border dummy and is statistically significant with a high degree of coefficient. As in the cases of many other studies, distance has a statistically significant but negative impact on export performance.

The column (5) of the same table includes Nepal's current expenditure (LNEPCUREXP) and Nepal's capital expenditure (LEPCAPEXP) in the estimations, in addition to the variables as presented in column (4). Both variables seem statistically insignificant, indicating that the role of current and capital expenditure is negligible in enhancing export efficiency. Similarly, Nepal's aid and revenue (LNEPAID and LNEPREV) are included in column 6 of the same table. Again, both variables are statistically insignificant, and both have negative signs. In column (7), foreign debt and domestic debt (LNFDEBT and LNEPDOMDEBT) are included in the estimation. The results for other variables are consistent in all estimations.

As stated earlier, Table 7.2 presents the estimated results for the set of equations, which include the regulatory quality (REGQ) of Nepal. This variable has interacted with the added fiscal variables as displayed in columns (8), (9), (10), and (11). The results for the other variables are consistent with the results of Table 7.1. The interactive terms are statistically significant in all respective columns. This means that if the governance quality is improved, that causes to increase in the role of both capital expenditure (column 8) and current expenditure (column 9) to enhance export efficiency meaningfully. The numbers suggest that if capital expenditure is increased with the improved regulatory quality by one percent, the export efficiency increases by about 0.70 percent, holding other variables in the model constant. This is almost similar in the case of current expenditure, but a bit lower, such as 0.55, with the same level of statistical significance.

Similarly, columns (10) and (11) present the estimated results for foreign debt and domestic debt. These coefficients for the interaction terms (NEPFDEBTxREPREGQ and NEPDOMDEBTxNEPREGQ) are statistically significant at the one percent level of significance, indicating that either foreign debt or domestic debt, both, will work only if the regulatory quality is improved.

Table 7.1 Gravity model's estimation results

Dependent variable: LEXPORT: Nepal's exports-log	*(4)*	*(5)*	*(6)*	*(7)*
LNEPGDP: Nepal GDP-log	0.173	0.173	0.406*	0.169
	(0.107)	(0.187)	(0.246)	(0.119)
LNEPPOP: Nepal population-log	2.338***	2.726***	2.386***	2.196***
	(0.496)	(0.716)	(0.538)	(0.602)
LPARGDP: Partners' GDP-log	0.486***	0.481***	0.496***	0.484***
	(0.068)	(0.068)	(0.069)	(0.068)
LPARPOP: Partners' population-log	−0.042	−0.043	−0.045	−0.038
	(0.077)	(0.077)	(0.078)	(0.078)
LDIST: distance Km-log	−0.373**	−0.371**	−0.375**	−0.371**
	(0.181)	(0.181)	(0.182)	(0.181)
Border-dummy	2.132**	2.128**	2.137**	2.136**
	(0.886)	(0.884)	(0.889)	(0.886)
LNEPCUREXP: Nepal current expenditure-log		−0.046		
		(0.144)		
LNEPCAPEXP: Nepal capital expenditure-log		0.060		
		(0.069)		
LNEPAID: Aid in Nepal-log			−0.022	
			(0.042)	
LNEPREV: Nepal revenue-log			−0.185	
			(0.185)	
LNEPFDEBT: Foreign debt of Nepal-log				−0.023
				(0.043)
LNEPOMDDEBT: Domestic debt of Nepal-log				0.023
				(0.049)
Sigma	*0.565****	*0.561****	*0.570****	*0.565****
	(0.109)	*(0.109)*	*(0.109)*	*(0.109)*
Gamma	*0.854****	*0.848****	*0.862****	*0.853****
	(0.160)	*(0.160)*	*(0.160)*	*(0.160)*
Sigma squared	*1.76****	*1.75****	*1.76****	*1.76****
	(0.191)	*(0.191)*	*(0.193)*	*(0.191)*
Log-likelihood	*-1971*	*-1971*	*-1970*	*-1971*
Number of observations	*1652*	*1652*	*1652*	*1652*
Number of groups	*106*	*106*	*106*	*106*

Note: ***, **, and * indicate the results are significant at 1%, 5%, and 10% level of significance. The standard errors are reported in parentheses.

Table 7.2 Gravity models with regulatory quality estimation results

Dependent variable: LEXPORT: Nepal's exports-log	*(8)*	*(9)*	*(10)*	*(11)*
LNEPGDP: Nepal GDP-log	0.018	0.350	0.019	0.109
	(0.165)	(0.222)	(0.165)	(0.167)
LNEPPOP: Nepal population-log	1.692*	−0.535	1.981**	0.676
	(0.940)	(1.069)	(0.967)	(1.073)
LPARGDP: Partners' GDP-log	0.533***	0.569***	0.550***	0.553***
	(0.073)	(0.065)	(0.073)	(0.073)
LPARPOP: Partners' population-log	−0.016	−0.023	−0.025	−0.022
	(0.082)	(0.082)	(0.082)	(0.082)
LDIST: distance Km-log	−0.447**	−0.462**	−0.460**	−0.458**
	(0.189)	(0.189)	(0.190)	(0.190)
Border-dummy	2.225**	2.234**	2.205**	2.224**
	(0.900)	(0.898)	(0.897)	(0.901)
LNEPCUREXP: Nepal current expenditure-log		0.552***		
		(0.195)		
LNEPCAPEXP: Nepal capital expenditure-log	0.693***			
	(0.249)			
LNEPFDEBT: Foreign debt of Nepal-log			0.542**	
			(0.227)	
LNEPDDEBT: Domestic debt of Nepal-log				0.329**
				(0.156)
NEPREGQ: Nepal's regulatory quality-index	−18.07***	−22.40***	−14.38**	−8.97**
	(6.916)	(6.112)	(5.858)	(4.328)
CAPEXPxNEPREGQ	0.877**			
	(0.341)			
CUREXPxNEPREGQ		1.045***		
		(0.288)		
NEPFDEBTxREPREGQ			0.735**	
			(0.304)	
NEPDOMDEBTxNEPREGQ				0.454**
				(0.226)
Sigma	*0.534****	*0.549****	*0.541****	*0.543****
	(0.116)	*(0.116)*	*(0.116)*	*(0.116)*

(*continued*)

Table 7.2 (continued)

Dependent variable: LEXPORT: Nepal's exports-log	*(8)*	*(9)*	*(10)*	*(11)*
Gamma	*1.192****	*1.219****	*1.200****	*1.201****
	(0.157)	*(0.156)*	*(0.157)*	*(0.157)*
Sigma squared	*1.71****	*1.73****	*1.72****	*1.72****
	(0.1970	*(0.201)*	*(0.199)*	*(0.199)*
Log-likelihood	*–1421*	*–1418*	*–1422*	*–1423*
Number of observations	*1311*	*1311*	*1311*	*1311*
Number of groups	*105*	*105*	*105*	*105*

Note: ***, **, and * indicate the results are significant at 1%, 5%, and 10% level of significance. The standard errors are reported in parentheses

A key lesson from the findings of the estimations is that fiscal variables without linking to the quality of governance cannot enhance export efficiency. The main policy inference from the empirical analysis is to focus more on improving the regulatory quality in the country so that the role of fiscal policy variables would be more influential in enhancing export efficiency. Therefore, the quality of governance is a key condition for influential fiscal policy in terms of export performance.

7.5.2 *Robustness Check*

For the robustness check, I conducted many alternative specifications' estimations of the gravity model as displayed in the different columns of Tables 7.1 and 7.2. The estimated coefficients for the variables of interest, particularly the fiscal variables, are not meaningfully different in all specifications unless they are interacted with the quality of governance. The magnitudes of the coefficients are slightly changed in different specifications, but the levels of significance have maintained a level of consistency, indicating the estimated results are robust and the findings are credible. The post estimation statistics in the lower panels of the tables show that estimated coefficients are standard and credible. These results have remained meaningfully the same, even though the covered period is reduced, ranging from 1996 to 2023.

7.5.3 Export Efficiency and Export Potential

In the next step, the technical efficiency is calculated. We find that the most efficient export destinations are Germany and the USA (98%), Bhutan and Switzerland (97%), India and the UK (96%), and Canada, Turkey, and the Central African Republic (95%). In case of technical efficiency and export potential, we find that Nepal has more export potential with China, about 85%, followed by Saudi Arabia, 76%, Brazil, 74%, Israel, about 74%, the Russian Federation, 72%, and Korea Republic, 70%. Notably, Nepal has a potential trade of more than 50% with a total of 25 trading partners. It means very little compared to the potential that has been traded. Nepal has done the maximum possible trade (above 95%) with Germany, the United States, Bhutan, Switzerland, India, the United Kingdom, Canada, Turkey, and the Central African Republic (Table 7.3 in Appendix). This calculation indicates that there is a big room to improve Nepal's export performance and efficiency in the future, and this is possible by linking the quality of governance with the fiscal policy targeting a good business environment in the country.

7.6 Conclusions and Policy Inferences

7.6.1 Conclusions

This section concludes with a summary followed by recommendations for policy inferences from the findings of this chapter. The primary objective of this chapter is to investigate the impact of fiscal policy variables on export efficiency, with a focus on export performance, as concerns have been raised by various stakeholders regarding the country's persistent poor export performance. For this purpose, a thorough analysis of the association between exports and fiscal policy variables has been conducted using an advanced econometric methodology for trade flows analysis.

The results suggest that all the major fiscal variables, such as government revenue, current and capital expenditure, domestic and foreign debt, and foreign aid, do not have a direct association with export efficiency. Nepal's export performance seems to come through partners' GDP and Nepal's population for the longer period. Interestingly, all these fiscal policy variables' impact seems to be very influential if the governance quality is improved. Therefore, improving the quality of governance helps to increase the impact of these variables on export efficiency, and it will eventually increase the proper utilization of government resources to increase productivity, and then export efficiency is possible. In the shorter period, Nepal's GDP and Nepal's populations' role seems not be consistent with the longer period study. Therefore, in the demand side, partners' GDP (market size) and in the supply side, the quality of governance linked with fiscal policy jointly contribute to export efficiency of Nepal.

In case of technical efficiency and export potential, we find that Nepal has more export potentials with China, about 85%, followed by Saudi Arabia, 76%, Brazil, 74%, Israel, about 74%, the Russian Federation, 72%, and Korea Republic, 70%. Notably, Nepal has a potential trade of more than 50% with a total of 25 trading partners. It means very less compared to the potential that has been traded. Nepal has done the maximum possible trade (above 95%) with Germany, the United States, Bhutan, Switzerland, India, the United Kingdom, Canada, Turkey, and the Central African Republic.

7.6.2 Policy Inferences

The main policy inferences from this chapter are fourfold. First, Nepal should focus and producing to meet the demand of major importing partners. Second, lowering the trade costs associated with the distance may be another priority to boost export efficiency. Third, if the quality of governance is not improved, Nepal's fiscal policy variables do not have a direct significant association with export efficiency. Therefore, improving the governance quality, particularly the regulatory quality, is an important step to seek the fiscal policy's influence in export performance. Fourth, Nepal has a good export potential with its neighbour, China, followed by Saudi Arabia, Brazil, Israel, the Russian Federation, Korea Republic and many other countries.

Appendix

Table 7.3 Export Potentials with Nepal's trading partners

Trading Partner	*Export Potential %*	*Current export efficiency% %*
China	85	15
Saudi Arabia	76	24
Brazil	74	26
Israel	74	26
Russian Federation	72	28
Korea, Rep.	70	30
Poland	69	31
Indonesia	69	31
Ireland	68	32
Greece	68	32
Thailand	68	32
Finland	65	35
Kuwait	63	37
Malaysia	62	38
Japan	58	42
Norway	56	44
Luxembourg	55	45
Argentina	54	46
Qatar	53	47
Slovak Republic	52	48
Vietnam	51	49
Kazakhstan	51	49
Hungary	51	49
Sweden	50	50
Chile	50	50
United Arab Emirates	48	52
South Africa	47	53
Mexico	44	56
Bangladesh	43	57
Portugal	42	58
Bahrain	39	61
Philippines	38	62
Hong Kong, China	38	62
Morocco	35	65
Ukraine	33	67
Macao	32	68
Slovenia	32	68
Spain	31	69
Peru	30	70

(continued)

Table 7.3 (continued)

Trading Partner	*Export Potential %*	*Current export efficiency% %*
Australia	29	71
Denmark	28	72
Croatia	27	73
Lithuania	26	74
Colombia	26	74
Algeria	26	74
Myanmar	24	76
Ecuador	24	76
Kenya	23	77
Oman	23	77
Estonia	22	78
Egypt, Arab Rep.	22	78
Uzbekistan	22	78
Latvia	22	78
Jordan	22	78
Iran, Islamic Rep.	22	78
Iceland	22	78
New Zealand	21	79
Uganda	21	79
Cote d'Ivoire	21	79
Occ.Pal.Terr	21	79
Bulgaria	21	79
Albania	21	79
Yemen	21	79
Mauritius	21	79
Angola	20	80
New Caledonia	20	80
Bosnia and Herzegovina	20	80
Afghanistan	20	80
Dominican Republic	20	80
Cambodia	20	80
Tunisia	20	80
Barbados	19	81
Madagascar	18	82
El Salvador	18	82
Pakistan	18	82
Fm Sudan	18	82
Brunei	18	82
Malawi	17	83
Mauritania	17	83
Tanzania	17	83

(*continued*)

Table 7.3 (continued)

Trading Partner	*Export Potential %*	*Current export efficiency% %*
Belarus	17	83
Mali	16	84
Maldives	15	85
Guyana	14	86
Nigeria	14	86
Seychelles	13	87
Czech Republic	13	87
Lebanon	13	87
Netherlands	12	88
Italy	11	89
Sri Lanka	11	89
Burundi	9	91
Ghana	9	91
Belgium	9	91
France	7	93
Singapore	6	94
Austria	6	94
Central African Republic	5	95
Turkey	5	95
Canada	5	95
United Kingdom	4	96
India	4	96
Switzerland	3	97
Bhutan	3	97
United States	2	98
Germany	2	98

Source: Author's calculation based on stochastic frontier analysis based technical efficiency.

References

Arestis, P. (2012). Fiscal policy: a strong macroeconomic role. *Review of Keynesian Economics*(1), 93–108.

CEPII. (2025). *The CEPII Gravity Dataset*

Conconi, P., Sapir, A., & Zanardi, M. (2016). The internationalization process of firms: From exports to FDI. *Journal of International Economics*, *99*, 16–30.

Dao, M. Q. (2014). Exports, imports, government consumption and economic growth in upper-middle income countries. *Progress in Development Studies*, *14*(2), 197–204.

Dehshiri, H., Renani, H., & Mirfatah, M. (2013). Analysis the impact of good governance on the non-oil export of oil exporting countries. *Journal of Economic Policy and Research*, *8*(1), 1–10.

Emran, M. S. (2005). Revenue-increasing and welfare-enhancing reform of taxes on exports. *Journal of Development Economics*, *77*(1), 277–292.

Epaphra, M. (2016). Determinants of export performance in Tanzania. *Journal of Economics Library*, *3*(3), 470–487.

Girma, S., Kneller, R., & Pisu, M. (2005). Exports versus FDI: an empirical test. *Review of World Economics*, *141*(2), 193–218.

Gupta, A. S. (2007). Determinants of tax revenue efforts in developing countries. *IMF Working Papers*, *2007*(184).

Ilegbinosa, I., Uzomba, P., & Somiari, R. (2012). The impact of macroeconomic variables on non-oil exports performance in Nigeria 1986–2010. *J Econ. Sustain. Dev*, *3*(5), 27–40.

Isard, W. (1954). Location theory and trade theory: short-run analysis. *The Quarterly Journal of Economics*, 305–320.

Jongwanich, J. (2010). Determinants of export performance in East and Southeast Asia. *World Economy*, *33*(1), 20–41.

Kahrl, F., & Roland-Holst, D. (2008). Energy and exports in China. *China Economic Review*, *19*(4), 649–658.

Kalirajan, K., & Paudel, R. (2015). India's trade deficit with China: will free trade agreement (FTA) work for India? *Global Economy Journal*, *15*(4), 485–505.

Kaushal, L. A. (2022). Impact of regional trade agreements on export efficiency – A case study of India. *Cogent Economics & Finance*, *10*(1), 2008090. https://doi.org/10.1080/23322039.2021.2008090

Lipsey, R. E., & Weiss, M. Y. (1981). Foreign production and exports in manufacturing industries. *The Review of Economics and Statistics*, 488–494.

Morlin, G. S. (2022). Growth led by government expenditure and exports: public and external debt stability in a supermultiplier model. *Structural change and economic dynamics*, *62*, 586–598.

Morrissey, O. (1993). The mixing of aid and trade policies. *World Economy*, *16*(1), 69–84.

Nepal Rastra Bank. (2025). *Current Macroeconomic and Financial Situation.* Baluwatar, Kathmandu, Nepal

Nguyen, S. T., & Wu, Y. (2020). Governance and export performance in Vietnam. *Journal of Southeast Asian Economies*, *37*(1), 1–25.

Paudel, R. C. (2019). Exports Performance of Nepal: What Can Be Done? *Applied Economics and Finance*, *6*(5), 92–103.

Paudel, R. C., Acharya, C., & Thapa-Parajuli, R. (2020a). The Role of Cooperatives, Remittances, and Infrastructure in Export Performance of Nepal: ARDL Approach of Cointegration. *Sumerianz Journal of Economics and Finance*, *3*(10), 151–159.

Paudel, R. C., & Bhusal, T. P. (2021). Role of Workers' Remittances in Export Performance of Nepal: Gravity Modelling Approach. *NRB Economic Review, 33*(1 & 2), 1–13.

Paudel, R. C., & Burke, P. J. (2015). Exchange Rate Policy and Export Performance in a Landlocked Developing Country: The Case of Nepal. *Journal of Asian Economics, 38*, 55–63. https://doi.org/10.1016/j.asieco.2015.04.003

Paudel, R. C., & Cooray, A. (2018). Export performance of developing countries: Does landlockedness matter? *Review of Development Economics, 22*(3), 1–27.

Paudel, R. C., & Thapa-Parajuli, R. (2018). Gulliver Effect in Macroeconomic Policies of Landlocked Developing Countries: A Comparative Study. *Economic Journal of Nepal, 41*(1–2), 18–34.

Paudel, R. C., Thapa-Parajuli, R., & Alharthi, M. (2020b). Electricity Consumption and Export Performance: Evidence from Nepal. *International Journal of Energy Economics and Policy, 10*(6), 529–535. https://doi.org/10.32479/ijeep.10524

Paudel, R., & Verma, R. (2016). Fiscal Policy on Economic Growth: Endogenous Models from Sri Lanka. *SCMS Journal of Indian Management, 13*(2).

Rob, R., & Vettas, N. (2003). Foreign direct investment and exports with growing demand. *The Review of Economic Studies, 70*(3), 629–648.

Rodrik, D. (1995). Taking trade policy seriously: export subsidization as a case study in policy effectiveness. In J. Levinsohn, A. V. Deardorff, & R. M. Stern (Eds.), *New directions in trade theory* (pp. 347–384). The University of Michigan Press.

Roper, S., & Love, J. H. (2002). Innovation and export performance: evidence from the UK and German manufacturing plants. *Research policy, 31*(7), 1087–1102.

Tagkalakis, A. O. (2015). Fiscal policy, net exports, and the sectoral composition of output in Greece. *International economics and economic policy, 12*(4), 521–539.

Tinbergen, J. (1962). *Shaping the World Economy; Suggestions for an International Economic Policy.* The Twentieth Century Fund, New York, USA.

World Bank. (2025a). World Development Indicators. https://data.worldbank.org/ (accessed 25 January 2025).

World Bank. (2025b). *World Integrated Trade Solution, WITS database*

Zhang, K. H., & Song, S. (2001). Promoting exports: the role of inward FDI in China. *China Economic Review, 11*(4), 385–396.

CHAPTER 8

Conclusions

8.1 Summary

The main objectives of this research book are to make a systematic analysis of the key political-economic issues related to the economic development of Nepal from a current macroeconomic perspective and to document suitable policy inferences in the respective areas. In addition, these major objectives are followed by six specific objectives allocated to six specific chapters (Chaps. 2, 3, 4, 5, 6, and 7). These are: to analyze the circular nexus of remittances, banks' credit to the private sector, and trade deficit, to analyze the role of governance quality on expert performance, considering the COVID-19 pandemic period in Nepal, to analyze the role of integrated agriculture and manufacturing sectors for potential high economic growth in the background of jobless slow economic growth, and to highlight the synergy effects from agriculture and manufacturing sectors in the background of economic structural problems of the Nepalese economy, to analyze the revenue efficiency, examining its determinants of Nepal, to analyze the role of democracy and economic development in the quality of governance, and to examine the determinants of export performance from fiscal policy perspective and to analyze the technical efficiency of exports, respectively.

To achieve the objectives mentioned in this book, it employs chapter-specific quantitative research methods based on secondary data collected

R. C. Paudel, *Essays on Key Issues of Development in Nepal*,
https://doi.org/10.1007/978-981-95-7715-6_8

from as many authentic sources as cited accordingly in the relevant places. Chapters 2, 4, 5, and 6 have used time series data but employed different methods of estimation. For example, Chaps. 2, 4, and 6 are based on the ARDL approach to cointegration. Chapter 5 is also a time series analysis, but it uses stochastic frontier analysis (SFA) following a standard technique. Chapter 3 is based on panel data and uses the gravity modeling technique with fixed and random effect estimations. Chapter 7 uses the SFA version of the gravity modeling technique in panel data. The results are reported in the standard format in the respective chapters using tables and figures with appropriate interpretation.

8.2 Findings

The findings from this book, based on different chapters (Chaps. 2, 3, 4, 5, 6, and 7), are discussed in the respective places in more detail. The key points from all findings are: first, the governance quality is the most important aspect to be integrated with the fiscal policy variables to realize the effective results in trade, growth, and social welfare of the country. The quality of governance is equally important in the situation of a pandemic, crisis, or normal times. The better quality of governance would help to trade more with export dominance, improve exports and revenue efficiency, break the nexus of remittance, banks' credits to private sectors, and trade deficits, and help to increase the productivity and national output, accelerating the economic growth rate.

We can conclude by being chapter-specific. First, as concluded in Chap. 2, remittance, the main source of a foreign reserve and household expenditure, to be directed towards more productive sectors and investment so that it would help to reduce the alarming trade deficits. The dominance of import trade turns to be export dominance. Focusing on manufacturing activities based on endogenous products, updating their production technologies is the best way of mobilizing the remittances into investment for cottage, small, and medium-scale industries.

Second, as stated earlier, as the key message from this book, the governance quality is very critical for enhancing the export performance. The export creation market needs to be reformed well and be disciplined, as the export volume has indicated that it increased during the peak time of COVID-19. Without improving the quality of governance, the exports do not flourish, as concluded in Chap. 3.

Third, a synergy effect from the integration of the agriculture and manufacturing sectors is very important for a speedy economic growth rate in the country. The agriculture sector, as it is now, for consistency and the scattered manufacturing sector, cannot contribute to accelerating economic growth. Here, the synergy from the integration of agriculture and manufacturing can be linked to service sectors, such as tourism, financial, health, and education sectors, too, in rural to urban areas. It will also help to upgrade the production technology in the country, as found in Chap. 4 of this book.

Fourth, as of now, revenue collection has not met the target of the government historically with some exceptions in a few years. As we are standing at a critical juncture of global politics, other sources like foreign aid and soft loans have become a tough job, and it seems the situation remains the same for at least a few more years. At the same time, the developmental needs cannot be fulfilled without public spending. Therefore, revenue efficiency is a very crucial issue because the heavy requirements of development resources cannot be managed unless the revenue is increased substantially. The revenue base needs to be expanded, and numerous policy shifts related to governance quality are necessary to enhance revenue efficiency as found in Chap. 5.

Fifth, as the quality of governance is a multifaceted determinant of economic development, this needs to be enhanced throughout the country with priority. Therefore, strengthening the local democracy and civil society participation are major tools to improve the quality of governance. This suggests investing more in building institutions and second-generation reform, with priority in the country as discussed in Chap. 6 of this book.

Sixth, as examined in Chap. 7, export efficiency is one of the most crucial issues in this globalization and reform era. To improve export efficiency, all fiscal policy variables must be integrated with the regulatory quality of governments; without enhancing governance quality, fiscal policy instruments have become ineffective. Therefore, special focus is needed to improve the regulatory quality and, side-by-side, a thorough analysis of the potential market dynamics with the trading partners' income status. Nepal can do better in terms of export performance using the untapped potential from its close neigbhbour, China, and other emerging trade partners, such as Saudi Arabia, Brazil, Israel, Russia, Korea Republic, Poland, Indonesia, etc. Human resources should be provided with an understanding of these needs of trade and growth.

8.3 Recommendations

Based on the findings from the key chapters of this book, several policy recommendations can be made to enhance the economic development issues of the country. These recommendations are derived from both the descriptive and quantitative analyses conducted in this book.

Based on these findings from Chap. 2, it can be said that the appropriate policy may not be to limit the remittance flows but to learn to enhance exports by developing compulsory saving and investment provisions. Also, looking at the nature of bank credit and considering the positive impact on trade deficits, it is probably a good time to develop a sound credit policy for the private sector with some provisions to maintain compulsory flows to the productive sector, such as manufacturing and industries. In addition, focusing on these types of credit flows to agriculture, hospitality, import of capital goods such as machinery and types of equipment, healthcare and hygiene, and small and medium scale industries to be specially considered. Doing this will help to increase exports and control imports.

Based on the findings from Chap. 3, a proactive and strategic effort to promote exports in neighboring and regional markets is needed to sustain the economy in times of crisis. The number of products has seen a positive growth in terms of exports in the international market, so a long-term strategy is needed to maintain sustainable exports of these products, which are high in price and light in weight. India is the market for more than half of Nepal's exports, which is governed by the bilateral trade treaty.

Exploring exports to China, which is the largest market in the world and is not a significant player in the case of Nepal's exports, is another way to boost exports in the background of Nepal's weak export diversification for a long time now.

Another important point of recommendation is to focus on connectivity and trade capacity building, which can help to promote exports both during a time of crisis and in normal situations. Nepal's weak connectivity to neighbouring and regional markets has always been a challenge to flourishing trade and reducing trade costs. Therefore, it is very important to focus on improved connectivity, quality infrastructure, quality of governance, and trade capacity building so that the supply chain for both imports and exports would not be an issue, and export performance can be improved.

Based on the findings of Chap. 4, it is recommended that Nepal should focus on a proper integration of the agriculture and manufacturing sectors. Doing this helps to create synergy for economic growth. For this purpose, Nepal needs to develop incentives for collaborative projects linking with both sectors, invest in infrastructure to support these industries, implement training programs to enhance the skills of the workforce, and explore several potential financing options from the banking sector in such activities. These will help to create a synergistic environment that fosters economic growth and resilience of the economy.

Chapter 5 recommends with a background that no technical efficiency gain is realized for the selected period of about five decades. Out of the 48 years used in the estimation, only in one year, the revenue efficiency is found above 80%, that is the year 2016, with an efficiency of about 87%. The rest of the years, the efficiency remains below 80%. These facts should be kept in mind by policymakers to prepare a suitable revenue policy. The base of the revenue is to be expanded, and enhancing the quality of governance, logistics, and required infrastructure to make digital revenue administration should be in priority.

Chapter 6 recommends promoting democratic exercise by promoting civil society's rights to participate, and it would be a meaningful contribution to further improve the quality of governance. It is important to invest more in the education sector and more rational expenditure in promoting democratic and civil society rights to improve the quality of democracy and improve the quality of governance in Nepal. Education and income growth need to be tied up further to improve the quality of governance to a new height.

Chapter 7 suggests that Nepal should focus and producing to meet the demand of major importing partners. Lowering the trade costs associated with the distance is another priority to boost export efficiency. Most importantly, if the quality of governance is not improved, Nepal's fiscal policy variables do not have a direct significant association with export efficiency. Therefore, improving the governance quality, particularly the regulatory quality, is an important step to seek the fiscal policy's influence on export performance. Nepal has a good export potential with its neighbour, China, followed by Saudi Arabia, Brazil, Israel, the Russian Federation, Korea Republic and many other countries. Nepal should focus on grabbing the benefits from the untapped export potential to these countries.

8.4 Limitations and Future Research

Despite this book's comprehensive analyses, a few limitations better to be acknowledged. Firstly, the data used for both qualitative and quantitative studies were primarily drawn from secondary sources, which may not fully capture the nuances of those respective sectors. However, we do not have any option other than the cited sources. Additionally, the study's focus on specific economic indicators like per capita GDP growth, governance quality, and trade openness, while insightful, may overlook other critical factors influencing financial development, such as political stability and technological advancements. I believe that these limitations do not reduce the credibility of the findings from the empirical analyses in the chapters of this book.

Future research may consider incorporating primary data through field studies and surveys to obtain more granular insights and validate the findings of this book as a robustness check of the secondary data, as well as the findings. Moreover, longitudinal studies examining the long-term impact of implemented policies on the banking sector's growth would provide valuable insights. Expanding the scope to include comparative studies with similar emerging economies could also enhance understanding and offer broader policy implications.